How Economics Can

'Angner shows that economics is a deeply moral endeavour that should give us hope that many of our most pressing problems can be solved' Niall Kishtainy, author of *A Little History of Economics*

'This book is a success, bucking the trend by prescribing practical solutions to humanity's biggest challenges and explaining the economic rationale behind them with refreshing – and highly readable – clarity' James Wilson, Tortoise Media

'A brilliantly clear explanation of how, in the right hands, the insights of economics can be used to make the world a better place' Rohini Pande, Henry J. Heinz II Professor of Economics and Director of the Economic Growth Center, Yale

'This optimistic new voice offers useful rules to help understand the world around us and how to make it a better place. Angner's writing is refreshingly human, filled with intellect and dry humour, this book is as enjoyable to read as it is serious about inspiring change' Professor Klaus Schwab, Founder and Executive Director of the World Economic Forum

'Provides an optimistic outline for improving society and our lives. With pristine clarity, good humour and solid authority, Angner sketches solutions to the most stubborn problems, both small and large, from poor retirement planning to poverty itself' J. D. Trout, John and Mae Calamos Professor of Philosophy, Illinois Institute of Technology

'This wonderful book demystifies economics and explains the practical tools it provides for thinking about challenges we all face in everyday life – from getting small children to go to sleep to doing what we can to tackle climate change' Diane Coyle, Professor of Public Policy, Cambridge University

'A fun and engaging read, designed to help us make better choices, lead better lives and make a better world' L. A. Paul, Millstone Family Professor, Philosophy and Cognitive Science, Yale

'Angner blends economic history, theory and practice wonderfully to draw out how powerful economics can be. Written in an accessible and engaging way, this book is full of lessons to show how economics can practically make your life, and the world around you, a better place' Jack Meaning and Rupal Patel, authors of *Can't We Just Print More Money?*

'A book brimming with beautiful explanations of important ideas and surprising discoveries' Tore Ellingsen, Stockholm School of Economics, former Chair of the Committee for the Prize in Economic Sciences in Memory of Alfred Nobel

'A fascinating, playful approach to a subject that can so often seem complicated and unrelated to the challenges of everyday life. With an engaging, entertaining style, Angner blends the practical and theoretical to leave the reader informed and inspired to put this way of thinking into practice' Eloise Skinner, author of *But Are You Alive?*

'Did you know that economics has a lot to say about building communities, figuring out how to avoid fooling ourselves, and may even possess the key to being happy in life? Angner makes a case for all these points and more. He is the perfect tour guide to economics' Jay Bhattacharya, Stanford University

'Makes the convincing case that economics is about so much more than money . . . whether that means helping people make better decisions about how to spend our limited time, or developing a more effective way to encourage organ donations, or figuring out how to sift through contrary parenting advice and find the approach that works. All these things, Angner explains, are economics in action. And what's more, we can use these principles in our own lives to make the world a better place' Kirsty Sedgman, author of *On Being Unreasonable*

'An excellent book for people who want to know what economists do' Robbie Mochrie, Senior Lecturer, Heriot-Watt University

'A fun and highly informative read' *Irish Times*

'A really nicely done introduction to economics and what it can do. It's a great book for a young adult or teenager considering studying economics, or perhaps an adult who has always wanted to know what economics is but never quite dared to find out' Five Books

ABOUT THE AUTHOR

Erik Angner is Professor of Practical Philosophy at Stockholm University, where he directs the Philosophy, Politics and Economics (PPE) programme. He has taught economics and philosophy at multiple universities for some twenty-five years, and is an appreciated lecturer and keynote speaker. He is the author of two previous books as well as multiple journal articles and book chapters on topics in the intersection of philosophy and economics. He lives in Stockholm with his wife and their three children.

How Economics Can Save the World

Simple Ideas to Solve Our Biggest Problems

ERIK ANGNER

PENGUIN BOOKS

PENGUIN BOOKS

UK | USA | Canada | Ireland | Australia
India | New Zealand | South Africa

Penguin Books is part of the Penguin Random House group of companies
whose addresses can be found at global.penguinrandomhouse.com.

First published by Penguin Business 2023
Published in Penguin Books 2024
001

Typeset by Jouve (UK), Milton Keynes
Printed and bound in Great Britain by Clays Ltd, Elcograf S.p.A.

The authorized representative in the EEA is Penguin Random House Ireland,
Morrison Chambers, 32 Nassau Street, Dublin D02 YH68

A CIP catalogue record for this book is available from the British Library

ISBN: 978–0–241–50271–6

www.greenpenguin.co.uk

Penguin Random House is committed to a
sustainable future for our business, our readers
and our planet. This book is made from Forest
Stewardship Council® certified paper.

To Elizabeth

Contents

Preface

I never meant to be an economist.

If anything, I meant to be the opposite of that. My impression of the discipline was shaped by the economists I saw on TV and in the news. They did not impress.

I went into philosophy of science in part because I was interested in the nature of science and the scientific method, the proper use of science in the policy process, and the boundary between science and pseudo-science. Economics struck me as intriguing, with what I saw as its gap between pretension and actuality.

To make sure I knew what I was talking about, I decided to take PhD-level courses in economics on the side. The experience was eye-opening. The material bore little resemblance to what I had expected. Modern economics is famously inaccessible. I experienced a culture shock not unlike the one I got when I studied abroad in Florence. Economics, like Italy, has its own norms, rules, and practices – including a language of its own. But once I got past my preconceptions I discovered a world of fascinating and useful ideas. And the people I met were not only kind and charming but also genuinely interested in making the world a better place.

In the end I learned two things. One, the public perception of economics is out of whack. (I blame mainly the economists themselves, by the way, for being terrible at describing what they're up to.) Two, economics offers not only thoughtful analyses about where we are and how we got here, but also actual tools that can help us make the world a better place – a place more fit for human flourishing.

My goal with this book is to discuss what economics *is* by showing what it *does*. My point is not that modern economics is perfect. There are many ways in which the orthodoxy can be improved. I'm certainly not defending the economics profession, whose performance leaves much to be desired.

I'm defending the idea that economics as a science can be applied for the good of humankind and the planet. Tossing it aside would be an own goal. Insofar as the theory, practice, and profession can be improved, fixing it is a moral imperative.

I'm not trying to inspire more people to become economists, although I would be delighted if they did. Instead, this is what I hope: to reach people who are not economists, but who care about the future of humankind and the planet, who vote, who believe in social change, and who could use economic methods, ideas, and theories to make the world a better place.

Let me tell you how. Economics is too important to be left to economists.

Introduction: How to Save the World

When Covid hit in early 2020, the most terrifying and destructive global event of a generation brought life as we knew it to a halt. We were all desperate for answers and solutions. Everyone from government leaders to average citizens searched for people who had the knowledge to help. Epidemiologists, virologists, physicists, even engineers were called upon to explain it all – and to hurry up and fix it.

Few thought to ask economists. They should have.

Economists were, in fact, well situated to help. Economics helps us understand many of the problems we're facing – as individuals and as a society. But better yet: economics offers solutions. It gives us hope that improvement is possible and within reach.[1]

Early reports suggested that the virus had emerged in 'wet markets' in Wuhan, China.[2] These are markets where people trade animals and animal products for pets, food, decoration, and traditional medicine. Understanding how a novel coronavirus can emerge requires understanding how the markets for animals and animal parts are organized, why they exist, and how they operate. Why people desire animals for pets, food, decoration, and medicine has to do with personal preferences and local culture. Why people provide animals for sale has to do with the need to make a living and the availability of alternative career paths.

This is economics.

If the virus had stayed in Wuhan, it wouldn't have caused a global pandemic. We probably wouldn't even know about it. But it didn't, and now we do. A virus can't move around on its own. It doesn't have to. It'll hitch a ride.[3] Understanding how a virus can spread across the world from a single location requires understanding how people travel and migrate. How much people want to move around reflects long-standing and fleeting desires as well as Instagram trends. How much they *can* move around reflects states of war and peace, how rich people are and how the riches are distributed, oil prices, and government regulation.

This is economics too.

Government officials rallied to prevent and control the spread of the virus. They imposed travel bans and deployed various other 'non-pharmaceutical' interventions.[4] That's washing your hands. Staying at home. Socially distancing. But people don't always do as they're told. Understanding how and when people comply with instructions requires an understanding of behaviour patterns, norms, and all sorts of beliefs and attitudes. Knowing whether people follow instructions requires tracking compliance. That in turn requires measuring things like movement patterns, behaviours, and habits – on a large scale and in real time.

This also is economics.

People wanted to take action – to stop the spread of the disease, encourage good behaviour, distribute vaccines, and compensate people who were suffering through no fault of their own. Figuring out what can and should be done requires figuring out what would happen if we took action – or if we did nothing at all. That involves not just predicting how people will react, but judging the merits of each alternative course of action. Making an all-things-told judgement requires us to compare the good and the bad in some systematic way. We probably want to put some numbers on things. Those numbers can be in dollars or pounds, but they don't have to be. Units of happiness or 'utility' will do too. We could call it cost–benefit analysis, because we're weighing costs and benefits.

Yes, this is economics.

Once the virus was gradually brought under control, people wanted to relax restrictions and return to normal. But many realized that we could improve on business as usual. The pandemic didn't just cause new problems, it exacerbated existing ones: inequality, health disparities, poor housing, lack of access to health care, and so on. The existing problems made us more vulnerable. They should have been fixed a long time ago. Building back better requires understanding the conditions that apply – both opportunities and limitations. A massively complex economy requires millions and millions of people to coordinate their activities – not the least so that producers will want to produce what consumers want to consume. Understanding how to make this work requires figuring out how to coordinate the activities of the entire economy.

It's all economics.

This book is about how economics can help us make the world a better place.

It's not just pandemics. Economics can help us address a remarkable range of problems, challenges, and crises. Economics is about individual behaviour and social consequences. The big challenges facing humankind are all, in part, caused by human behaviour, either individually or in groups. War, climate change, pollution, discrimination, etc., are caused by human beings. Even if they weren't, the solutions would involve human behaviour. Fixing problems requires getting people to act differently: to stop fighting wars, discriminating against people with a different background, burning fossil fuels, or whatnot. Finding the best solution requires assessing costs and benefits. Implementing it requires coordination between lots and lots of people.

Every big problem has an underlying physical reality. The physical reality constrains the paths of development and the range of solutions. There will be other scientists studying that reality. We should listen to them. Other scientists study social and political realities. We should listen to them too. (I'm not saying we should listen to economists *only*.) But no physical, medical or political science can address the big questions *on its own*. Understanding how the challenges facing humankind appeared, trying to predict what's going to happen next, preventing future disasters – all of this is economics.

What is economics?

Economics has always been about fixing the world – making it a better place, more fit for human flourishing.

This may surprise you. Many people believe economics is about predicting the stock market, in the best case, or promoting the interests of the ruling class, in the worst case. There are economists who do such things. But as a general matter, it's not true. Economics has wide scope. It's not only, or even primarily, about making predictions. It's not just about the stock market, unemployment indicators, and such. And economists' proposals are quietly radical. They're often focused on improving the lives of the least well off – liberating the poor and oppressed, making their lives more bearable and their futures brighter.

What *is* economics? Where did it come from? What good is it?

Cambridge economist Arthur Cecil Pigou is known as the father of welfare economics. He tried to answer those three questions a century ago. Pigou said that some sciences aim to bear light, while others aim to bear fruit. Some give us knowledge that we want for its own sake; some give us knowledge that we want because it helps us make the world a better place. Some satisfy a purely intellectual craving; some satisfy a desire for social or other improvement. To Pigou, economics falls squarely in the second category. He wrote: 'It is not wonder, but rather the social enthusiasm which revolts from the sordidness of mean streets and the joylessness of withered lives, that is the beginning of economic science.'[5]

As Pigou emphasized, economics was born from frustration with misery and destitution. It's driven by a desire for social improvement. It thinks of improvement in terms of human welfare. Welfare, in this sense, is what you have when your life is going well. Welfare is what's good for a person. It's something that you have – not something that you're on. So, at a fundamental level, welfare is the subject matter of economics. It's what economics is *about*. Improving economic welfare is the central task of economics. It is also what economists are trying to promote in their policy recommendations. It is the fruit of economists' labour, when things go well. And welfare is the standard of evaluation – the measuring rod by which we can tell if economics is a success or a failure. Economics is, in Pigou's view, a deeply moral enterprise.

Pigou was keen to emphasize that economics is a *science*. It is the sort of thing that tells us what is and what is not, like physics and biology. It is not the sort of thing that tells us what ought to be and what ought not to be, like theology. Economics itself does not – indeed cannot – tell us that misery and destitution are bad. Pigou cites the great French positivist thinker Auguste Comte: 'It is for the heart to suggest our problems; it is for the intellect to solve them.'[6] Once the heart rebels at the sordidness of mean streets and the joylessness of withered lives, as it should, economics can tell us how to fix things. Pigou compares economics to medicine. It's a science. It's guided by its relevance to immediate practical problems. It seeks 'knowledge for the healing that knowledge may help to bring'.[7] Economics, he believed, could cure what ails human society in the same way that medicine can heal the human body. Pigou was writing in the immediate aftermath of World War I, when the need for healing – societal and individual – would have been on everyone's mind.

Austrian economist Friedrich A. Hayek could not agree more. He wrote: 'It is probably true that economic analysis has never been the product of detached intellectual curiosity about the *why* of social phenomena, but of an intense urge to reconstruct a world which gives rise to profound dissatisfaction.'[8] The ambition to fix an imperfect world helps explain the wide scope of economics. By that I mean the behaviours and phenomena that are fair game for an economist to study. Economics is not just about the pursuit of wealth and the institutions (such as the stock market) that permit it. The scope of economics is as wide as it needs to be to make the world a better place. Economics is a science all right. But it springs from a passionate desire to improve a world that is evidently and painfully imperfect. And its task is to rebuild the world to make it better than it was before. Economists left to right have shared the sentiment. Karl Marx famously said that the point is not just to interpret the world, but to *change* it.[9]

Pigou's predecessor Alfred Marshall called economics 'a study of mankind in the ordinary business of life'. The wording reminds us that economics is not just about higher ambitions and aspirations. It's not just about lower urges either. It is not only about money and riches – although it is about those too. Economics, to Marshall, is about any and all human desires, behaviours, and activities connected to human welfare. With the right kind of effort, he hoped that not only poverty but also ignorance would gradually be extinguished:

> Now at last we are setting ourselves seriously to inquire whether it is necessary that there should be any so-called 'lower classes' at all: that is, whether there need be large numbers of people doomed from their birth to hard work in order to provide for others the requisites of a refined and cultured life; while they themselves are prevented by their poverty and toil from having any share or part in that life.[10]

Marshall thought poverty and ignorance could be eliminated. He thought well-being was within reach for all – with the judicious application of economic science.

One of the most influential views of economics belongs to Lionel Robbins of the London School of Economics. His *Essay on the Nature and Significance of Economic Science*, first published in 1932, may be the most famous text in economic methodology ever. He wrote: 'Economics is the science which studies human behaviour as a relationship between ends and scarce means which have alternative uses.'[11]

Economics is about human behaviour in a situation when things are scarce. That just means there's less than people want. Money is scarce. When you pay rent, you have less money to spend on food. And when you spend it on food, you have less to spend on gifts for your mother or spouse. Money is scarce even for the super-rich. The Musks and Bezoses cannot at the same time keep, donate, and plough all their money into another pointless vanity project. Time is scarce. An hour when you work is an hour when you're not sleeping. And every hour you're asleep is an hour when you're not going to the movies. Attention is scarce too. We only have so much of it, and have to decide in some way how to use it. Governments face scarcity as well. As with individuals, there are limits to how much money they can spend on butter when they've spent so much on guns – and the other way around. Governments can borrow to fund deficit spending in a way that you and I can't. But as long as there are *some* limits, there's scarcity.

Under scarcity, people and countries can't get everything they want. They must make decisions, and such decisions require tradeoffs – giving up one thing in order to get another. If you decide to sleep late, there are other things you can't do: go to work, finish the novel you were reading, or enjoy the sunrise. How you should trade one thing off against another depends on your ends, goals, and purposes. Economics has little to say about those. Goals can be high or low, material or immaterial, and so on. What makes a choice *economic* is just that tradeoffs have to be made – that one thing has to be sacrificed in order that some other thing be attained. When you're doomscrolling, you're sacrificing some time that could be used to read books. And when national defence accounts for 10 per cent of all federal spending, as it does in the US, there are many other things you can't afford.[12]

The economic sphere, therefore, is not limited to questions of money or even material things. Arts and culture, war and peace, labour and leisure are all examples of the economic in Robbins's sense. When artists make art, they're making sacrifices in terms of time, effort, and attention. When politicians start wars, they're making sacrifices in terms of other people's lives. When families decide that one parent will stay home to take care of the newborn child, they're sacrificing some income and the equality that comes with being a dual-earning family. The result of these choices will reflect the specific sacrifices that were made. Robbins went out of his way to specify that economics even includes what he called 'indulgences to commit what would otherwise be regarded as offences against religion or morality' – basically, sex and drugs and rock 'n' roll.[13] Decisions to engage in prostitution, to take illegal drugs, to practise or enjoy music are all choices under scarcity. So is the decision that a community faces about legalizing gambling and marihuana. It's all economics.

Pigou's, Hayek's, Marshall's, and Robbins's vision shaped modern economics in fundamental ways. Economics is about individual choices under scarcity – but also about the consequences of those choices for society as a whole. Economics is about small things. It's about the little decisions people make every day about life, work, and play. It's also about big things: questions such as why some countries are poor and some countries are rich, and how to best deal with the risk of climate catastrophe. It is always about what's good for people – what makes their lives worth living – and about how to improve the world in which they live. Its tight focus on improving the world makes economics different from many other disciplines.

Importantly, economics is not just about understanding how the world works – it's about changing it. Far from a disinterested, cool, and calculating project, economics sprang from deep disappointment with the state of the world – and a passionate desire to improve it. Far from a technocratic effort to tinker around the edges of the economy, economics hopes to rebuild the world and make it better – including eliminating poverty and ignorance. Far from a narrow pursuit focused on money and riches, it is about everything that humans want and need. It's about everything that helps humans live satisfying, rewarding, fulfilling lives – lives worth living.

The economic way

This book is about how economics can help us build a better world – a world in which people live better, more meaningful lives. Economics delivers. It offers real, actionable, evidence-based solutions to big problems. Its proposals can help in our private lives, in our communities, in business, and in politics. The solutions are distinctive, innovative, and often counterintuitive. They're quite different from what's on offer elsewhere, for example in the other social and behavioural sciences.

I don't expect you to take my word for it. Each chapter focuses on a big challenge facing us, as individuals and communities. It also outlines how economists propose we deal with it. I'll describe the economic way to end poverty and reduce inequality; improve parenting without harming yourself; address antisocial behaviour; save lives; become happy, humble, and rich; build community and save resources; and more.

The solutions won't make the world a better place magically and on their own. If you demand nothing less than magic wands or silver bullets, I'll direct you to the fiction aisle. (Not that there's anything wrong with fiction, mind you.) The next best thing, and the best we can realistically hope for, is to find solutions supported by evidence. That's what economics delivers. The evidence gives us reason to act, and reason to think our actions will make a difference. Obviously, economic advice needs to be implemented with caution and care. It needs, above all, to be coupled with a decent ethics. That includes a vision of the good life and a good society. I'd say it also needs to be applied with a view to aesthetics. If we're building a better world anyway, we might as well make it beautiful, with the help of poets, painters, and artists.

The solutions may surprise you. Some people expect economists to 'solve' every problem by means of privatization, deregulation, or liberalization. Economists do, indeed, sometimes suggest such measures. But sometimes they actively oppose them. The specific advice will depend on the problem to be solved, as well as the context in which it appears – including the values of the people involved. There are problems that economists wish to solve by raising taxes, giving money to the poor, promoting equality, boosting humility, or empowering communities. One thing that these solutions tend to have in common is that they're far from conservative, in the sense of defending the status quo. Economic solutions are quietly radical – and frequently liberating. They are often designed to promote the interests of the least well off, not the rich and powerful.

You may be tempted to ask: 'Is this really economics?' The range of problems economists address and the solutions they propose is wide indeed. But the answer will be an enthusiastic 'Yes!' You may have to remind yourself that economics is about anything and everything related to human well-being. People sometimes complain about economists' 'imperialism' – which is a way of saying that they're mucking about where they're neither invited nor welcome. But to a great extent the alleged imperialism of economics is merely a reflection of its broad scope. That's a feature – not a bug. Then again, the most exciting economics these days is interdisciplinary. It's economics, but not economics alone, and it draws on a wide range of influences from psychology, neuroscience, and beyond, all the way to literature and theology.

The tools of economics

How do economists know what works? It's a fair question, especially now that social and traditional media are overflowing with 'experts' on every conceivable topic. I'll give you an idea of what makes serious economics different from that. Economists' solutions – unlike those of some opinion holders I could name – aren't just pulled out of thin air. I won't be able to review the entire empirical record underlying the various solutions.[14] But I'll outline both where economists' solutions come from, and what makes economists think their proposals will work.

The key is to understand the *tools* that economists deploy to investigate and improve economic reality. There are many such tools. *Laboratory experiments, field studies, field experiments*, and *surveys* all allow economists to gather data about people's beliefs, preferences, and behaviours under a wide range of circumstances. *Econometrics* – statistics for economists – makes the data speak. *Theory* and *models* help the economist paint a picture of the world, provide structure for the empirical data, and offer guidance when making inferences. The number and sophistication of tools that economists use to investigate the world keep increasing. The standard toolkit now includes futuristic brain-imaging techniques borrowed from neuroscience. Such techniques allow us to peek under the hood, as it were, of the brain making choices.

The economist's toolkit also includes a certain way of looking at the world. It's the *economic way of thinking*.[15] The economic way of thinking is a collection of heuristics or rules of thumb. Heuristics don't in and of themselves tell us anything about the world. They tell us, instead, how to approach it. One central heuristic tells us to think of social phenomena as the unintended and perhaps unanticipated outcome of individual choices. Some people see conspiracies everywhere. The conspiracy theorist assumes that everything that happens must reflect some devious design or other. But the economist knows that many social phenomena emerge without there being any design at all. Other heuristics tell us to treat people as fundamentally equal, to think on the margin, to look for opportunity costs, to think about the long term, to solve for the equilibrium, and so on. We'll talk about what these heuristics mean in practice, why they offer the right way to think about many challenges we're facing, and what they tell us about the best way to address them.

The tools of economics – especially the economic way of thinking – help explain what economics is, what economists do, and what makes economists' solutions distinctive. You can think of studying economics as a matter of becoming acquainted with the tools in the toolbox. You can think of a full-fledged economist as somebody who's attained mastery of them. The consistent application of the tools of economics is what makes economic proposals recognizable *as economics* – as opposed to psychology, sociology, literature, or whatever. By the time you're done with this book, you too will be on your way to being something of an economist – if you weren't already. (And that's not a bad thing.)

Why care?

Why should we care? Why pay attention to economics at all? The most obvious reason is that we care about ourselves, other human beings, human communities, and the world that we live in. It's not as though economics can answer every question and solve every problem – certainly not by itself. I don't expect it'll fix your love life, and it won't remove pesky pilsner stains from your lederhosen. But insofar as economics can help us improve ourselves, our lives, our communities and the world around us – and it can! – everyone who cares has reason to try to learn what economics can teach.

You may not care about each and every challenge that I talk about in this book. Maybe you have no interest in getting happy and rich, favouring instead other goals and pursuits. That's fine. I'm not telling you what your ultimate goals and purposes should be. But I'm pretty sure you care about *some* of the challenges. If you care about *any* of these problems, you should care about real, actionable, evidence-based solutions to them. If you care about *none* of the challenges – not climate change, not happiness, not community, etc. – chances are you have bigger problems than can be addressed in a book.

The fact that economics delivers solutions – and not just understanding – is particularly important in an era when we're bombarded with information about the problems facing human-kind. Economics can offer some degree of hope, where hope is in desperately short supply. There's a term for the specific form of helplessness or paralysis that people experience after hearing the facts about climate change. The term is 'climate despair'. Some report feeling similarly dejected when reading about hunger, inequality, pollution, discrimination, and so on. This is alarming. Becoming more informed about a challenge shouldn't leave us less motivated to do something about it. If scientists communicate their knowledge about a problem in a way that makes people *less likely* to fix it, the scientists have failed. I'm not saying we should stop talking about problems. I'm saying we should frame our discussion, if possible, in a manner that inspires action. You might never have thought of economics as uplifting. And yet, as a thoroughly policy-oriented and problem-focused discipline, it can be.

Learning more about economics is good for another reason: it allows *you* to make its solutions better, more responsive to human needs. Economic policy requires input from the community and other stakeholders. Economic science, in and of itself, can't tell us what the most urgent problems are. That's for the heart (and philo-sophical reflection) to say. Nor can economics tell us what solutions are morally permissible. It can't tell us what values are most import-ant, or what considerations should go into its cost–benefit analyses. To be as good as it can be, economics requires community input. Even a well-considered economic policy won't work in practice with-out some degree of buy-in from the people on the receiving end. And if it's going to be implemented at all, it needs to be endorsed by policy makers and the population to which they're accountable.

Learning about economics is equally useful no matter what your politics. If you consider yourself right wing, you'll find suggestions that comport with pre-existing conceptions. But you'll also learn that there may be something to be said for interventions that you might associate with the left – giving money to the poor, for example. The same thing is true if you're left wing. A decent left-wing society can't be run off of unicorn fluff. It still needs to solve problems of production and distribution. If there are going to be resources that can be used to help the poor and downtrodden, somebody must produce those resources. Managing a decent society – a society you'd be proud of living in – requires economics.

There's good news. Given where we are, even just a little bit of study might yield a large increase in understanding. If you haven't already had the chance to learn about what economists have been up to, your learning curve will be steep. Even a small investment of time and effort can give you a lot of new knowledge. As economists might say: on the margin, your return on investment will be solid.

And here's a final reason to care. Learning about what economics *does* allows us to assess it as a discipline. Economics has always had more than its fair share of critics. From the very beginning, it's been shadowed by a movement denouncing its practitioners, attacking its assumptions, rejecting its conclusions, and protesting its influence.[16] Historian of economics William Oliver Coleman calls the movement *anti-economics*. Anti-economists don't just disagree with or criticize specific theories or practices within economics. They want to dispense with the entire enterprise and start over again. But here's the thing. Whether economics is good or bad depends on what it does: what challenges it can meet, and what problems it can solve. Until we have the answer to those questions, we're in no position to answer the question of whether economics is good or bad.

The questions you need answers to are: 'What can economics do? What can it deliver?' I will argue: 'A lot'.

Looking ahead

Over the course of ten chapters, you will learn ways in which economics can help make the world a better place – a place more fit for human flourishing. You'll learn about fixes to problems big and small. You'll see that economics can fix the world in much the same way that medicine can heal the body. You'll see why the anti-economists are quite mistaken. You'll learn the tools of economics and, in the process, become something of an economist yourself. To help you master the lingo, you'll find a glossary on page 227. (The secret handshake I'll just have to teach you in person.)

Pigou and his fellow travellers were right. Economics is not perfect, but relying on it is better than not. Economics is a science – yes, like physics. Calling it a 'moral science' is not an oxymoron. It helps explain and predict things that would otherwise be puzzling. And not only that. It upholds the promise of improving our own lives and of making the world a happier, better, and more just place for us and our children. This is particularly true when it comes to the poor and dispossessed – the people whose misery caused Pigou and his fellow travellers to revolt a century ago.

Economics really can save the world.

How to Eliminate Poverty

My grandmother was poor. She was born during World War I, the fifth of six children. At the age of sixteen, she was diagnosed with tuberculosis. The disease was a leading cause of death at the time, especially among the less well-off. Her mother and grandfather succumbed, but my grandmother survived. She lived – to her amazement – to be ninety-two. The disease left her permanently disabled, though, and in need of continual hospitalization. She cried when I got my tuberculosis vaccine, knowing I wouldn't have to suffer in the manner that she did.

My grandmother had little formal education or professional training. She was at the top of her class until she had to drop out of school. Her passion for learning remained total and complete until the end. She collected dictionaries and encyclopedias from estate sales and second-hand stores, so she'd never be ignorant of a word or a fact. She studied multiple foreign languages for fun. Although she never got around to learning French herself, she was able to help me with my French homework by extrapolating from her knowledge of other languages and the principles of etymology. She studiously read the newspaper every day, took notes, and called me to discuss. When I lived in a different time zone as a graduate student, she took pleasure in being able to phone me at 3 a.m. (her time) when she had the urge to talk about international politics or whatever she had just heard on the BBC World Service.

There's no mystery why she was poor. She was every bit as smart, curious, and entrepreneurial as anybody else in the family. She was poor because she didn't have any money. She didn't have any money because her parents were themselves struggling, and because her disability made her mostly unable to work. A limited social-welfare net meant that my mother (born during the next world war) grew up intermittently homeless, when she wasn't in the foster-care system. Nor is it a mystery what my grandmother would have needed to alleviate her poverty – to live a better life and to provide for her daughter. She needed money for food, shelter, and her child's education. With more money, their quality of life would have been vastly improved.

In a legendary exchange, F. Scott Fitzgerald said: 'The rich are different.' Ernest Hemingway replied: 'Yes, they have more money.'[1] The exchange never actually took place, but never mind. The principle applies to my grandmother. What she lacked, above all, was money – not better character, morals, or genes. There's no knowing what she could have accomplished if she hadn't been so poor for so long.

As it happens, the same applies to the economic approach to poverty. Poverty and destitution have been central concerns of economics since the very beginning. The economic approach to poverty is, basically, to give poor people money. If it isn't money, it's other kinds of resources and opportunities. The economic approach starts from the assumption that poor people are fundamentally the same as everybody else, except for that one thing. Their problem is not ultimately bad character, bad morals, or bad genes. Economists believe the poor are about as good at managing money as everyone else – neither better nor worse. Give poor people money, resources, and opportunity – and the problem of poverty will be solved.

This chapter describes the economic approach to poverty. I'll talk about what it is, where it comes from, and what evidence supports it. We'll learn how economists study it with the methodology of the randomized controlled trial. We'll see that economics is more responsive to scientific developments and to empirical evidence than many people think. We'll also learn why economics is slurred as the 'dismal' science. I'm pretty sure those who use the term – often progressives sceptical of economics – have no idea where it comes from.

As I'll explain, the origin of the term could not be more racist. It was used to slam economists who had teamed up with moral reformers to abolish slavery. Pro-slavery apologists claimed Black people were fundamentally inferior and consequently fit to live only under a 'beneficent' whip. Apologists *hated* economists for arguing that all humans were fundamentally equal, and therefore equally deserving of freedom and prosperity.

The economic approach to poverty gives us a window into the soul of economics – what it is and what it tries to accomplish. In historical context, the economic approach to poverty helps us see why it's not an oxymoron to call economics a 'moral science'.

Give them money

British prime minister Margaret Thatcher once grew impatient. A fellow Conservative was arguing that the party should move to the political centre, threading the needle between capitalism and socialism. Thatcher would have none of it. She reached into her briefcase, grabbed a copy of Hayek's book *The Constitution of Liberty*, slammed it down on the table, and said: 'This is what we believe.'[2] Hayek was known for his vigorous defence of the free market as a means to distribute goods and services. He won the Nobel Memorial Prize for Economics in 1974.[3] He remains something of an icon among libertarians and conservatives. Thatcher was a fan. So was US president Ronald Reagan.

Hayek thought the government should give money to poor people. It was 'wholly legitimate', he wrote, for the government to provide the 'assurance of a certain minimum income for all'.[4] By minimum income, he meant a level below which people like my grandmother should not be allowed to fall, if and when they are unable to provide for themselves. Hayek didn't think everyone should be equally rich. He just wanted everybody to have the income required to live a minimally good, dignified life. He believed that governments should fork over cash to the poor, even if it involved taking from the rich. Hayek understood that such redistribution was compatible with the free market. One can be for both. One can even argue that the free market *works better* if everyone has some money to spend. If some people are so poor that they cannot engage in market transactions, after all, the market cannot do its thing.

I don't know if Thatcher and Reagan read those parts of Hayek's work. As far as economists go, though, there's nothing unusual about Hayek's views.

The economics of poverty is a vibrant subdiscipline of economics. There is no better introduction to this area than two books by 2019 Nobel laureates Abhijit V. Banerjee and Esther Duflo. Both teach economics at the Massachusetts Institute of Technology (MIT). The books – *Poor Economics* and *Good Economics for Hard Times* – are great reads.[5] Unsurprisingly, there's a lot going on in this subdiscipline. I can only touch on a tiny sliver of it here.

So much of that work, though, supports the idea that we should just give money to poor people. In a chapter titled 'Cash and Care', Banerjee and Duflo cite data from almost 200 developing countries in which the government transfers money to poor people.[6] Most of these countries deploy some *unconditional* cash-transfer scheme. That's a system in which everyone who satisfies basic eligibility criteria gets a certain amount of cash in hand. There are no strings attached. Recipients can spend it on whatever they want. The total number of people enrolled in at least one of the programmes in the study was one billion. That's a lot of people. It's a lot of data.

Programmes that give poor people money with no strings attached have obvious advantages, as Banerjee and Duflo make clear. The system is cheap and easy to manage. Sending cash is much easier than distributing grain, milk, or other bulky and perishable products. Unconditional transfers require little screening or monitoring. Making sure that recipients are deserving and responsible is tricky, and risks accidentally excluding people. Moreover, unconditional transfers allow people to spend the money on whatever they need the most. Some people need food; others need medicine. Some need shelter; some need investment in the family business. When funds are unrestricted, the individual is free to get the biggest bang for the buck. Unconditional transfers are arguably fair, since everybody gets the same benefit. Unconditional transfers also don't stigmatize, in the manner that some targeted interventions can. And allowing the less fortunate to make their own spending decisions respects their autonomy and dignity.

The danger, of course, is that cash with no strings attached will be spent unwisely, irresponsibly, or immorally. Nothing prevents the recipient from spending it on tobacco or alcohol, instead of food, medicine, and shelter. Unconditional transfers could have other untoward effects too. Free money could undercut people's willingness to work. If so, it risks making people dependent on handouts and restricting economic development. Such an outcome could be even more harmful than the problem the transfers were originally designed to fix. Economists are, in general, highly attuned to the possibility of unintended and undesirable consequences. Hayek is famous for his writings on these themes, among others. These fears must be taken seriously.

To figure it out, economists such as Banerjee and Duflo look at data – massive quantities of it. The conclusion is that fears are unwarranted. In their words:

> What is very clear from all these experiments is that there is no support in the data for the view that the poor just blow the money on desires rather than needs. If anything, those who get these transfers *raise the share* of their total expenses that go to food . . . nutrition improves and so does expenditure on schooling and health. There is also no evidence that cash transfers lead to greater spending on tobacco and alcohol. And cash transfers generally increase food expenditures as much as food rations . . . There is no evidence that cash transfers make people work less.[7]

The numbers reported in the study are averages. We can safely assume there are many irresponsible, immoral, and lazy individuals among the one billion. There are likely many families in these countries who did not benefit from these schemes. And no matter how carefully a programme is implemented, there is no guarantee that giving a household or a village free money will help it. Banerjee and Duflo's point is that, *on average*, the schemes appear to have done real good, with few downsides. Unconditional cash-transfer schemes still cost money. The cash has to come from somewhere. But the data suggest they do a lot of good and result in little harm or waste. Hayek would have been delighted.

Reflecting on the lives and choices of people around the globe, Banerjee and Duflo find it striking how similar even the very poorest are to everybody else. Poor people have less money – some very much less – but other than that, they are no less rational than anybody else. If anything, Banerjee and Duflo write, the opposite is true. 'Precisely because they have so little, we often find them putting much careful thought into their choices: They have to be sophisticated economists just to survive.'[8] The poor aren't lacking in intelligence, curiosity, character, or desire to live. They're lacking in money, resources, and opportunities. When smart policy gives them what they need, they can live better lives. And when the lives of the poor are improved, all of us get to live in 'a better, saner, more humane world'.[9]

Randomize it

How do you know, though? Suppose you notice that there are a lot of newborn babies around the time that storks appear. You know better than to suppose that the storks brought the babies, but you also know that the two events could have a common cause. The regular cycle of seasons might have something to do with it. The connection could, in principle, run the opposite way too. The babies

22

could be attracting the storks. The point is that two things tending to happen together doesn't allow you to infer that the one thing is the cause of the other. *Correlation* doesn't imply *causation*, as economists say.

It's a silly story, but the general problem is a big deal in economics. Suppose you notice that women who have children end up with less prosperous careers. Why is that? One obvious hypothesis is that having babies causes careers to slow down. Maybe there's discrimination against working mothers in the workplace. Maybe the labour market is in some other way less hospitable to them. But there could be a common cause. Maybe women who are less ambitious are simultaneously more likely to have kids and also less likely to perform at work. If so, it's the lack of ambition that causes the less successful careers, not the children. It's also conceivable that a slower career causes the children. A woman who feels that her career is about to stall might be more likely to have children than a woman who does not. A mere correlation doesn't tell us what caused what.

Suppose you notice that poor people in countries with unconditional cash-transfer schemes do better than poor people in other countries. An obvious explanation is that free money helps them live better, more meaningful lives. But there could be a common cause. Maybe countries with unconditional cash-transfer schemes have better governance, more honest politicians, less corrupt civil servants, a better educational system, more social capital, and a more dependable rule of law. If so, any combination of these factors could explain why poor people there do better than poor people elsewhere. It's also conceivable that the causal relation runs in the opposite direction. Maybe the fact the poor are doing relatively well in a country inspires politicians there to help them along by sending cash.

The problem is not unique to economics. The same problem appears in medicine. Suppose you give sick people medicine, therapy, surgery, or holy water. Suppose also the patient gets better over time. Maybe the intervention – whether it was medicine or holy water – made the difference. But we can't infer that just from tracking people's recovery over time. In medicine, the problem has long been solved with the help of the randomized controlled trial.[10] The method is held in such high esteem that it's referred to as the 'gold standard'. Here's how it works. You recruit a group of participants. Ideally, you want it to be large, and also representative of some even larger population of interest. Then you divide the participants randomly into two groups. The 'test' group gets the intervention. The 'control' group does not. If you randomize correctly, the two groups will be statistically identical. As far as you can determine, there will be no differences between them before the intervention. If it turns out that the test group does better than the control group afterwards, you have evidence to think the intervention made the difference. Otherwise, not.

Economists have enthusiastically adopted the randomized controlled trial. From the outside, economics may seem monolithic and unchanging, but once economists started experimenting with the randomized controlled trial, they quickly made it part of the standard toolkit. The 'gold-standard' methodology gives them a new way to figure out what causes what. It allows them to answer long-standing economic questions of many different kinds. That includes questions about discrimination in the workplace. It also includes questions about poverty reduction. Results from randomized controlled trials help shape economists' answers to old questions. They've inspired new questions too.

Economists may not be able to divide people into test and control groups randomly. Doing so might be impracticable. It might also be unethical. Suppose you want to know what babies do to a woman's career. For reasons I just explained, it's not enough to compare women who happen to have had a baby to women who haven't. You also can't procure a few hundred babies and hand them out at random to women in the workforce.

But ingenious economists can often find workarounds. You may not need to randomize, if nature has already done it for you. Some years ago, Petter Lundborg, Erik Plug, and Astrid Würtz Rasmussen realized that fertility treatments work the same way. The economists used data from 18,538 Danish childless women who had undergone *in vitro* fertilization (IVF). The procedure sometimes works; it sometimes doesn't. Success is practically random. At least, there's no reason to think it depends on previous career trajectories and the like. The economists were able to compare two large groups of women who were statistically identical, except for the fact that some had children whereas others did not. The comparison showed that having a child did affect women's earnings. It also showed that women who had babies did, in fact, have less prosperous careers. The authors described the effect as 'negative, large, and long-lasting'. That's true even though Danish parents enjoy generous maternity leave and subsidized child care.[11] The authors also tried to explain the effect. Their main finding is that women with children move to lower-paying jobs closer to home. The study provided solid evidence for the hypothesis that having children causes careers to slow down, as well as a plausible mechanism to explain it.

The naturally occurring randomized controlled trial, then, answered a long-standing question of intense economic interest, even in the presence of practical and ethical obstacles.

Economists interested in poverty have it easier, in a way. Unlike children, money can in fact be handed out randomly to people. There are no insurmountable practical or ethical obstacles. My colleague Johannes Haushofer did it. He teamed up with another economist, Jeremy Shapiro, and a non-governmental organization called GiveDirectly.[12] The organization gives money with no strings attached to poor households in developing countries. Together, they ran a randomized controlled trial in rural Kenya. Randomly selected households in randomly selected villages received money. The other households did not. To be eligible, households just needed to satisfy a basic eligibility criterion. The amounts were sizable, corresponding to several months' worth of expenditure for the average family.

What happened? The researchers checked back in after nine

months. They found that households receiving the unconditional transfer consumed more and saved more. They spent more on food. They increased their food security, meaning they had more dependable access to foods that met their needs and preferences. Recipients made more investments, in things like metal roofs and livestock. The investments paid off, in that they led to more business and agricultural revenue. Receiving cash increased people's psychological well-being, and appears to have increased female empowerment. Meanwhile, households that received cash did not spend it on 'temptation goods', like tobacco and alcohol.[13] In all, the consequences were good. And the perverse effects that one may legitimately fear simply did not materialize.

The randomized controlled trial gives solid evidence for the efficacy of unconditional cash transfers. Again, the results are averages. There were almost certainly individual households that did not in fact benefit from the transfers. All Haushofer and Shapiro's conclusions say is that, on average, the consequences were desirable. Moreover, the fact that cash transfers work in rural Kenya doesn't *necessarily* mean that they'll work in Bangladesh or Fiji. But then no scientific evidence is ever 100 per cent conclusive. There's always a possibility that the results don't hold up, or don't travel. The analysis offered by Haushofer and Shapiro is pretty much as good as it gets. It gives us a very good basis for making informed choices about the anti-poverty policy.

'Good economics alone cannot save us,' Banerjee and Duflo remark. 'But without it, we are doomed to repeat the mistakes of yesterday. Ignorance, intuitions, ideology, and inertia combine to give us answers that look plausible, promise much, and predictably betray us.'[14] If we want to solve poverty, we're better off with economics than without it. Now, unconditional cash transfers won't help everyone, and they certainly won't fix every problem magically and on their own. Cash needs to be coupled with 'care', in Banerjee and Duflo's lingo. It may not be ideal to hand people money and just walk away. So, what else can be done?

The feeling of scarcity

Behavioural economists Sendhil Mullainathan and Eldar Shafir come at the problem of persistent poverty from a different angle. Their 2013 book *Scarcity* focuses on more psychological aspects of the problem.[15] Mullainathan was born in a small farming village in India. He now teaches at the University of Chicago, by way of Harvard and MIT. Shafir is an American economist who has long been a leading light of behavioural decision research and behavioural economists. He's at Princeton University. The two co-founded ideas42, a New York-based non-profit that designs behavioural solutions to difficult social problems.

Mullainathan and Shafir point out that many anti-poverty programmes are based on the idea that poor people simply don't try hard enough.[16] The thought is that they need to be motivated or incentivized if they are to feed and educate their children, look for work, and lift themselves out of poverty. A lifetime limit on the number of years a person can receive welfare payments is an example. Other anti-poverty programmes come with conditions or restrictions that prevent poor people from spending money as they see fit. Food stamps in the US cannot be used to buy hot food, for example. The thought is that conditions and restrictions build character, or at least prevent people from excessive and irresponsible spending.

Mullainathan and Shafir think these programmes are getting it precisely backwards. To them, poor people are not lacking in motivation or responsibility. The problem is different. Mullainathan and Shafir think there are *psychological* reasons why the poor don't just lift themselves up by their bootstraps. The solution is to make the lives of poor people easier – not harder.

Mullainathan and Shafir use the term 'scarcity' a little differently from other economists. You know how the term is usually used: to refer to a situation in which there's less to go round than people want. Mullainathan and Shafir, by contrast, are interested in the *feeling* of scarcity. That's the subjective experience of not having enough. 'By scarcity, we mean having less than you feel you need,' they write.[17] The feeling of scarcity could be, and often will be, due to a lack of money. But it doesn't have to be. It can also result from a lack of food, time, energy, health, employment, relationships – or anything else that a person cares about and wants more of. You don't have to be poor to experience scarcity in this sense. But being poor obviously makes a person vulnerable to an intense feeling of scarcity – lacking in many of the things that make life worth living.

The feeling of scarcity is a powerful mental force, according to Mullainathan and Shafir. It has far-reaching consequences for the way we think and act. They write:

> When we experience scarcity of any kind, we become absorbed by it. The mind orients automatically, powerfully, toward unfulfilled needs. For the hungry, that need is food . . . For the cash-strapped it might be this month's rent payment; for the lonely, a lack of companionship. Scarcity is more than just the displeasure of having very little. It changes how we think. It imposes itself on our minds.[18]

The feeling of scarcity has a tendency to remain top of mind. As such, it influences what we notice, what we focus on, how we deliberate, what we value and desire – and ultimately how we choose to live our lives. Scarcity *captures* us.

Being captured by scarcity can be a good thing.[19] It can make us more attentive and more efficient. When time or some other resource is about to run out, scarcity can make us more mindful, and more focused. Scarcity is the reason why meetings become more effective closer to the end. It is why some of us become more productive, creative, and prolific on deadline. (Ask me about it!) It can also make us more careful, and less prone to making silly mistakes.

Being captured by scarcity can also be bad. Once the feeling of scarcity becomes sufficiently intense it can overwhelm us. It can reduce our ability to notice, focus, deliberate, and choose. Mullaina-than and Shafir use the term *bandwidth* to refer to our mental capacity. Scarcity reduces bandwidth – sometimes dramatically. Scarcity interferes with our fluid intelligence, that is, how well we process information and make decisions. It messes with executive control, which keeps the tendency to act impulsively in check. It makes us less insightful, less forward-thinking, less controlled.

How do researchers study scarcity? An example will give you an idea. Laurel Aynne Cook and Raika Sadeghein were interested in how feelings of scarcity make people take out payday loans.[20] These short-term loans with very high interest rates can be useful to deal with an occasional crisis. But they're very costly indeed. It is common for clients to borrow more than they need, and more than they can pay back. Then they may find themselves in a cycle where they have to take out a second payday loan to pay off the first one. A cycle like that can be very hard to escape. Payday lenders target people with a lot of perceived scarcity. (People who don't experience scarcity wouldn't usually dream of borrowing money on these terms.)

Cook and Sadeghein recruited American adults online for their study. All the participants were told that they needed $500 to cover expenses. Participants were randomized into different groups. Some were told to imagine that they were broke; some were told to imagine that they had just been paid. Some were told that they were about to lose something they valued, such as their car; some were told that they were now unable to afford something they had planned to buy. Some were told the payday loan was their only opportunity to get cash; others were told that they had other sources of funds but might choose to take out a payday loan anyway.

The researchers predicted that people with a lot of perceived scarcity would be more likely to take out a large payday loan. They expected a particularly large effect among people facing what they called a *triple threat*. That's a situation in which people are broke, are facing a loss, and have few other options. And, indeed, participants who faced a triple threat *overborrowed*. They borrowed even more than they needed to cover expenses. These individuals borrowed an average of $725 in order to cover a $500 expense.[21] The researchers concluded that those consumers with the greatest degree of perceived scarcity are likely to make bad decisions – decisions that will prove costly, and that would further compound the treacherous financial situation of somebody already in trouble.

As an aside, the social and behavioural sciences have recently been rocked by something called the *replication crisis*. A replication is an attempt to do a study over again, in the hope of getting the same results. Replications are a form of quality control, where independent researchers check the work of the study's original authors. The 'crisis' is that a surprising number of famous studies failed. Failed replications are embarrassing to the author and cast doubt on the quality of their work. Although its record is far from perfect, economics has come out looking better than its related disciplines.[22] And Cook and Sadeghein's study has, in fact, been successfully replicated.[23]

What does scarcity have to do with persistent poverty? The answer is that scarcity has a tendency to perpetuate itself. If scarcity has compromised your ability to think straight and act rationally, you're likely to make a mess of things. You may not notice signs of problems to come, you may misinterpret the signs, you may be unable to think things through, and consequently you may fail to take proper action. Afterwards, you may not even realize that you messed up. Mistakes when managing limited resources create even more scarcity. This, in turn, reduces your bandwidth even more – and further degrades your ability to think straight and act rationally. 'Scarcity creates its own trap,' as Mullainathan and Shafir put it.[24]

Cook and Sadeghein studied this process by examining complaints filed with the US Consumer Financial Protection Bureau.[25] They analysed 200 randomly selected complaints from people who had taken out payday loans. Many of the complaints came from people who experienced the triple threat. They needed cash. They needed it urgently, often to prevent some loss in terms of health, housing, or transportation. And they had few other options. Many complaints described having to take out a payday loan to pay off a previous one. The complaints described a large emotional toll of borrowing money at high interest rates. The emotional toll was made worse by harassment from lenders, who in some cases would call frequently with threatening messages at home and at work. The complaints also described lenders who withheld information about the loan amount, interest rate, payment history, and so on. Without that information, borrowers have even more trouble making payments on time. Missing payments lead to additional fees and charges, additional stress, and even worse decisions. Thus, already vulnerable people find themselves in a vicious cycle where scarcity engenders scarcity – and all the rest of it.

Mullainathan and Shafir go out of their way to point out that the poor are no different from other people.[26] They weren't born with less bandwidth than everyone else. They have the same visual system, cognitive apparatus, processing power, and so on. The difference between the poor and the rich is that the poor are more likely to experience scarcity among multiple dimensions. Scarcity reduces their bandwidth, which interferes with their ability to think clearly and to act wisely. This makes them more prone to unwise decisions, especially with respect to money, which leads to more scarcity and even less bandwidth. They remain poor in part because of the psychological stresses of living under scarcity in a world of plenty – not because of defective genes or other innate differences.

Understanding scarcity gives us practical ideas for helping people out of poverty, loneliness, and despair – and for helping them avoid it in the first place.[27] People who are short on bandwidth are unlikely to benefit from things like informational campaigns or incentives. Interventions like that work only if people have the ability to take the information in and rationally change their behaviour accordingly. What the poor need is more bandwidth. Interventions need to focus on alleviating the feeling of scarcity. That means making their lives easier to navigate. It means designing programmes that are more forgiving for people who make mistakes. Solutions might include financial products, logistical assistance, and improved working conditions. Such interventions can help reduce the financial volatility that poor people experience, cushion against the most intense feelings of scarcity, and give them back the bandwidth they need to improve their lives.

Cash transfers can obviously have the effect of alleviating the feeling of scarcity. By giving poor people both purchasing power and bandwidth, cash transfers serve to empower them and enhance their autonomy. But sometimes it's better to just give poor people what they need. Child care, for example, is critical to allow the working poor to get back on track.[28] If you give them money, they can buy child care in the market. But that requires shopping around: analysing the options, figuring out what they cost, and trying to assess which is best for each child. The process can be stressful. It requires bandwidth. For somebody already experiencing scarcity, it may be better to have a highly subsidized child-care programme provided by a government that also does quality control.

You may think that making poor people's lives easier, you'll undercut personal responsibility. Mullainathan and Shafir maintain that the opposite is true.[29] Getting more bandwidth allows people to take responsibility for their lives and to succeed even if the scarcity trap causes occasional slip-ups.

Again, these interventions won't fix poverty magically and by themselves. They won't help every single poor person. But helping people get out of the scarcity trap will, on average, make a difference to their lives – and to persistent poverty.

The dismal science

'Not a "gay science", but a rueful, . . . no, a dreary, desolate, and indeed quite abject and distressing one; what we might call, by way of eminence, the *dismal science.*'[30] British nineteenth-century historian Thomas Carlyle was against economics. For a long time, the phrase 'dismal' had been associated with the Devil.[31] In its modern use, 'dismal' has to do with misfortune and disaster; doom and depression; the dreary, dark, gloomy, woeful and cheerless. His smear – 'the dismal science' – has stuck.

What was it about economics that so triggered Carlyle? Was it the lack of grace and sophistication among its practitioners? Was it the focus on vulgar, material things – such as wealth and riches? Or was it the way economists had displaced traditional authority, such as religion?

It was none of these things. It was *slavery*. Economists were against it; Carlyle was for. He smeared economics as dark and devilish because economists spoke up for the rights of dark-skinned people.

John Stuart Mill was a philosopher and economist during a period when the two disciplines were not yet neatly separated from each other. He is famous not least for his book *Utilitarianism* and its defence of the Greatest Happiness Principle.[32] Every action and every organization, Mill argued, should be evaluated by the amount of happiness that it generates. Everything we do, and everything we say, should be guided by this idea of 'the greatest happiness of the greatest number'. The turn of phrase is due to Mill's fellow philosopher/economist Jeremy Bentham.[33] Utilitarians such as Mill and Bentham enjoin us to engage in a sort of calculus, computing how much happiness there would be if we act in various ways – and to choose accordingly.

A crucial feature of this utilitarian calculus is that it assigns the exact same importance to each and every individual. Your happiness counts for the same as mine; the priest's for the beggar's; the king's for the outcast's. It doesn't matter who you are or where you are from – whether you were born in Scotland (like Carlyle), England (like Bentham and Mill), Africa, India, or the West Indies. 'Society between equals,' Mill wrote, 'can only exist on the understanding that the interests of all are to be regarded equally.'[34]

The utilitarian calculus moved Mill and Bentham to advocate radical social reform and to promote various emancipatory causes. Mill was a vocal defender of women's rights. He abhorred 'the legal subordination of one sex to the other', which gave a husband rights over his wife and control of her property.[35] Mill wanted nothing less than 'perfect equality'. Bentham wrote a treatise defending what we now call gay rights. At the time, sodomy was considered a crime against nature, punishable by death. Bentham argued homosexual acts between willing partners should be legal, on account of generating no pain but plenty of pleasure. Both Mill and Bentham were against slavery. Bentham deplored 'the evil of slavery' – arguing that the suffering of slaves cannot possibly be outweighed by any commensurate benefit to the master.[36] All their arguments took the happiness of the disenfranchised, dispossessed, and vulnerable to be every bit as important as everyone else's.

Mill and Carlyle were close friends in the 1830s. They would later drift apart, for reasons that will become obvious.[37] Mill helped Carlyle pursue a literary career, suggesting that he write a history of the French Revolution and providing him with important source materials. Their friendship even survived an unfortunate episode when almost the entire manuscript was incinerated after Mill left it sitting around the house.

Carlyle was well aware of Mill's views about equality and emancipation, and simply would not stand for them. In 1849, he published a broadside attack on 'the science of supply and demand'. It first appeared in *Fraser's Magazine for Town and Country*, where it was attributed to one Dr Phelim M'Quirk. It was republished four years later under Carlyle's own name. The treatise, which runs to about fifty pages, is *viciously* racist. The very title is unprintable. The purpose is to defend slavery in the West Indies. The language is atrocious. The piece describes slaves as subhuman, calling them 'two-legged cattle' who require a 'beneficent whip' – for their own good, of course. Economists such as Mill would argue that some nations were rich and some were poor because of their different histories and institutions, but Carlyle disagreed. To him it was all about race. Abolishing slavery would have no chance of working. Freeing the slaves would only turn the West Indies into 'a Black Ireland', he said, which, like its 'white or sallow' counterpart, would be 'sluttishly starving'. The Devil is in idleness. Carlyle concluded that the white man had the right – nay, the duty! – to let the whip fly.

Carlyle was particularly incensed by the manner in which economists had joined forces with a group of evangelical Christians who used to gather at Exeter Hall in London. The evangelicals opposed slavery on the grounds that all people are made in the image of God. After introducing the term 'the dismal science', Carlyle continues:

> Exeter Hall Philanthropy and the Dismal Science, led by any sacred cause of Black Emancipation, or the like, to fall in love and make a wedding of it, – will give birth to progenies and prodigies; dark extensive moon-calves, unnamable abortions, wide-coiled monstrosities, such as the world has not seen hitherto!

Carlyle was protesting too much. But he got his point across. Treating black-skinned people, white-skinned people and the Irish (whom Carlyle considered to be non-white!) as equals would lead to miscegenation, abomination, idleness, horror, and chaos. Economists were for that sort of thing? A dismal science indeed.

Analytical egalitarianism

The idea that science should treat people as fundamentally the same has a fancy name. It's called *analytical egalitarianism*. The term is due to two historians of economics, Sandra J. Peart and David M. Levy.[38] It's *analytical* because it tells us how to analyse things. And it's *egalitarianism* because it tells us to treat people at bottom as equals. It's not a law of nature. It's a rule of thumb telling us how to go about studying the world and the people in it.

Analytical egalitarianism has long been part and parcel of the economic way of thinking. Peart and Levy have traced the historical roots of the notion all the way back to the early days of the discipline. Here's Adam Smith in his *Wealth of Nations* – in certain ways the founding document of modern economics:

> The difference of natural talents in different men is, in reality, much less than we are aware of; and the very different genius which appears to distinguish men of different professions, when grown up to maturity, is not upon many occasions so much the cause as the effect of the division of labour. The difference between the most dissimilar characters, between a philosopher and a common street porter, for example, seems to arise not so much from nature as from habit, custom, and education. When they came into the world, and for the first six or eight years of their existence, they were perhaps very much alike, and neither their parents nor playfellows could perceive any remarkable difference. About that age, or soon after, they come to be employed in very different occupations. The difference of talents comes then to be taken notice of, and widens by degrees, till at last the vanity of the philosopher is willing to acknowledge scarce any resemblance.[39]

Smith believed that all people are fundamentally the same, and he insisted that our analyses treat them that way. He does not deny that there are differences – for example, between an elevated philosopher and a lowly street porter. His point is that dissimilarities are due mainly to differences in 'habit, custom, and education'. If we want to account for the fact that one person is *this* and another person is *that*, it is unsatisfactory to talk about innate differences. Such talk, Smith thought, would accomplish little beyond stroking the ego of the upper classes. Rather, we must explore what differences in habit, custom, and education made people this or that way.

Mill agreed. His commitment to the idea that people should be treated the same is highly evident not least in his reply to Carlyle, which also appeared in *Fraser's Magazine*.[40] There's never been 'a doctrine more damnable', Mill writes, than the idea that 'one kind of human beings are born servants to another kind'. The idea that every observable difference between human beings is due to some 'original difference of nature' is, to Mill, 'a vulgar error'. If one tree is taller than another, are we compelled to infer that one seed must have been stronger than another? Do soil, climate, humidity, exposure, pests, grazing animals, meddlesome humans, and mere chance make no difference at all? To Mill, it would be absurd to think so. Superficial differences notwithstanding, people are fundamentally the same and should be treated that way. If one is poor and the other one rich, it is not because the former is inherently inferior to the latter. Differences between black and white, rich and poor must be explainable in terms of 'external influences'. If any of these influences are under our control, improving the lot of humankind is both possible and desirable. To Mill, as Peart and Levy remark, race is 'analytically irrelevant'.[41]

In Mill's work, the moral and the methodological are intertwined. He started out with a *moral principle* according to which each and every person is worth the same. That's the utilitarian principle. The moral principle inspired a *methodological rule of thumb* telling scientists to treat everyone as fundamentally the same in their analyses. That's analytical egalitarianism. The methodological rule of thumb serves to bring into focus the external influences that determine why one person is fortunate and another one is not. Knowing what these external influences are, the scientists know how to improve the lot of humankind. When they are guided by the moral principle, they will do so. The moral principle in combination with the methodological rule of thumb is what will help scientists fix the world – including abolishing slavery.

The idea that people should be treated the same has been a crucial ingredient in economics since the days of Adam Smith and John Stuart Mill. It continues to shape both economists' efforts at understanding the world and their work to improve it.

Anti-egalitarianism today

There are scientists who don't think people should be treated as fundamentally the same. Such scientists go looking for individual differences whenever they see inequality. One particularly famous example is the book *The Bell Curve*, by Richard J. Herrnstein and Charles Murray.[42] It first came out in 1994 and caused a major controversy that has not subsided. The authors are not economists. One was a psychologist and the other is a political scientist.

Herrnstein and Murray begin by noting that American society is increasingly stratified. People who already have a lot keep getting more, whereas those who have little get less and less. Stratification has led to segregation, with the richer classes increasingly physically removed from the poorer ones.[43] Understanding stratification and segregation, they say, requires the courage to accept that people are fundamentally different – especially with respect to intelligence. If we don't, bad things will happen. 'To try to come to grips with the nation's problems without understanding the role of intelligence', they say, is 'to grope with symptoms instead of causes, to stumble into supposed remedies that have no chance of working'.[44] Stratification and segregation, the authors write, must be understood as driven by differences in intelligence. Cognitive differences are 'the decisive dividing force', and so 'social standing is bound to be based to some extent on inherited differences'.[45] The rich are just smarter than the poor. Because there's little we can do to remedy fundamental differences in intelligence, trying to eliminate stratification and segregation is useless at best – and harmful at worst.

There are, in fact, differences between individuals. At least some of those differences have a biological basis and are in part heritable. Individual differences can have consequences for society as a whole. All of this is open to scientific investigation. You don't have to be racist or in any other way a bad person to acknowledge all this, or to be interested in the scientific study of such phenomena.

My point is that methodological choices have consequences. How scientists go about studying the world affects what they find. Different methods serve to bring different aspects of the world into better focus. What they see in turn influences the solutions that they come up with. If scientists look for innate differences – as Herrnstein and Murray, and Carlyle before them, did – it should not be surprising if that's what they find. And we should not be surprised if, at the end of the day, the scientists infer that there's little that can be done to improve things other than shielding the more fortunate from the hopes and aspirations of the less so.

A moral science

The economic way of thinking reflects a deeply moral impulse. The idea that the poor, enslaved, disenfranchised, and vulnerable should count just as much as everybody else goes back to the early days of the discipline. The idea has helped shape the manner in which economists study the world and the people in it. It remains deeply entrenched. It's reflected in economists' efforts at understanding the world. It's also reflected in their proposals to improve it. The idea that poor people and rich people are fundamentally the same is also a *result* of economics. It's a conclusion that economists came to after decades or centuries of work on poverty, its causes, and its consequences.

Economists have every reason to be proud of this history. Carlyle was viciously racist, and the institutions he defended were inhuman and unjust. Bentham and Mill were on the right side of history, whether we are talking about women's rights, gay rights, or the abolition of slavery. You don't have to be an economist to think that people should be treated the same. You don't have to be a bad person to study individual differences – or to criticize economics. I can only assume that people who deploy Carlyle's smear 'the dismal science' are unaware of its virulently racist history.

The episode should be better known. The fact that it isn't is a missed opportunity for economics. Understanding the original moral impulse tells us a great deal about what economics is – and what makes it different from other ways of studying the world. Its commitment to treating people the same inspired the smear 'the dismal science'. But that very commitment helps economists to see what prevents people from living their best lives. It suggests ways to improve those conditions, especially for the most vulnerable. Far from being a pallid, dispassionate, and technocratic enterprise, economics is and has always been a deeply moral science. In the best case, it can inspire compassion for the poor and dispossessed, a desire to do something about their situation, and real, actionable strategies to fix it.

There is nothing dismal about the economics of poverty. It's inspiring, uplifting – and useful.

2

How to Raise Happy Children and Remain Sane

When our oldest daughter was about three, she didn't sleep much. Neither did we. She had trouble falling asleep in the evening, and she didn't stay asleep at night. We got more and more tired. Sleep deprivation is awful. It affects your thinking and concentration, memory and mood – even your immune system. Being unable to sleep at night makes it hard to function at any time of the day. And when two people who live together are both irritable and unable to think straight, the atmosphere easily gets strained. (If, as a young person, you thought your parents were stupid and boring, you might have been right – and it could have been your fault.)

Something had to be done. We were running on fumes. Since my wife and I are both social scientists – with three PhDs between the two of us – we did what we were trained to do. We bought a stack of parenting guides and sleep-help books. We ploughed our way through them.

Reading those books was a frustrating experience. I can only assume the authors were well-intentioned. But their advice was mostly unhelpful. First off, it was contradictory.[1] The advice we got was sometimes diametrically opposed. Some books said you had to carry your child around until they fall asleep, and pick them up immediately if they wake up. Others said you had to put your child down when still awake and not pick them up again until morning, even if they cry. But the contradictory advice was only one of the problems with the literature.

The second problem was that the books offered little by way of evidence. The various writers resembled each other, not in the conclusions they had come to, but in the confidence they displayed. As social scientists, my wife and I wanted to know how the authors could be so sure. We wanted data. We found precious little. Authors would often just refer to 'my 30 years of experience as a paediatrician', or some such. It made us wonder what three decades of experience is good for if two equally prominent physicians ended up with completely opposite conclusions.

The third problem was maybe the worst. The books left us with the impression that we could cause lasting damage to our child, ourselves, or our relationship if we didn't follow *the specific instructions* they favoured. Proponents of carrying the baby around, for example, suggested that letting a child cry unattended could stunt their emotional development, blunt their parents' emotional response, and ruin the child's attachment.

The books, all told, were worse than useless. They left us with the distinct impression that we could ruin our child's future if we made the wrong choices. And yet they gave us little idea of what the right choices would be. They instilled in us a fear of doing harm, but gave us little sense of how to avoid it.

Frustration inspired me to do a search in PubMed. That's a huge public database of biomedical science maintained by the US National Library of Medicine. A recent paper from the prestigious journal *Pediatrics* popped up.[2] It was exactly the sort of thing I was looking for. It was a study of measures that parents can take to help their children fall asleep in the evening and stay asleep at night. And it told us what we needed to know.

The study was a randomized controlled trial, the same methodology that we came across in the last chapter. The researchers recruited families with infants and divided them randomly into three groups:

1. A control group was not told to do anything in particular. They were just given an informational booklet about

infant sleep patterns and some tips for dealing with kids having trouble falling asleep. (The other groups received the same information.)

2. A second group was instructed to try something called *Ferberization*. (The name comes from Richard Ferber, who invented the method.) Instructions said to put the child down while still awake, and then leave it alone for a preset period of time – even if it cried. Parents were then invited to return to the child, soothe it briefly without picking it up or turning the lights on, and leave it alone again. This was to continue until the child fell asleep. The first night, parents were supposed to leave the child alone for only a few minutes at a time. On subsequent nights, they were supposed to increase the period of time that the child was left alone. The child would ultimately, after a week, be left alone for about half an hour at a time. The idea behind Ferberization is that children need the opportunity to learn to soothe themselves.

3. A third group was asked to try something called *bedtime fading*. Instructions said to put the child down while still awake, and measure how long it takes for it to fall asleep. If it took more than fifteen minutes, parents were instructed to put it down thirty minutes later on the next night. If it took less than fifteen minutes, parents were instructed to put it down thirty minutes earlier on the next night. This was to go on until the child hit a sweet spot where it consistently fell asleep in less than fifteen minutes. The idea behind bedtime fading is to adjust the child's internal clock to help it fall asleep dependably at the right time.

The results were clear. Children in the two treatment groups (groups 2 and 3) fell asleep earlier, woke up less frequently, and got more sleep than children in the control group (group 1). Both methods for sleep training worked. They worked equally well, in fact, as far as the researchers could tell. But what about the emotional toll? The researchers measured stress levels in children and parents during the study. Stress levels, if anything, went down over the course of several months as the children slept better. And what about the bond between parent and child? The researchers put it to the test after a year had passed. They found no differences in attachment between the different groups, no differences in emotional or behavioural problems among the children, and no detectable negative consequences for either child or parent – or for their relationship.

The study told my wife and me a lot about sleep training. It left us reassured too. Once the child is old enough, sleep training appears to work whichever method you use. It has no real negative consequences. As a parent, you should feel free to use whichever method you want. You do not need to fear causing damage to your child, yourself, or your relationship. The result didn't *guarantee* that sleep training would work for us, or anyone. A single study will never be the last word on the matter. But to us, this one paper beat the entire stack of baby-sleep books. It gave us reason to try sleep training, and the confidence that we were doing everything we could. A free search on PubMed turned out to be more dependable – and more calming – than hundreds of dollars' worth of parenting books.

This chapter explores how economics can make you a better parent. Economists have advice about everything from breastfeeding to sleep training. They can help you develop strategies you can use, for the benefit of your child, in every stage of your child's life. There are no *guarantees* that the advice will help. But unlike most advice you'll get as a parent, it's supported by data. The data give you reason to try, and reason to think it might work. Parenting can be stressful, even under the best of circumstances. I imagine it always will be. But, luckily, economists have advice for the parent too. It's designed to help you stay sane, even happy, while doing right by your children. And that's not all. Economics can help resolve tension in discussions about parenting. These conversations can be surprisingly fraught. Tensions can run so high that people unironically talk about 'mommy wars'. One thing economics teaches us is that what's good for one person doesn't need to be good for another. Circumstances matter, as do personal preferences. In many cases, there is not going to be a one-size-fits-all solution. Moreover, when it comes to personal preferences, we have good reason to defer to the parents. Often enough, Mommy (and Daddy) really do know best.

I'd forgive you for being sceptical. You may reasonably point out that the literature on parenting is already vast. You may infer that economists have little to add. You could equally reasonably remark that economists don't typically deal with children in a professional capacity. You may conclude that they will always be at a disadvantage compared with doctors and nurses who do. And yet the sleep-help literature suggests that doctors in their actual practice possibly don't learn quite as much as they think, or as much as one would hope, about things like sleep training, even after decades of experience. Be that as it may. Economists do, in fact, have much to contribute.

I'm not saying economists, or the individual parents involved, always know best. Nor am I saying that we should stop listening to medical doctors, nurses, public-health officials, and other medical professionals. But economists have insights to share, if you want to be a better, happier, less-tired parent – and maybe avoid unnecessary conflict too. I promise not to be insulted if you don't take *my* word for it. You don't have to.

The parenting economist

Emily Oster is Professor of Economics at Brown University in Providence, Rhode Island. Her original field was development economics. That's the branch of economics that studies why some countries are poor and some countries are rich. But she's famous outside economics for her two books about pregnancy and child-rearing: *Expecting Better* and *Cribsheet*.[3] Both are massive best-sellers – indicating that parents of all kinds find her books both helpful and reassuring. Both promise practical advice based on actual data.

What makes Oster think she has something to say about parenting? She's a parent herself, but that's not the point. The point is that her training as an economist puts her in a good position to help new parents deal with challenges that they're facing.[4] One challenge is a flood of information – from friends, family, and strangers on the internet. The advice is often contradictory and bewildering, even if well intentioned. It hits you when you're already overwhelmed and sleep deprived. What you need to do is to sift through all the information, get rid of the useless stuff, and figure out what the rest *means*. That's where economics comes in.

Economists are trained to distinguish information that's trustworthy from information that's not. Trustworthy information comes from well-designed studies; untrustworthy information is anecdotal and unsystematic. Economists are also trained to tease out what the data say about *causality*, that is, what causes what. When we look at data on breastfeeding, for example, we don't just want to know that breastfed children tend to have better outcomes. We want to know if they have better outcomes *because* they were breastfed – or for some other reason, maybe because they had better-educated mothers. Economics can help new parents deal with information overload by eliminating information that's not worth our attention, and by extracting actionable insights from what remains. We'll only look at a small number of examples here, but it will give you an idea.

Is breastfeeding good? The question is surprisingly fraught. There is a lot of information floating around. Its quality is mixed and provenance often unclear. Oster wants to know what the evidence says. She reviews benefits for the nursing child, the nurser, and the world. She finds compelling evidence that breastfeeding lowers the risk of infant eczema and gastrointestinal (GI) infections.[5] When researchers in a randomized controlled trial encouraged parents to breastfeed, the probability of eczema went from about 6 per cent to 3 per cent. The probability of gastrointestinal infections went from about 13 per cent to 9 per cent. Oster also finds strong evidence that breastfeeding lowers the risk of breast cancer for the mother, possibly by as much as 20–30 per cent.[6] She notes that formula is made from cows' milk, and that milk production is responsible for generating methane gas, which is bad for the climate. Many alleged benefits have not been systematically studied, or else the evidence is mixed. But even so, there are in fact benefits all round.

All this makes breastfeeding sound great – maybe even a no-brainer. But not so fast, says Oster. The fact that there are benefits does not mean breastfeeding is necessarily right for you. Some uncertainty always remains. None of the studies is perfect, and some may be wrong. Some benefits and costs may never have been studied at all. We can't say for sure that breastfeeding doesn't affect a baby's personality or the quality of its parents' social life, for example – only that we do not, at this time, have compelling evidence that it does. The uncertainty should be factored into a rational decision. Moreover, scientific evidence is not the only thing that matters to rational decision making. Situational factors in combination with personal preferences matter too. Some people really don't want to breastfeed. Others simply can't. If that applies to you, it is not a disaster for baby, you, or the world.

Borrowing a term popular elsewhere in economics, we can put it this way: breastfeeding is a good *default option*. It's a good starting point for most people, absent compelling reasons not to. We have good reason to make the world more accommodating to people who want to nurse, by providing them with the liberty, time, space, and other resources that help them nurse whenever they want. But! If nursing doesn't work out for you, there is no reason to feel guilty. Nor is there any reason to look down on – or shame – people who don't. The possible harms associated with not breastfeeding – eczema and GI issues – are not super serious. Moreover, the chances that a child will experience those consequences as a result of not being breastfed are low. The drop from 6 per cent to 3 per cent is large in relative terms: it's a reduction of 50 per cent. But it's still low in absolute terms: it's a reduction of only 3 percentage points. Again, if breastfeeding works out for you: great! If it doesn't, it's not a tragedy.

Oster also looks at co-sleeping, having baby sleep in the parents' bed. The current recommendation is to avoid co-sleeping, and to let the baby sleep alone in a cot or cradle. The main reason is sudden infant death syndrome (SIDS), or 'cot death'. SIDS is the unexpected death of an infant less than one year old. Oster reviews the evidence and finds that co-sleeping does, in fact, increase the probability of SIDS. There are factors other than co-sleeping that matter too. Breastfeeding lowers the probability of SIDS; parents smoking and/or drinking increases it. When a breastfed baby whose parents do not smoke or drink co-sleeps, SIDS rates go from 0.08 to 0.22 deaths for every 1,000 live births. When a bottle-fed baby whose parents smoke and drink co-sleeps, SIDS rates go from 1.77 to 27.61 deaths for every 1,000 live births.[7]

Considering the data, not co-sleeping is a great default. It's a good starting point for parents, absent compelling reason to do so. We also have good cause to help new parents make it work. All Finnish parents receive a free 'baby box', which is full of baby supplies and which doubles as a cradle. The BBC reports that the box may have helped Finland achieve one of the world's lowest infant mortality rates.[8] Oster recognizes that there are reasons why parents might want to depart from the default and co-sleep after all. The calculus looks a little different from the previous one. The probability of harm is still low. SIDS remains thankfully rare, in absolute terms. But the harm that might befall the child if unlucky is super serious. The sudden death of their child is every parent's worst nightmare. For this reason, you should think the decision through very carefully, and make sure you have a compelling reason to co-sleep. You should also take every other precaution. Above all, you should avoid smoking and drinking.

Selfish reasons to have more kids

Oster is far from the only economist to have turned their attention to parenting. Bryan Caplan is Professor of Economics at George Mason University, just outside Washington, DC. He works on big policy questions about immigration and higher education. He is perhaps most famous for a graphic novel on the science and ethics of immigration, with illustrator Zach Weinersmith.[9] One of his books is titled *Selfish Reasons to Have More Kids*.[10] You don't need to be selfish to enjoy the book. You don't need to want more kids either. The subtitle tells you what the book is about: *Why Being a Great Parent is Less Work and More Fun Than You Think*.

Caplan is particularly impressed with research in *behavioural genetics*. That's the study of how genes and environment influence behaviours and attitudes. To tease out the effect of genes on behaviour and attitudes, scientists study children and adults who were adopted as infants. This allows the scientists to separate the contribution provided by the biological parents (the genes) from the contribution provided by the adoptive parents (the environment). Here's what Caplan concludes:

> When adopted children are young, they resemble both the adopted relatives they see every day and the biological relatives they have never met. However, as adopted children grow up, the story has a shocking twist: *Resemblance to biological relatives remains, but resemblance to adopted relatives mostly fades away.*[11]

The environment in which a child is raised – including the parenting styles of the adoptive parents – has an effect on the child. That effect is largely temporary, though. In the long run, behaviour and attitudes are mostly determined by genes. And this is true not only for things like height and weight: it is also true for 'smarts, personality, achievements, values, and so on'.

All this, to Caplan, means that we're doing parenting wrong. Reflecting on the findings from behavioural genetics has far-reaching implications for how we think about raising children. And the implications are liberating.

One, lighten up![12] Parents worry too much, experience too much guilt, and as a result are much less happy than they could be. There's a lot of pressure to provide an environment full of educational toys and materials, and to fill the schedule with physical and other activities. If your kids needed all of your time, attention, and money to succeed, there would indeed be a lot of pressure. But they don't, and there isn't. Kids do not need Einstein-branded toys to turn out well. Nor do they need ballet lessons, piano lessons, soccer practice, and language lessons. The guilt that many parents feel about not being able to provide their kids with more *this* or more *that* is mostly uncalled for. If you're basically fine yourself, your kids will likely be basically fine too – even if you give yourself a break. Caplan puts it best: 'Odds are, your kids will painlessly inherit your brains, success, charm, and modesty.'[13]

Two, treat your kids with kindness and respect. Being stern will not help your kids build character. Being kind will not make them soft. The manner in which you treat them will have limited effect on their behaviour and attitudes. But it will influence how they experience their childhood and how they remember you. Your parenting style matters in the moment. Focus on the journey, not the destination. 'Raise your children with love, control your temper, and enjoy family time,' Caplan advises.[14]

Three, you count too![15] There's no clear tradeoff between parents' happiness and their kids' future. Because your efforts matter less than you think, you can give yourself a lot more slack. Once you give up on the idea that you need to keep the kids busy at all times, you'll have much more time and energy to do things *you* enjoy. Start by dropping activities that nobody likes. If you and your child enjoy the activities, great! If you don't, you can ditch them without feeling bad. Then give the kids more 'me time' – time for unstructured play – so that you can have yours too. All of this should be unbelievably easy, once you think of it. As Caplan says, 'once you know how laborious modern parenting has become, making parents happier is like finding hay in a haystack'.[16] There's an added bonus. Your happiness in the moment will rub off on the kids. They'll notice that you're less stressed out and more fun. Don't worry; be happy.

To be clear, Caplan is not advocating a completely *laissez-faire* attitude to raising children. Most of the research was done with middle-class families in first-world countries. The conclusions hold only within the normal range of conditions that kids experience within such families. You need to provide your kids with a standard amount of food, drink, shelter, care, love, affection, time, attention, and so on, in order for the argument to kick in. You will want to keep your kids safe from violence and abuse. Those are real problems for many kids. But the sort of thing that many parents worry about – abduction by a stranger, for example – are *extremely* unlikely. Kids have, on the whole, never been safer. Not counting babies, Caplan says, 'children are the safest people in the United States', and children are so much safer than they were, say, back in the 1950s.[17] Moreover, because parenting styles can have short-term effects, you may have good reason to take a more activist approach to raising your children. If *some* structure and even discipline make the kids better behaved, it can make your life easier – and theirs too.

Four, have more kids! When you learn that you don't have to sacrifice all your money and every waking moment, kids come across as a pretty good deal. You can have all the adorable cuteness, the satisfaction of being part of the circle of life, and so on, at a fraction of what you thought was the cost. Caplan is keen to point out that there's no optimal number of children for all people. Individual circumstances and personal preferences matter. 'I'm here to provide information, not run your life,' he says. His point is that if you have any inclination to have kids at all, you can probably have one or two more than you think you want.

Part of the problem is that people are considering the decision in the wrong way.[18] Kids require a large up-front investment. When they're little, they demand a lot of your time and attention – and money too. They are costly, not the least in terms of sleep. Many people are *myopic*, in the sense that they lack foresight. The up-front costs loom very large. Suppose that, when you're young, you think you can only handle two kids. If you're myopic, you may base your decisions entirely on these up-front costs. But the number of kids you want may increase over time. In middle age, when your kids are teenagers and too cool for school, you may want three, to have somebody to hang out with. And in old age, maybe you need four, to have a decent chance of grandkids and a sufficiently steady stream of visitors. If so, Caplan proposes that you maybe should average it out and aim to have three, while the myopic version of you would have only two. Thinking about it rationally requires weighing the up-front costs against a lifetime of rewards – including grandkids.

Caplan's work illustrates so many of the ways in which economics can help new parents. It helps us sift through and make sense of the information available to us. That includes the data coming out of behavioural genetics. Without Caplan spelling it out for us, we might not have been aware of its existence – and we almost certainly would not have thought of its implications for parenting. Economics also helps us make wise decisions, on the basis of the best available information, even if limited. In particular, it tells us a lot about how to think about time in the context of decision making – and how to avoid myopia. And economics underscores how individual circumstances and personal preferences matter, which means that '[diverse] parenting styles deserve our respect'.[19] The economic perspective encourages us to give ourselves some slack, feel less guilt, enjoy ourselves and our time with the kids more, and be less judgemental of parents who make choices different from our own. This is pretty good.

The economics of it

You may ask why any of this is economics? The work of Oster and Caplan is so different from what might otherwise come to mind when you think about the discipline. Nurseries are very different from limited liability corporations, and parenting light years from investing. But parenting is part of the ordinary business of life, in Marshall's phrase. Having a child may feel like a miracle to the people involved. But forming a family, having children, and raising them are things humankind has been doing continuously for as long as it's been around. You can think of parenting as 'big business' even, considering the amount of time, money, and attention that people invest in it.

Parenting is also individual behaviour under scarcity, as Robbins used the term. The resources available to parents – in terms of time, money, attention, etc. – are in fact scarce. Many parents are intensely aware of how little time there is in a day, and how much money it costs to raise a child. In the US, that's $200,000–300,000 per child up to age seventeen.[20] That figure can easily double once you include the cost of a college education. The choices that parents make are clearly economic. They are massively consequential for parents and children. And the choices have effects for the community and for the economy as a whole.

It is true that economists historically have given more attention to traditionally male pursuits and activities. Stereotypically female ones, including raising children, have been underplayed. This is unfortunate. The fact that an activity has traditionally been considered women's work does not make it less economic, or any less worthy of study by economists. Luckily, that's changing – as the economics of parenting illustrates.

The economics of parenting, in fact, offers a good view of the inner workings of economics. I've already mentioned economists' fluency with numbers, and their ability to tease information out of data. The fluency comes from their training in econometrics. Econometrics is one of the most important tools in the toolbox. It's a core element of any serious economics curriculum. Econometrics is often about causality – distinguishing situations where one thing happens *because* of another from situations in which two things happen to occur together. Without that kind of knowledge, we're unlikely to make progress. We're unlikely to get out of the pickle where equally competent and experienced professionals tell us to do completely opposite things. You don't have to be an economist to be able to interpret data, but it helps.

Economists can also help you determine what to do in light of the information. Knowing what the data say and do not say won't by itself tell us what to do. Meteorologists can tell you the probability of rain, and they can explain why it rains at all. That information is relevant to your decision to take an umbrella when you leave the house in the morning. But knowing the probabilities doesn't make the decision for you. What you should do depends not only on what the probabilities are but also on your goals and values. How bad is it to be caught in the rain without an umbrella? How bad is it to schlep one around on a sunny day? Meteorology won't answer those questions.

Economics emphasizes that decisions must be made in light of *individual circumstances* and *personal preferences*.[21] Individual circumstances are facts that apply to you, that need not apply to anybody else, and that nobody else may be familiar with. Scientific data matter to your decision, but so do individual circumstances. Preferences capture the things we want. Parents' preferences will often concern their children. We want certain things for our children – things like health and happiness. They matter. Preferences should also concern the parents. We want certain things for ourselves. Sleep and mental health will be high on the list for many parents, for example. They matter too. Reasonable people may have not only different individual circumstances but also different preferences. Such differences mean that the approach that's best for you need not be best for me.

This is no more strange than the fact that you and I can look at the same menu in a restaurant and decide on different meals.

Translating scientific results into actionable advice can be especially tricky when there's uncertainty. Parenting is *full* of uncertainty. Parents will rarely, if ever, find themselves in a situation when they know everything they'd like to know. Not only do we not know for a fact what will happen if we do this or that: we may not even know what the probabilities are. And yet children can't wait. They require our attention *now*. We have to make choices anyway. In some cases, those choices will be massively consequential.

Luckily, economics is, among other things, a science of individual behaviour. Economists are well situated to figure out what we should do with the scientific information. A theory of rational choice is another central tool in the toolbox. Every economist has studied that theory. It tells you precisely what you should do, given your beliefs and preferences. It tells you how to deal with risk and uncertainty. If you're trying to make decisions in light of the best available evidence, this theory is one place where you can look for guidance.

The theory can help us choose more wisely even when we do not have complete and total information. It tells us how to make the best use of the information that we have, and how to come to a decision in spite of what we don't. Economists are trained to deal with this sort of thing. You don't have to be an economist to make good decisions. Some economists make terrible decisions. (I know people whom I suspect became economists *because* they were bad at making decisions.) But the theory of rational choice can be a useful tool nonetheless.

Finally, economics can help determine what's good for you, in a manner that respects individual differences in circumstances, goals, and preferences. A theory of preference sits at the core of the economic theory of choice. The injunction to 'consider people's preferences' is part and parcel of the economic way of reasoning. Preferences figure importantly when economists try to explain what people are doing. But they also figure when economists are trying to determine what's good for a person. Is breastfeeding good for you and your family? The answer will depend on many things. It will depend on general facts about breastfeeding. It will depend on your specific circumstances. But it will also depend on your preferences – what you want for yourself and your family. How important is breastfeeding to you and your child? Equally, how important are the things you'd have to give up in order to make breastfeeding happen?

The story is not just that your preferences are relevant to your decision, although they are. The story is that your preferences help *define* what's good for you, at least when you're well informed. To do well, in this picture, is simply to have satisfied, well-informed preferences.

The theory explains what economists mean by 'utility', by the way. The term is often misunderstood. When economists talk about 'utility', they mean the degree to which a person's preferences are satisfied. Utility is not something you experience, or something floating around in your head. 'Maximizing utility' just means 'choosing whatever you prefer'. Having a lot of utility is good for you, because getting what you prefer is good for you.

The story about preferences is important. It tells us at least two things.

First, it underscores that what's good for you need not be good for me. There won't normally be a one-size-fits-all solution. The preferences that count for your well-being are yours, not mine. Yours may be different from mine. Maybe you like coriander, while I hate it. If you like coriander and get it in your soup, you're thereby better off. If I hate it and I get it in my soup, I'm thereby worse off. The same thing is true for breastfeeding, co-sleeping, and having more kids. What's good for you and your family need not be good for me and mine.

It seems to me, anyway, that so many discussions about parenting are based on the assumption that there's one correct answer to questions such as 'Is breastfeeding good?' Oster suggests that notion may be a large part of what drives the 'mommy wars' and what makes discussions about parenting so fraught. If there's one correct answer for all people, and you and I disagree, then one of us must be wrong. Economics is here to tell you that's not necessarily true. You and I can both be right. What works for you need not work for me, and vice versa. There may not be that much to be warring about.

Second, the story suggests the best judge of a person's preferences is the person concerned. There are exceptions, of course. And the full story is far more complex. But as a first approximation, nobody is ultimately in a better position to know what your preferences are than you. To the extent that what's good for you depends on your preferences, then, you be the judge of that. What's good for you may depend on things other than your preferences, like the facts, and you may not be the best judge of them. But preferences matter. Who's to say if your preferences ultimately favour breastfeeding or not? You, that's who.

What if we tried to keep these two points in mind? What if we tried to remember that what's right for you need not be right for me? And what if we tried to keep in mind that you're the best authority on your preferences, and that I'm the best authority on mine? I confess I have no hard data to report. But I want to believe that many discussions would be less fraught, more respectful, and more productive. Recognizing that what works for me need not work for you might allow us to relax a little – and to be less judgemental of others. Realizing that preferences matter might encourage us to be a little more deferential to other people's needs, goals, and purposes. Believe it or not, economics can help with that.

Yale or jail?

The global financial crisis of 2007–2008 was a major disaster. Queen Elizabeth paid a visit to the London School of Economics in the aftermath. She was incredulous. If the crisis was so big, she asked,

'Why did no one see it coming?'[22] The question resonated. If there is *one* thing economics is good for, you might think, it is to predict ginormous economic disasters. And yet economists had failed to foresee the crisis of a lifetime. They came across like Captain Ahab not noticing the giant white whale crashing into the hull of his ship. To many observers, it was an emperor's-new-clothes moment. The purported Queen of the Social Sciences was revealed – by a real queen, no less! – to be wearing no clothes at all.

The economics of parenting illustrates why none of this is particularly embarrassing. It helps us see what economics is *not*.

You already know economics is not, in the first instance, about things like financial markets. There are economists studying such things. But the vast majority of economists don't. Economics is so much more than that.

Economics is also not primarily about predicting the future. When Oster says breastfeeding is associated with a reduction in the risk of GI issues, what she's saying is something like this: if you took a very large group of babies, breastfed one half and bottle-fed the other half, then babies in the former group would have fewer GI issues. This is a kind of prediction, and it may be useful. Hayek called this kind of prediction 'pattern prediction', because it allows us to predict a pattern that might emerge in some larger group.[23] But this is very different from saying that you can predict if any one individual child will go to Yale or jail, or if any one country will experience a financial disaster in 2033. Economists do not, in general, believe that they can do that.

None of this makes economics unusual among the sciences. Consider seismology, the science of earthquakes and the like. No serious seismologist will claim to know exactly when the next major earthquake will hit San Francisco. Economists and seismologists would love to be able to predict future crises and disasters. But the fact that they can't doesn't make economics or seismology any less of a science. Science has many virtues other than prediction. Explanation is one. Informing decision making is another. Economics, like seismology, can help us build a better, more resilient world, even without being able to predict when the next crisis will happen.

Economics and tolerance

Just a few years ago, the economics of parenting was not a thing. Now it is. Serious economists like Oster and Caplan put it on the map. This work is interesting – and indeed fun. And it may well help you! Unlike some parenting books I could name, *Cribsheet* and *Selfish Reasons to Have More Kids* don't tell you there's one strategy that fits all – and they don't threaten you with consequences if you don't follow it. The work is data-driven and evidence-based. It's about breastfeeding and co-sleeping. It's about relaxation and screen time. It's about raising happier, better-adjusted children and enjoying being a parent in the process. It's also about creating a society in which it is possible to do so. It is not about predicting whether your child will end up at Yale.

As you can imagine, I have not read too many other parenting books since that experience with the sleep-help literature. I'm probably missing out on a lot. I hope I won't cause my kids lasting damage as a result. I just found the economics of parenting so much more informative and reassuring.

Many people are surprised to hear there's even such a thing as the economics of parenting. And yet, having and rearing children clearly falls within the purview of the discipline. The topic is approached using all the standard tools in the toolbox, including econometrics and the theory of rational choice – not least the story about preferences. The theory reminds us that what works for you need not work for you, and that sometimes Mommy and Daddy know best.

If the economic approach to poverty can inspire a measure of compassion, the economic approach to parenting can inspire a measure of tolerance.

3

How to Fix Climate Change

'Global climate change is a serious problem calling for immediate national action.' That's the first line from an open letter published in 2019. The letter says climate change is real. It says climate change is caused by human activity. And it says that climate change must be countered by swift, radical action.

The line could have been penned by any climate-change activist group. But two things make the letter unusual.

First, it was published in the name of the US economics profession. The title was 'The Economists' Statement on Carbon Dividends'.[1] It appeared in the *Wall Street Journal* in January 2019, a fortnight after the biggest annual American academic conference for economists. At the time of writing, it's been signed by 3,623 US economists. The authors describe it as 'the largest public statement of economists in history'. No cause has generated a more robust response from the profession, it seems. The number could have been even higher. They rejected my signature, in case you're wondering why it's not on there. I'm American enough, as a naturalized US citizen who earned my PhD in Pittsburgh. Maybe I was disqualified because I'm active outside of the country. Anyway, the number of signatories should have been at least 3,624.

The signatories otherwise are no fringe characters. They include twenty-eight Nobel Memorial Prize laureates and four former Chairs of Federal Reserve. But what's most remarkable about this group is its ideological diversity. Signatories include economists from left to right, including fifteen former Chairs of the influential Council of Economic Advisers under Republican and Democratic presidents.

Second, the letter doesn't just say something must be done. It outlines a plan to deal with the problem. The plan is to make polluters pay something called a carbon tax. That's a fee that fossil-fuel companies must pay for their carbon emissions. The tax is called Pigouvian, after the Pigou we met in the Introduction. The basic idea has been kicking around for 100 years. Anyone who's taken an introductory microeconomics course should be familiar with it. The carbon tax punishes polluters. It hits them where it hurts. Meanwhile, the plan says to hand the money back to the American people. The cash will, for most people, compensate for rising energy prices. Benefits will be particularly noticeable for the least affluent, and for people whose lifestyles don't generate a lot of emissions.

Economists are sometimes accused of 'market fundamentalism'. That's the belief that economic and social problems are best solved by unregulated markets, free from government interference. But every serious economist recognizes that unregulated free markets don't always deliver the best results. Every economist also knows that government intervention sometimes can improve on what the markets deliver. The market for fossil fuels is a prime example. Unregulated free markets in fossil fuels are part of the problem. They encourage producers to produce too much. They encourage consumers to consume too much. The result is climate change. The fix is a tax.

This chapter describes the economists' proposal to fix climate change. I'll discuss what it is, and how it works. There's a logic to it. To understand the proposal and its virtues, you have to understand the economic logic. Understanding the economists' solution to climate change will shed light on the economic mode of analysis, as well as on some of the preferred policy solutions. The solution is quite general. It can helpfully be deployed to deal with things like alcohol abuse, passive smoking, antibiotic resistance, pollution, and more.

I wouldn't be surprised if you've never heard of the economists' proposal on climate change. Most people I talk to haven't. I know people who *work on* climate science and climate policy who aren't aware of its existence. That's a shame. The problem of climate change is large enough, and urgent enough, that every serious solution deserves a hearing. The proposal is not a magic wand. It's not guaranteed to work. Nobody is saying it'll fix the problem on its own. The proposal needs to be coupled with other kinds of action. But it just might make a difference, and either way it's a good start. Given the magnitude of the crisis, we should leave no stone unturned. More people should know about it.

The proposal

'The Economists' Statement on Carbon Dividends' appears on the website of an organization called the Climate Leadership Council.[2] Its website contains a great deal of additional information in a human-readable way. It's worth visiting. Citations and references to the proposal in this chapter come from the website.

The core idea is that carbon emissions can be controlled by a tax imposed on anyone who burns fossil fuels – whether coal, oil, or gas. The fee is paid by producers, not consumers. The amount is proportional to the carbon content of the fuel they burn. The more a company contributes to the problem, the more it pays.

The proposal works by giving producers an incentive to reduce their carbon emissions. The carbon tax will make it more expensive to burn fossil fuels, hence companies will economize on their use. The companies will also have an incentive to move towards more sustainable forms of production. At least some of the cost of carbon will be passed along to consumers. Carbon-intensive products will become more expensive. Consumers too will have an incentive to reduce their consumption of products with a large carbon footprint. They will also have an incentive to move away from such products, and towards more sustainable options. These shifts will spur innovation, as companies will compete to deliver less carbon-intensive goods. The tax will also encourage investment in more energy-efficient modes of production.

Carbon emissions will go down. The carbon tax will encourage producers and consumers to move away from a carbon-based economy. It will do so in part by shifting consumption patterns, and in part by stimulating innovation and investment.

Do we know exactly how large the tax needs to be to fix the problem? No. But we don't have to. Suppose you're trying to lose weight by reducing your calorie intake. You probably won't know exactly what your optimal calorie intake is. But you don't need to. You can start eating and drinking a little less. Then you can see what happens. If you're pleased with the result, great! If not, you can keep going. You stop when you're satisfied with the results. It would be defeatist to say: 'I won't try to go on a diet because I don't already know exactly how I need to reduce my calorie intake.'

The same thing is true for a carbon diet. You don't need to know by exactly how much you need to reduce your carbon footprint. Since we can't know exactly what the optimal tax is, the economists suggest starting with a 'robust' one and then gradually increasing it until the problem is solved. The economists propose a fee should start at $40 per ton. They expect such a fee will cut US emissions in half by 2035. It's possible that the dollar amount is too low. If the reduction in emissions isn't dramatic enough, or fast enough, the proposal suggests cranking up the fees until it is. It would be defeatist to say we shouldn't try a carbon tax because we don't already know the optimal number.

In order to make sure companies do not try to escape carbon fees by moving abroad, the economists propose a system of import duties imposed on goods from countries without a similar carbon tax. Since countries with a carbon tax would be exempt, it would give smaller countries dependent on US exports an incentive to impose a similar system at home.

The proposal goes on to argue that the money collected by the government should be returned to citizens. The point is to put the money in people's pockets, not government coffers. The authors estimate that a family of four will receive a lump-sum rebate of about $2,000 a year. For most families, that's a sizable chunk of money. A majority will come out ahead, even with rising prices. The effect will be particularly noticeable to low-income earners, who don't already have a lot of money, and to people with a small carbon footprint. They'll receive more money from the government than they'll lose through rising energy prices. The proposal will not only reduce carbon emissions and slow climate change. It will reduce inequality as well. It will make sure that the costs of climate action do not fall on those who can least afford them.

The rebate is there to make sure the interests of ordinary American workers and consumers are in line with the effort to fix climate change. The more radical the action and the higher the carbon tax, the more money will go to regular folk. 'This aligns, for the first time, the economic interests of ordinary Americans with climate progress,' the authors write.[3] The alignment should make it easier to build a political coalition in support of the proposal.

Behavioural scientists who study climate communication will tell you it's important to have a positive pitch. An article from the online magazine *Behavioral Scientist* makes the point effectively.[4] The author, Desmond Kirwan, points out that much climate messaging is negative. It is heavy on the doom and gloom, guilt and shame. Senders may believe that strongly negative messages are better at inspiring action. It's not as though the future is bright. But strongly negative messaging risks having the opposite effect of what was intended. Researchers recommend that we try to spur action by adopting a more positive and constructive frame. The economists' proposal gives us something to work with. The innovation, investment, and transitions to more sustainable consumption patterns offer real benefits to actual human beings. And the lump-sum rebate will give people – especially the poor and those with small carbon footprints – new options in life. The money may allow them to live lives that are simultaneously better for them and more sustainable. Emphasizing the potential gains of the transition, and not just the losses, may be more likely to spur the sort of individual action that we'd like to see.

The proposal has other benefits too. The economists suggest that a hefty carbon tax could allow us to streamline the existing patchwork of more limited and less efficient rules and regulations. Some of these rules would simply become redundant, provided the carbon tax is muscular enough. If so, they can just be eliminated. Fewer regulations could be good for both productivity and innovation. That said, the economists go out of their way to point out that many rules and regulations would need to remain in effect. Some are designed to fix problems that cannot be addressed by means of a carbon tax. Other emissions need to be controlled by means of alternative rules and regulations. Moreover, some rules and regulations are best seen as complements to a carbon tax. The economists mention energy-efficiency standards among the examples. They may do a lot of good even in the presence of carbon taxes.

Is the proposal guaranteed to work? No. Maybe it will fail, despite the economic logic and its many virtues. Suppose the proposal fails to control climate change. The carbon tax is still likely to generate innovation, investment, and more sustainable consumption patterns, all while reducing income inequality. If this is the worst-case scenario, I say bring it on. It's still pretty good – and a gamble worth trying. As long as it's introduced as a complement to other, effective forms of climate action, it's unlikely to do real harm. The proposal does not say that we should eliminate all other regulations, or that we should stop pursuing other reasonable avenues to control climate change.

The economics of externalities

The original proposal specifies that it's 'guided by sound economic principles'. What are those principles? It may not seem as though the proposal has much to do with economic theory. It's just a tax, right? Yet, there's more to this than meets the eye. The proposal is grounded in the theory of rational choice. It's coupled with the idea of thinking on the margin, which is a central element in the economic way of thinking.

Here's how the reasoning goes.

Look at the problem from the point of view of the producer. How much will they produce? Suppose the company finds that a barrel of oil brings in a lot more money than it costs to produce. They will almost surely try to increase production. The second barrel too will likely bring in more money than it costs to produce. But as the company produces more and more, extracting another barrel of oil is likely to get more and more expensive. At some point the cost of producing another barrel will exceed the amount of money that it brings in. That's when the company will stop ramping up production. Production will stabilize when the *marginal cost* to the producer – the cost of producing one more barrel – equals the *marginal benefit* – the benefit of producing one more barrel. At this point, the company can't increase their profits either by increasing or decreasing production. They're maximizing profits.

Suppose now that the production of oil affects other people. In economic parlance there is a *negative externality*. That's just a fancy way of talking about some undesirable effect on a third party. The third party is an innocent bystander, in the sense that they're not party to the transaction. Every time the producer delivers another barrel, the bystander suffers some injury. Many goods come with negative externalities. Alcohol consumption leads to car crashes that kill innocent bystanders. Cigarette smoking generates smoke that's unpleasant and hazardous. Factory farming, other than generating vast animal suffering, is an incubator for antibiotic-resistant strains of bacteria. Carbon emissions caused by fossil-fuel extraction is a classic externality. They harm people who were involved neither in producing nor consuming the barrel of oil.

In the presence of externalities, there's a *social cost* associated with each barrel that's produced. The social cost is the harm to the third party. It doesn't influence the producer's cost–benefit analysis. The producer who only cares about profits will keep raising production until the marginal cost to them (the private cost) equals the marginal benefit to them (the private benefit). If we can assume that oil production has no positive externalities, this means that the total cost associated with the last barrel will exceed the total benefit. The total cost is the sum of the private and social costs. That sum will exceed the total benefit. The last barrel will cause more harm than good. People will therefore produce and consume more than what would be best from the point of view of society as a whole. The *socially optimal* number of barrels is the point where marginal total cost equals the marginal total benefit. And they're producing more than that. In the presence of negative externalities, unregulated free markets will produce more than would be socially optimal.

Pigouvian taxes are designed to fix this exact problem. A Pigouvian tax is a fee, imposed by the government. The size of the tax, ideally, corresponds to the size of the negative externality. Unlike negative externalities, which affect a third party, a Pigouvian tax affects the producer. They'll pay attention. If it's dialled in right, the producer will ramp up production until they hit the socially optimal quantity – neither more nor less. The externality has been internalized, as economists say.

You may have heard that taxes introduce distortions and inefficiencies. The idea is that a free market tends towards efficiency, and that any 'interference with' or 'distortion of' the free market will reduce efficiency. That's often true, but when there are negative externalities, it's not the case. Standard economic theory, as I've described, says that you can make society more efficient by imposing a suitable fee. There's more to the story, of course. But the central point stands. I'll say it again: according to standard economic theory, a well-designed Pigouvian tax makes the world *more efficient*. Making polluters pay makes society better off.

The story can be derived directly from standard rational-choice theory. The inefficiencies can be identified graphically using a set of supply and demand curves: lines that represent how much consumers want to buy and how much producers want to produce at different prices. The curves can be derived directly from the assumption that consumers (and producers) are rational, in the economists' sense. The full story is more complicated than I suggest here. But the economics is sufficiently elementary that it is covered in every introductory microeconomics textbook. And that's true independently of whether the author is associated with the political right (like N. Gregory Mankiw) or left (like Paul Krugman). This helps explain how so many economists could line up behind the economists' proposal. The theory underlining it is perfectly standard.

But does it work?

There's a joke about economists, that they say: 'I know it works in practice. But does it work in theory?' Carbon taxes work in theory. That will satisfy many economists. As a normal person, though, you might still ask whether it works in practice. There isn't a metric ton of empirical evidence about the efficacy of carbon taxes. But there's reason to be optimistic.

Economist Julius J. Andersson notes that Sweden has been imposing a carbon tax since 1991.[5] It was one of the first countries to try using such a tax to curb climate change. Around the same time, Sweden extended its value added tax (VAT) to cover petrol and diesel. The carbon tax was introduced at $30 per ton. The number was gradually ratcheted up. It reached $132 in 2018. The tax mainly affects the transportation sector. So that's what Andersson studied.

What was the effect of the increased taxes on fuel used for transportation? Andersson compares actual Sweden to 'synthetic' Sweden – an imaginary country that's a lot like Sweden, except it did not impose these taxes during the relevant time frame.

The result shows that the carbon tax was successful in reducing emissions of carbon dioxide. After the imposition of the carbon tax, and the extension of VAT, carbon dioxide emissions from the Swedish transportation sector dropped by almost 11 per cent. The largest share of the drop was attributable to the carbon tax.

Meanwhile, Andersson found no evidence that the carbon tax was a drag on gross domestic product (GDP). There's an argument that carbon taxes will negatively affect GDP, and that emissions will drop because the entire economy slows down. And yet the data for Sweden show no such thing. In fact, GDP in actual Sweden was marginally higher than GDP in synthetic Sweden.

What works in theory appears to work in practice. The effect of the carbon tax may not have been large *enough*. Carbon taxes will need to be complemented by other interventions, including emissions standards. But on the margin, the imposition of the carbon tax did what it was supposed to do: it significantly reduced emissions of greenhouse gases.

Why trust an economist?

What is the contribution of economics to the discussion about climate change and climate policy? Standard economics – rationality assumption and all – accomplishes at least four things here. First, it proposes an intervention that's workable, in the sense that it is under the government's control. Imposing taxes is something the government can do, practically and legally. Second, it offers a stringent argument to the effect that such a tax, once it's dialled in, can make the world more efficient. If the theory is right, the fee will make society as a whole better off. Third, it offers empirical evidence to the effect that carbon taxes work in practice. A drop of 11 per cent is not bad. Fourth, the theory acts as a coordination device, allowing a diverse group of economists to agree on a workable proposal to solve an urgent problem. Getting such a large, varied group of people to agree on a proposal with teeth is a solid achievement. You don't have to be an economist to agree to climate action. Some economists don't. But economics offers resources that allow us to develop workable solutions – and vigorously defend them too.

There's also a deeper level at which the proposal reflects core principles of economic thinking. One is about the importance of thinking on the margin. We could, if we wanted, start off by thinking of an ideal world – a world of peace and justice and understanding. We could ask: 'How are duties and burdens and resources and joys supposed to be distributed in this ideal world?' 'How much should producers produce, and how much should consumers consume?' This mode of thinking is common in political theory, where it's referred to as *ideal theory*. There's nothing obviously wrong about this mode of thinking, although once we're done – if we're ever done – we still don't know very much, if anything, about how to get from *here* to *there*. Rather than starting with an ideal world, economists start with the world that we live in. They ask: 'Given where we are, how can we move in the right direction?' This is thinking on the margin. Their answers are designed to immediately address the question how to get *there* from *here*.

You could ask: 'If the proposal is so good, why hasn't it been implemented yet?' That's a great question. It's a political one, outside of my bailiwick. My point is that it's a worthwhile proposal, not that everybody appreciates it. The most common argument against the proposal, in fact, is that voters and politicians don't like it. But there's something weirdly defeatist about this argument. If we have to restrict ourselves to solutions that people already like, there won't be very many solutions left. Andersson points out, moreover, that public support for carbon taxes increases when people receive evidence that they work.[6] Maybe, just maybe, a lack of public support is due to the fact that voters and politicians don't know what carbon taxes are, what the underlying logic is, or what evidence supports the claim that they work. We could, instead of just giving up on the enterprise, try to explain how it works.

Rationality and irrationality

Two economists were walking down the street. The first one says: 'Isn't that a $20 bill?' The second one says: 'Can't be. If it were, somebody would have picked it up already.'

The exchange is available on any one of several websites collecting jokes at the expense of the economics profession. If it's funny to you, it's because you know about *Homo economicus* – rational economic man. The idea that people are rational in their private and public lives strikes many people as implausible – even laughable on the face of it. Just look around. People sure don't *seem* rational. They overeat and undersave; drink, smoke, and do drugs; pursue hopeless relationships and abandon fulfilling ones; vote for politicians whose policies would harm them; and shoot themselves in the foot and fall on their face both literally and metaphorically. None of this would make much sense if people really – truly – were rational.

Rationality remains central to modern economics. It's likely the first thing you will learn if you study economics. It is the first thing you'd come across, although in a more advanced form, as a new PhD student. The reason why the module on rational choice comes first is that so much of modern economics is built on top of it. Game theorist Ariel Rubinstein describes the module as a sort of 'induction ceremony into the world of economic theory'.[7] He thinks it should be accompanied by a presidential fanfare. Rational-choice theory has not only taken over modern economics, it has migrated too, occupying neighbouring disciplines such as political science, sociology, and even some branches of biology.

The case for carbon taxes is based on rational-choice theory. You may suspect this is a bit of a problem. People who are sceptical of economics often point out that its fundamental assumptions are false. They infer that this invalidates the entire project. How can we take carbon taxes seriously, when they proceed from the assumption that people are rational?

The thing is, this entire line of attack is misguided. You cannot determine if a scientific theory is right or wrong just by inspecting its basic assumptions. You have to assess what the theory does. Can the theory explain things you otherwise wouldn't understand? Can it help you predict things that matter to you? Can it help us construct and control things we care about – anything from bridges to health-care systems? These are the sort of questions you have to ask if you want to know if a science is any good – not whether its fundamental assumption strikes you, an outsider, as intuitively plausible or not.

Here's an example. Isaac Newton's theory of mechanics is one of the most successful scientific theories of all time. It is based on a small number of laws. The laws are so simple you can teach them in high school. They can be used to explain the movement of the earth, the moon, and other heavenly bodies; the regular movement of the tides; the swinging of a pendulum; and more. And yet! The fundamental assumptions of Newton's theory are plainly absurd. It assumes that all terrestrial objects and heavenly bodies are small. Not only kind of small, but *infinitely* small. The theory postulates the existence of an invisible force – gravitation – which works like magic with infinite speed across the entire universe. If Newton's theory could be assessed by the plausibility of its assumptions, it would have been firmly rejected immediately upon publication. (And if the fundamental assumptions of Newtonian mechanics are absurd, those of quantum mechanics are just *nuts*.) But none of this matters. Newton's theory is considered successful because of what it delivers. It helps us understand; it helps us predict; it helps us construct and control.

As in *The Great British Bake Off*, the proof of the pudding is in the eating. We don't, and we shouldn't, judge Newton's theory based on whether its assumptions conform to our unscientific intuitions and everyday observations. What is true for Newton's theory is true across the board – whether in physics or economics. What matters is what the theory allows you to *do*. That's what questions it can answer, what mysteries it can dissolve, what structures it helps us build, and what problems it can fix. Same thing for economics. The fact that some assumption or other strikes you as false is utterly and completely irrelevant to the question of whether economics is good science or bad.

Rational-choice theory looks weird on the face of it. But the reason economists keep it around isn't that they're deluded into thinking that it's literally true all the time. The reason they keep it around is that it delivers things we care about. Those things include workable solutions to climate change, solutions that can be supported by evidence. Properly understood and used right, rational-choice theory can help us understand a great deal of behaviour. It can help us understand where externalities come from – why there is so much pollution, for example. But, more importantly, it can help us fix some of the biggest challenges facing humankind – including climate change. Economics can trace a path towards a better world.

4

How to Change Bad Behaviour

Open defecation is the practice of pooping outside – in fields, behind bushes, in canals, or in other open spaces.[1] According to UNICEF and the World Health Organization (WHO), more than 5 per cent of the population in fifty-five countries practise open defecation. The practice has many bad consequences. It's unsanitary. It spreads disease. It pollutes waterways. It threatens children's nutrition and public health. Yet it has proven resilient, even when local governments have tried to eliminate it by providing latrines and informational campaigns.

Child marriage refers to a marriage where at least one of the spouses is a child under eighteen.[2] Before the Covid pandemic, UNICEF estimated that, over the course of a decade, 100 million girls would get married before they turn eighteen. After the pandemic, the number rose by 10 million. Child marriage is associated with multiple bad outcomes. Girls who marry before eighteen are more likely to suffer domestic violence. They're less likely to complete school. They're more likely to die as a result of pregnancy or childbirth. Their children are at greater risk too, as they're more likely to be stillborn or to die in infancy. In spite of dedicated efforts to end the practice, it remains prevalent.

Female genital mutilation (FGM) involves cutting off or injuring external female genitalia, for non-medical reasons.[3] It is mostly carried out on infants and girls under fifteen. The WHO estimates that three million girls are at risk every year. Two hundred million girls and women alive today have been subjected to FGM, a practice that has no health benefits but causes severe pain and can result in infection, bleeding, and death. Survivors may have to deal with the physical and psychological consequences for the rest of their lives.

What do open defecation, child marriage, and female genital mutilation have in common? They're all practices perpetuated by humans. They've been around for a long time. They're prevalent. They're hugely harmful. When they're so bad, you might think people would just agree to discontinue them. And yet they have proven remarkably resilient – even when people involved understand there are harmful consequences.

One of the people working to eliminate such practices is Cristina Bicchieri, director of the Philosophy, Politics, and Economics Program at the University of Pennsylvania. Bicchieri is a game theorist. That's the economic theory of strategic interaction. It covers decisions when several people are involved, and when whatever happens in the end reflects what everyone does. Game theory is foundational to much modern economics. Bicchieri has used it to build a theory of *social norms*. She's written two books about it: *The Grammar of Society* and *Norms in the Wild*.[4] She believes practices like open defecation, child marriage, and female genital mutilation need to be understood in terms of social norms. Even if such problems aren't a matter of social norms, she believes solutions can be. Her theory explains what norms are, and why people follow them. It explains why norms are so resilient, even when they're obviously harmful. Even more importantly, her theory suggests that change is possible. She believes her theory holds clues to real, lasting social change.

Bicchieri thinks many efforts to eliminate these practices go about it the wrong way.[5] Many well-intentioned efforts centre on providing resources. The Indian government, for example, has tried to curb the problem of open defection by building latrines. Sometimes efforts focus on providing information. When the Pakistan government tried to inform people about the health consequences of open defecating, the result was modest. Bicchieri believes that resources and information may be necessary, but that they rarely are sufficient. Instead, she urges, efforts to eliminate harmful practices should try to mould people's *expectations* – their beliefs about what other people do, and about what other people think is right and proper. Moreover, they should facilitate *coordination* – helping people change their behaviour in concert.

In the interest of eliminating harmful practices and promoting human rights, Bicchieri participates in a wide range of collaborations.[6] She's worked with the Gates Foundation to study social norms and sanitation in India. She's collaborated with UNICEF to understand the high rates of child marriage in Mali. She's collaborated with Chatham House to understand corruption in Nigeria. She also offers regular training sessions, among other things, for human-rights workers from across the world. These days, you'll find her training course offered for free on Coursera.[7] At the time of writing, the website says more than 100,000 have already enrolled. Bicchieri is obviously not the only one who thinks her approach shows real promise.

The theory can be applied both to any social problem caused by social norms, and to every problem that could potentially be solved by social norms. That's a lot. It doesn't offer quick fixes, but it gives you real, actionable advice. It can be used to address major social problems and minor annoyances. You can use it to deal with colleagues who leave dishes in the sink and people who get in your face.

Norms and behaviour

Why do people do bad things? We have many explanations. But everyday explanations of bad behaviour are often inadequate and sometimes malignant. Matthew 7:18 tells us that a good tree cannot bear bad fruit. Many of us harbour similar thoughts about each other. There are two kinds of people, in this view. Some are good; some are bad. Good people do good things; bad people do bad things. If we see somebody doing a bad thing, then that person must be one of the bad people. If we see somebody else doing a good thing, that person must be one of the good people. I'll call this the *folk explanation* of bad behaviour.

The folk explanation relates to something psychologists call the *fundamental attribution error*. When we explain other people's behaviour, we tend to point to their personality, character, or disposition – more or less stable features of the person. When we explain our own behaviour, by contrast, we tend to point to cir-cumstances, environments, and external pressures – more or less fluid features of our situation. So if a stranger is rude on the bus on the way to work, we might be tempted to say: 'The reason that happened is that he's a rude, obnoxious person.' If we ourselves act rudely in similar circumstances, we might instead be tempted to say: 'The reason that happened is that I had overslept and was run-ning late, and so I was completely stressed out!'

The folk explanation of bad behaviour can combine with the fundamental attribution error in unfortunate ways. The folk explanation makes us pin the blame for bad behaviour on bad people. And who are these bad people? The fundamental attribu-tion error makes sure it is not *us*. We are just stressed out, or having a bad day – never a bad person. The bad person must be somebody else. Who, exactly? Certainly, it's somebody who's dif-ferent from us. If our neighbourhood develops a litter problem, we're likely to infer that the guilty party must come from outside the neighbourhood, or that the composition of the neighbours must have changed. In the worst case, this mode of thinking encourages us to blame immigrants, people of a different religion or ethnic background, or the like.

But this is the wrong way to think about bad behaviour. Most or all of us are capable of doing harmful and antisocial things under the right (or wrong) conditions. It's by and large a mistake to blame people who are different from us. The theory of social norms explains why.

Social norms are informal rules that govern the behaviour of people living in groups and societies. We may think of ourselves as rational animals – at least much of the time. We may recognize that we are creatures of habit. But our behaviour is, to a very great extent, driven by social norms. Imagine that you find yourself at dinner in a restaurant in a foreign country. You have a whole table full of delicious dishes and eating implements in front of you. The problem is that you have no idea what sauce goes with which dish – and which implements to use and how. The first thing you would do, in all likelihood, is to look around and try to figure out what the locals do – and then do the same thing. You're trying to discover what the norm is so that you can follow it. You probably wouldn't even think about it. If you did think about it, you might come to visualize eating wrongly and the locals pointing and laughing. The mere thought of such a transgression might fill you with dread. That's the power of norms. Norms determine all sorts of behaviours – good and bad. Understanding why people do the things they do requires paying attention to social norms. So does changing the things people do – whether we want to eliminate small annoyances or fix big problems or both.

A central insight of Bicchieri's is that people by and large *want to* follow norms. If all the locals eat a certain way, chances are you want to eat that way too. If nobody else is littering, you're not going to toss your trash on the ground. Violating norms is the stuff of literal nightmares. You know that fear of finding yourself on stage during graduation and realizing that you're in your underwear? That's the fear of violating norms. We really, really don't want that.

But the desire to follow norms is *conditional*. Suppose you're headed to the pub for a pint. When you get there, the other customers are standing neatly, waiting for their turn to order. In those circumstances, you wouldn't dream of bellying up to the bar, waving your arms around, and hollering for attention. You'll join the queue and patiently wait for your turn. But suppose instead that when you got there you found the other customers in a scrum by the bar competing for the publican's attention. Now you wouldn't dream of lining up neatly at the back and waiting for your turn. You too would make your way to the bar, wave your arms around, and holler for attention. The example illustrates what it means to say that the desire to follow norms is conditional. Your desire to line up neatly depends on others lining up neatly. Your desire to push your way to the bar depends on others pushing their way to the bar. How you want to go about quenching your thirst depends entirely on how others do it.

The fact that our desire to follow social norms is conditional makes them different from *moral* norms. Moral norms are rules and principles of morality. 'Murder is wrong' is one example. If you genuinely believe that murder is wrong, you probably aspire to abstain from murder independently of what others are doing. Imagine that someone tosses a cigarette butt into your rose garden, and you feel like killing them on the spot. You're not going to decide whether to murder the person by first determining if your neighbours murder litterers in their gardens. When you're fully committed to the idea that murder is wrong, you don't even need to know. The same thing is *not* true for social norms.

The pub scenario I just described is an example of a *game*, in the technical sense. Each individual has to make a decision: to line up neatly or to belly up to the bar. What ultimately happens in the pub is a result not only of what one person does, but of what everyone does. Game theory applies.

In this game, you can expect one of two things to happen. Either everyone lines up neatly, or everyone mobs the bar. Economists say that the game has two *Nash equilibria*, named for mathematician John Nash, the main character in the film *A Beautiful Mind*. These are situations where no one player can improve their situation by changing their decision, *given everybody else's decision*. Or to put it differently: in equilibrium, everybody has already made the best decision they can in light of whatever the other players are doing. As long as everyone wants to do what everyone else does, either everyone will line up neatly, or they will all push their way to the bar. And these equilibria are *stable*, in the following sense. If you were to do the opposite of what everybody else was doing, you'd likely realize the error of your ways and quickly change your decision. Suppose that you're completely absorbed by whatever is on your phone, and that you accidentally jump the queue. As soon as you look up, you'll be horrified to learn that everyone is watching disapprovingly. You'd much rather go to the back of the line than insist on ordering ahead of your turn. The number of equilibria in a game need not be two, by the way. The number depends on the structure of the interaction, in combination with people's preferences.

Bicchieri's view is that social norms are equilibria of a certain kind. Not all equilibria are norms, but all social norms are equilibria. The rule that says that you line up neatly at the bar can be an example of a social norm. It's an equilibrium because of people's conditional preferences. Social norms are propped up by *expectations*. First, each individual expects that sufficiently many other people will conform to the norm. Bicchieri calls it an *empirical* expectation. One reason why I get in line is that I fully expect others to do so too. If I didn't, I wouldn't bother. (Again, this is where social norms differ from moral norms.) Second, each individual expects that sufficiently many other people judge that he or she *ought to* conform to the norm, and may punish any deviation. Bicchieri calls it a *normative* expectation. One reason why I get in line is that I expect others will disapprove if I don't. Moreover, I fear any violation of the norm might generate sanctions – and that their disapproval might translate into raised eyebrows, sneers, or verbal attacks.

I'm simplifying a bit, obviously, but this is the theory. Social norms are equilibria, characterized by conditional preferences, empirical expectations, and normative expectations. That is what *defines* social norms. But what is it that makes social norms such powerful drivers of behaviour? Bicchieri says it's because they tend to trump personal beliefs about right and wrong. She writes:

When personal beliefs and normative expectations disagree, I predict that normative expectations, not personal normative beliefs, will guide behaviour. This is in line with what social psychologists have observed: beliefs that are perceived to be shared by a relevant group will affect action, whereas personal normative beliefs often fail to do so, especially when they deviate from socially held beliefs.[8]

Imagine that my personal convictions tell me that doing X is wrong. Imagine also that there's a social norm that tells me to do precisely X. This means that I have an empirical expectation: I expect others to do X. It also means that I have a normative expectation: I expect others to judge that I ought to do X, and that they might penalize me if I fail to do X. These expectations, along with my conditional preferences, are much more powerful drivers of behaviour than my private conviction that it is wrong to do X. This explains why mere information is, by and large, insufficient to move the needle. Even if my private conviction changes, that's unlikely to translate into new behaviour patterns.

Social norms can support all sorts of behaviour, relatively independently of people's private convictions about that sort of behaviour. Sometimes the behaviour is good. Norms against littering help keep the environment clean – even in a society where there are individuals who don't have any principled objection to littering. Norms favouring honest dealing help promote well-functioning markets, even when individuals don't have any moral objections to cheating and stealing. Social norms, in such cases, are a force for good. But sometimes, the behaviour is not good – and can be very, very bad. Norms demanding honour killings as a response to 'bringing shame upon the family' are an example. Such norms can drive one vicious murder after another – even in a family where each individual would rather not. Social norms, in such cases, are a force for bad. They can prop up enormously harmful practices – and for a long time too.

Norms can change

Bicchieri's account has implications that are both intriguing and important.

Two groups, or societies, can behave completely differently even though they face the same interaction – play the exact same game – and have the exact same preferences. If you observe two groups of people following different norms, you cannot infer that their values and commitments are any different. People are quick to tie differences in behaviours to ethnic attributes, national character, or whatever. Doing so is a mistake, and can be a source of ethnocentric and even racist ideas. Italians will sometimes tell you: 'In Milan, traffic lights are instructions; in Rome, they are suggestions; in Naples, they are Christmas decorations.' Can you assume that Italians from the north, centre, and south of the country are fundamentally different? No. If you drive from Milan through Rome to Naples, your attitude to traffic lights will change too. When your fellow drivers treat them as Christmas lights you would be wise to do so too. Treating them as instructions when nobody else does would cause traffic accidents and lots of yelling. It is at least *possible* that people in different parts of the country play different equilibrium strategies in the very same game. Remember analytical egalitarianism from chapter 1? Don't assume that another group must be fundamentally different because they act differently from yours.

Large-scale social change can happen without any fundamental change to the structure of the interaction *or* people's preferences. Norms are stable, as I've said, in the sense that small deviations won't dislodge them. But if *sufficiently many* people suddenly change their behaviour, they can cause a cascade of deviations which ends with a new norm being established. Suppose that not one but half the people in the pub decide to ignore the queue and rush the bar instead. Under the circumstances, the norm would collapse. People who are still in line would abandon their expectations. They would no longer believe that others expect them to line up. They would also no longer believe that others judge that they *should* line up. Since it would be in their interest to join the scrum at the bar, they would. In brief, once a critical mass of people decide to switch to another equilibrium, everyone else will follow suit. In this scenario everyone changes their behaviour. And yet, there has been no change in the nature of their interaction, nor in their fundamental preferences. People have just switched from one equilibrium in the game to another.

There's some indication only about one-quarter of the group needs to change in order to dislodge an established norm or convention, at least in some cases.[9] A smallish but committed minority may be everything it takes.

You may think that social change must be preceded by a change in values. It can be, but it doesn't have to be. Yes, values do change over time – consider, for example, public attitudes towards gay marriage and adoption over the course of our lifetimes – and, if sufficiently many people change their preferences, they will change the nature of the game, and consequently the equilibria that people can and will play by. But social change can also occur simply because people switch from one equilibrium to another in the very same game. Sometimes the values change *after* the behaviour does, as we internalize ideas of what is right and proper on the basis of our own changing behaviour patterns.

Social change can be fast. You may think that things aren't improving quickly enough when it comes to attitudes to social justice, climate change, or whatever. You'd probably be right. Changing values can be a relatively slow process. Attitudes to gay marriage and adoption have shifted dramatically in my lifetime, but it's taken a generation. Switching from one equilibrium to another can be almost instantaneous. Here's another example. Think about a show where everyone is seated. If only one person stands up and dances along to the music, they'll block the view of people behind. Somebody might protest loudly enough that they will sit down again. But if *sufficiently many* people stand up and dance, others will stop protesting and join in instead. Even in a large space, this process can be completed in a matter of seconds. Rapid social change is possible.

How to change norms

The million-dollar question, though, is: *How do you get people to change?*[10] Bicchieri doesn't have a silver bullet, obviously. Nor does she have a one-size-fits-all solution. Sometimes the social norm is the problem. Then, the norm needs to be abandoned. Sometimes the problem is the absence of a social norm. Then, a new norm needs to be established. Sometimes one norm needs to be replaced by another. The solution will depend on these considerations, and a whole bunch of other factors. That said, Bicchieri has suggestions.

First, let's talk about some things that are *less* likely to work. One, changing people's fundamental preferences: 'You shouldn't enjoy driving a sports car; you should prefer biking to work.' 'You shouldn't want to leave dishes in the sink; you should enjoy washing up after yourself.' Instructing people that they shouldn't want what they want is not likely to have much effect – especially if your point is that they should want what *you* want. And even if you do manage to change people's preferences, this is a relatively slow process. Two, telling people they're doing something morally wrong: 'You're a bad person for leaving dishes in the sink.' 'It is morally objectionable to stand up in front of me during the show.' Even if you succeed in instilling in people the correct personal moral beliefs, we already know that they have limited motivating power. Personal moral convictions don't drive the behaviour. If there's a conflict between a personal moral conviction and a social norm, by and large the social norm will win. Three, just ordering people around: 'Sit down!' 'Clean up!' 'Don't litter!' Between the motivating force of one's own preferences and whatever social norm might apply, a person's desire to comply with your orders or instructions is likely to be much lower.

The key to changing people's behaviour is to focus on *expectations*. Social norms are propped up by expectations. If we can change the expectations, we can change the behaviour.

Sometimes it is enough simply to inform people what others expect. Binge drinking among college students is a major problem. Its most predictable effect is alcohol poisoning. It is also associated with many other bad outcomes, including rape and sexual assault. Research has found that many students overestimate how much other students drink. Trying to conform to what they think is the norm for alcohol consumption, they drink more than they would want. By doing so they inadvertently end up reinforcing other students' impression that students drink a lot. Students are stuck in a cycle where everyone drinks more than they would want. How do you fix this problem? It turns out that an information campaign may be sufficient. Just tell students how much (or how little) other students drink – and maybe also how much (or little) they would drink if they had their way.

The fundamental problem for the college students is something psychologists call *pluralistic ignorance*. You know the feeling. You're attending a lecture where you don't understand a thing. You'd really like to raise your hand and ask what's going on. But nobody else is raising their hands. You think they probably understand the lecture. They may even find it easy. You fear they will judge you for asking a question. So you don't. Now, it's possible that everybody in the audience feels the exact same way. Nobody gets it; nobody raises a hand; everyone gets the impression everyone else gets it. The example illustrates that we often cannot immediately observe other people's behaviours and attitudes. We don't know how many questions other people have, or how much they really drink. Pluralistic ignorance is probably common. When people suffer from pluralistic ignorance, dislodging the norm can be easy. Just fix their empirical expectations.

In other cases, merely informing people about what others do is not sufficient. Practices like FGM and child marriage, horrifically harmful as they are, are sometimes propped up by empirical expectations that may be broadly correct. Other parents do indeed subject their daughters to genital cutting and marry them off early. These practices are driven, in part, by the fear that an older, uncut girl will not succeed in getting married. And in a society where everyone else is following the norm, that might well be true. People are stuck in an equilibrium, whether they like it or not. As long as everyone follows the norm, everyone has a reason to do so, and nobody dares act differently.

The way to change a person's behaviour in such a scenario is to change *other people's* behaviour and expectations. Merely correcting misconceptions about other people's behaviours will not be sufficient. It sounds paradoxical, but it is not too far from the truth. The key is to change everyone's behaviour more or less at the same time. The main reason why it's hard to change bad behaviour is that the group is probably already in a stable equilibrium. You can't effect change one person at a time. Convince any one person to change their ways, and they'll quickly think better of it. But convince a sufficiently large group of people and – voilà! – you might find yourself in another stable equilibrium. With a little luck, the new one is better than the old one.

In the process, you may be helped by a quartet of principles. We can call them *principles of change*. First, the new norm you want to establish has to be common knowledge. Each person has to know what norm to switch to. But not only that. Each person has to be satisfied that other people know what the norm is, and that they know that you know, and so on. If you want to shift people to a new norm, you have to figure out a way to make sure the new solution is common knowledge. One way to accomplish this is to communicate in public. If you and I both hear a message, that message will immediately become common knowledge. It helps if the new norm is simple to understand and to follow. Second, people have to have a reason to change. You need to make sure that people understand that the new solution is *good for them*. If it's not in their interest to switch to a new norm, they will have no incentive to do so. They may even resist your efforts. Third, you have to address people's normative expectations. That means communicating that other people won't judge you for switching from one behaviour to another and punish you if you do. Even inefficient norms are propped up by the expectation of social sanctions. That could be anything from a raised eyebrow to social exclusion or worse. Fourth, you can take advantage of *trendsetters*. They're people who forge their own path, rather than following everybody else's. And they're people that others seek to emulate.

As an example of these principles, Bicchieri describes successful programmes targeting open defecation.[11] What these programmes have in common is that they involve an active, collective change in personal beliefs and social expectations. For example, a facilitator might lead participants through an area where people defecate in the open, triggering feelings of disgust. The facilitator might place faeces next to food items, and point out that flies make return trips between them. Or they might smear charcoal on their hands, try unsuccessfully to wipe it off, and then shake the hands of the participants. A structured conversation might move from feelings of disgust to the desirability of change, and then to collective means of addressing the situation. The fact that the conversation takes place in public can help shift normative expectations – beliefs about what others think is right and proper. Such a shift can in turn dislodge empirical expectations – beliefs about what others do. With a little luck, such a shift can result in the community moving to another equilibrium.

Applying these principles of change is not automatically going to fix your problems with other people's behaviour – whether it's about dirty dishes in the sink, toilet lids in the upright position, or corruption in politics. But they're good to keep in mind. Here's one modest example. When I teach, I tell students that if they're puzzled or confused, they should never hesitate to ask a question. If you're confused, I say, it's likely that there are others who are confused too – and who would be grateful if you asked. This is my way of dislodging pluralistic ignorance – and trying to prevent any norm discouraging participation from getting established. It's also a way to communicate that others don't judge people who ask questions, and that the student won't be socially penalized for it. It's a cheap and fast intervention that can work.

Solving for the equilibrium

A local newspaper recently reported on what it described as a paradox.[12] The city of Stockholm had decided to crack down on illegal parking. It invested in parking enforcement. City officials expected to see fewer cars parked illegally. They also, apparently, expected increased revenue from parking fines. The paradox is that the investment led to fewer fines and less revenue. How could this be?

Let us first ask under what conditions the outcome would seem paradoxical. I expect the city (or at least the journalist) expected a chain of events like this:

1. The number of parking enforcement officers goes up.
2. The number of citations goes up.
3. Revenues go up.

So far so good. If this is the entire story, we should in fact expect revenues to increase when parking enforcement is beefed up. And it would be paradoxical if they went down.

But it's not the entire story. The chain of events doesn't stop at 3. Our analysis can't stop there either. We should expect things then to proceed along the following lines:

4. Drivers realize they're more likely to get a ticket when parking illegally.
5. Drivers decide to abide by parking rules more consistently.
6. The number of citations goes down.
7. Revenues go down.

Once you think things through, meaning all the way from step 1 to step 7, you realize that any increase in revenue will be temporary. Step 3 can't be where the story ends. Drivers have every reason to make sure the story doesn't end there. They will adjust their behaviour accordingly. When they do, in due time, revenues will decrease.

Economists will tell you to 'solve for the equilibrium'. This just means thinking through what happens when people adjust to changing conditions, including other people's behaviour. Whoever expected increased revenues didn't solve for the equilibrium, because they didn't consider what would happen as people adapt. Solving for the equilibrium means asking, for each participant, do they have reason to change their behaviour? If the answer is yes, the analysis can't end there. Solving for the equilibrium means thinking through the consequences of people adapting until nobody has reason to change their behaviour any more. Doing so is an essential part of what it means to think like an economist.

Bicchieri's work shows the power of solving for the equilibrium. Her entire account of social norms is built around the concept of an equilibrium. It helps her develop an analysis that's clean, neat, powerful, and sometimes surprising. It's a great example of what can happen when you think like an economist.

Maybe you too desire social change. If you do, you have reason to solve for the equilibrium as well. If the situation or scenario that you wish to see is not an equilibrium, you may find it hard to get there – and almost impossible to stay.

Economics as social science

The economics of social norms illustrates something else that's important about economics: the way in which it is a *social* science. The word 'economics' has Greek roots, relating to household management. We still use 'economy' to refer to the way in which resources are managed – whether within a household or within the larger community.[13] The aim of modern economics is to explain and predict economic phenomena. The phenomena tend to be features of *groups* of people. The groups could be families, businesses, non-profits, markets, and the like. They could also be entire countries – or the whole world. Consider economic growth, GDP, unemployment rates, interest rates, etc. They're all properties of a country, region, or community. It would make no sense to talk about *my* unemployment rate or *yours*. You and I can be employed, or not. But an unemployment *rate* has to do with groups: it is the number of unemployed people in a group divided by the total number of people in the group.

The story about social norms is a story about social things: the rules and practices that govern the behaviour of people living in societies. It explains why people in one place and time act one way, whereas other people in another time and place act another way. Like the economics of poverty, it does not assume that every difference at the level of groups must reflect some corresponding difference at the level of individuals. It describes norms, rules, and practices as genuinely social phenomena. The fact that economics is a social science is explicit in definitions of the discipline, by the way. Some definitions make reference to individual choices. But those definitions go on to specify that economics covers the consequences of such choices for the economy as a whole.

It might come as a surprise, then, that modern economics is often described as *individualist*. There is a sense in which economics is indeed individualist. The way the term is normally used, individualism is the view that all explanations of group-level phenomena must ultimately be in terms of the behaviours and attitudes of the individuals in the group. This is called 'methodological' individualism. Bicchieri's story about norms is individualist in this sense. At the end of the day, she wants to explain what norms are and how they change over time in terms of individual preferences and behaviours. It is possible to think of norms as something that cannot be explained in such a way. For example, you can think of norms as existing independently of human beings. Such explanations can capture the force with which norms constrain individual behaviour. But they have trouble accommodating changing norms – in particular, norms that change because individual expectations change. And, as we know, social norms can collapse, and quickly too.

But none of this means that economics is not a social science. Economics recognizes that people are part of social networks, that those networks influence behaviour, and that individual decisions are interdependent. These insights are all built into the theory. Game theory is used as the foundation for so much of modern economics precisely because people's behaviour is interdependent. Game theory tells us the behaviour of a group is not simply the sum of individual behaviour. In fact, the story says that two groups that are exactly identical in every way may end up behaving very differently.

Hope and change

The economics of social norms recognizes that humans sometimes do very bad things and for very long periods of time – but also that they are able to change, sometimes dramatically and quickly. The theory tells us how we can effect social change, and thereby promote human rights and human flourishing. It points out that some efforts that might come naturally to us in the face of entrenched antisocial behaviour are unlikely to work, and will yield only frustration. But it also offers actionable advice about how best to encourage people, groups, and societies to improve.

Although individualist, in a technical sense, the story is based on the recognition that humans are social beings, part of a densely woven fabric of human relations. The economics of social norms gives us a powerful reason to do the right thing – whether we're talking about littering, voting, or avoiding corruption. Pro-social actions may have direct, salutary effects on the cleanliness of the environment, level of corruption in government, and election outcomes. But the indirect effects on *other people*'s behaviour are important too. Indeed, they can swamp the direct ones. Other people's behaviour depends on their expectations about my behaviour and attitudes. You and I both have reason to act in such a way that we reinforce the expectations that we want other people to have.

By explaining norms ultimately in terms of individual behaviours and attitudes, economics allows individuals to be in charge of their destiny. Bad norms are ultimately propped up by *us*, as individuals. We don't have to do that. The story about social norms can inspire hope, even in the face of harmful norms and practices that have been in place for centuries. If the economics of poverty can inspire a certain measure of compassion, and the economics of parenting a certain degree of tolerance, the economics of norms offers a degree of hope that rapid social change is sometimes not only desirable – but also possible.

5

How to Give People What They Need

On 22 February 2022, surgeons at the Cleveland Clinic removed a kidney from my friend Deb. She wasn't sick, and there was nothing wrong with her kidney. It had served her well for just short of seventy-two years already. It didn't have to be removed, and the surgeons hadn't asked her to. Deb had volunteered for the procedure. She had two reasons. One, there was somebody else who needed her kidney more than she did because his own kidneys were failing. She and the recipient didn't live in the same state, and they had never met. Deb's kidney was expected to give him many years of life – and high-quality life to boot. The second reason was that Deb has a granddaughter who needs a kidney. Deb would gladly have donated directly, but the two aren't compatible. Her granddaughter's body would reject Deb's kidney, and the entire process would be for naught. By donating to a stranger, Deb can increase the chances that her granddaughter finds her own match. She says she's started thinking of herself as 'grandma spare parts'.

Human kidneys are in screechingly short supply. At the time of writing, there are some 92,000 people on the waiting list in the US alone.[1] Many of them will die before they find a donor. Kidneys can be recovered from the recently departed: people who, when they were alive, consented to donating their organs – or at least did not expressly refuse to do so – after their death.[2] But there are nowhere near enough deceased kidney-donors to go round. This is where living donors come in. Most people need only one kidney to live a full, long life. They could donate one of their healthy kidneys to a person who has none. Some people donate a kidney simply out of the goodness of their heart. Such donations are called 'altruistic'. Some people donate to a specific person. Such donations are called 'directed'. This scenario typically involves a relative (or even friend) who volunteers a kidney to save a loved one. Directed donations have a complication, though. Like Deb and her granddaughter, the prospective donor and recipient are not necessarily compatible. As a result, there are people out there who are willing to donate but who cannot, and many, many people who need a donation but who can't get one.

In economics speak, the problem is one of inefficiency. It's not just an abstract problem. People are dying because of it. Inefficiencies really get economists fired up. Economists talk about 'Pareto inefficiency', after the early twentieth-century Italian economist Vilfredo Pareto.[3] A situation is Pareto inefficient when it is possible to make at least one person better off without making anybody else worse off. That's true for the kidneys. If we figure out a way to make one more donation possible, we can help two people along without harming anybody else. The donor, who is willing to donate a kidney if it could save a life, and the recipient, one of the thousands and thousands of people who need a kidney to survive and who faces the prospect of never getting one. You can think of the problem as a mismatch. A major reason why economists talk so much about Pareto efficiency is that it is relatively uncontroversial. If it really is possible to improve one or more people's lives without harming anybody in the process, doing so will often be desirable. Few people would have grounds for complaint, anyway.

One economist who got fired up by the kidney situation was Alvin E. Roth. At the time, he was teaching at the University of Pittsburgh, down the street from Deb's house. He sought a smarter way to distribute kidneys available for donation. He also wanted to inspire more people to donate. The key was to develop a scheme that would incentivize healthy people like Deb to donate by linking her donation with increased chances that her loved one could get a kidney too. Roth decided to attack the problem with the entire economics toolkit: from formal modelling to laboratory experiments. He developed a system that allocates kidneys more efficiently. He worked with transplant surgeons and other medical professionals to implement it. Roth tells the story in *Who Gets What – and Why*, a highly readable book that offers a fascinating peek into his work and mindset.[4]

Roth has helped build an entire subdiscipline of economics. *Market design* – or, more broadly, *mechanism design* – asks a simple question: 'How can we build markets (or mechanisms) that make good things happen?' The 'good things' could be anything, but often involve giving people something they need: a kidney, a home, an educational opportunity, etc. In a way, market design inverts the work order of traditional economics. Economists often ask questions such as this: 'Given a market of a certain kind, what do we expect to happen and how good or bad is it?' Market design turns the question round. Instead of starting off with a market of a certain kind and asking what will happen, market designers start off with what you *want* to happen and ask: 'What kind of market (or mechanism) would deliver this outcome?'

If you think about it, there are many situations where you can't legally go out and buy what you need – even if you have the money. A kidney is just one of many such items. A job is another. You can't just go work as an astronaut, no matter how much you want to. You have to be hired. Educational opportunities too. You can't just go enrol your child in the most prestigious primary school, no matter how much you'd like to. Your child has to be admitted. Situations like this are a lot like getting married. You can't just marry your favourite singer or film star. They have to agree to marry you first. These sorts of situations are called *matching problems*. Assuming bribes are out of the question, you can have one of these things only when the person or people on the other side of the market reciprocates. Matching problems don't necessarily solve themselves, as the organ shortage illustrates. Their solution is a mechanism that helps people find their match. Such mechanisms are called *matching markets.* Market design looks for solutions to matching problems.

It's not as though market design is a brand-new activity. Humans have exchanged things since before recorded history. Organized markets and bazaars in which exchanges took place have existed for almost as long. In a way, all of us have experience with mechanism design. You know the common system of dividing up a cake between two kids? Ask the first to cut the cake in two roughly equal pieces. Ask the second to choose first. When kids proceed in this way, the two pieces are as similar in size as they could possibly be, and both kids are happy. So are you, since the potential for conflict has been eliminated. Notice how this works. You lay down the rules. The kids maximize their share ruthlessly. The outcome is both equitable and fair – and experienced as such by everyone involved. This is a good mechanism.

Although the basic concept is old, the method is new. Mechanism design has taught us a lot about how markets work. It's led to multiple Nobel awards. More importantly, it's made the world a better place – one market at a time. Economists' solutions have given regular people work and educational opportunities by the boatload. Not the least, market designers have saved thousands of lives.

A mechanism for kidneys

Deb's daughter Wendy – herself a professor at the University of Pittsburgh – also donated a kidney. Her reasons were similar to Deb's. She says she feels 'fortunate' to have been able to help a stranger get a new lease of life. Wendy's donation, though, didn't benefit just one person. It set in motion a series of transplants that ended up giving *three people* unknown to her new kidneys. How is this even possible, when she didn't have more than one kidney to give? Al Roth is how.

Roth got his PhD in operations research at Stanford. Operations research is about organizations – how they're managed and how they can be managed better. He was puzzled by the fact that the discipline focused so much on *things*, rather than people. It described in great detail how inputs and outputs moved around factories and warehouses. It offered formal models that represented how things flow around and how such flows could be optimized. But Roth felt that it overlooked the people involved: their goals and purposes – and how success and failure can depend on having the right person in the right place at the right time. He was drawn to game theory because it focuses on the roles played by the people involved. In particular, he liked how game theory explores the ways in which people organize themselves to accomplish their goals – and the ways in which they fail to do so.

Roth had spent time playing around with a formal model developed by two older game theorists: Lloyd Shapley and Herb Scarf.[5] The model imagined a world in which there were *indivisible* goods. These are things of value that can be exchanged but which cannot be divided up between people the way a gallon of milk can. Much of economics is focused on *commodity markets*, in which it is generally assumed that goods are infinitely divisible – divisible in infinitely small shares. So the sort of situation Shapley and Scarf were studying was rather different. They imagined that everyone had one unit, that everyone wanted one unit, but that not everyone wanted the unit they happened to have. The model was a purely intellectual endeavour, in the sense that the authors didn't have an application in mind. To have a language in which to describe their results, Shapley and Scarf called the goods 'houses'. Houses that people live in are roughly indivisible, and each household needs about one residence, so that worked – kind of. But Shapley and Scarf weren't really interested in real estate. That was not the point.

Roth's central insight was that the model captures the kidney situation perfectly. Just think of each donor–recipient pair as one unit. Let the 'houses' be kidneys. Each pair has one kidney to spare. Each pair also needs one kidney. In the best case the donor and

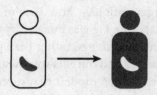

Figure 1: Kidney donation

recipient are compatible. Then the donor can offer their kidney to the recipient. Figure 1 shows this situation, although not in an anatomically correct manner. The individual on the left (drawn in outline) has one kidney more than they need to live a long, full life. The individual on the right (drawn in solid) needs one. The pair is satisfied with what they have.

Not every donor–recipient pair is compatible, however. Such a pair still *has* one kidney. It still *needs* one kidney. But the pair cannot make do with the kidney that it has. (If the donor and recipient were compatible, they wouldn't be in the market for another kidney; the donation would already have taken place.) To make things more interesting, Shapley and Scarf's model assumed that it was, for whatever reason, impossible to exchange 'houses' for money. That's not true for actual residences, which are bought and sold for sometimes astronomical sums. But it *is* true for kidneys, because most countries have made it illegal to buy and sell human kidneys. The reason is moral. People across the world feel that some things should not be bought and sold and that markets for such goods should not exist. Roth calls such unacceptable markets *repugnant*.[6] Which specific markets are repugnant differs by region, but in most places it is likely to include such disparate things as drugs, sex, dog meat for human consumption – and human body parts. Giving up a kidney for free is widely considered acceptable, and having your expenses covered is fine too. But getting money in exchange for the kidney is not.

Roth's insight meant that a formal model that used not to have an economic application suddenly did. This, in turn, meant that the model could be interpreted as applying to the real world. And all the formal results became at least potentially applicable to real-world problems.

Shapley and Scarf had been studying various ways in which you could effect an exchange that would leave people better off than they were before, without harming anybody else in the process. The most obvious way to do so is to find two pairs, each of which is willing to trade their house for the other's. Suppose the Joneses like the Smiths' house more than they like their own, and vice versa. The Joneses and Smiths could just swap. The swap would leave both better off, and it wouldn't harm the Muhammads, Berkovitzes, or Jansens. It would be a *Pareto improvement*.

Figure 2 shows this situation for kidney donations. The pair on the left has a kidney that the pair on the right could use, and the other way around. The donor on the left offers a kidney to the recipient on the right, while the donor on the right offers a kidney to the recipient on the left. The swap leaves both pairs better off.

In other cases, no two-way exchange would be possible. But! You could find a situation where the Muhammads like the Berkovitzes' house, the Berkovitzes like the Jansens', and the Jansens like the Muhammads'. In such a case, you could effect an exchange involving

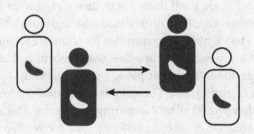

Figure 2: Two-way kidney exchange

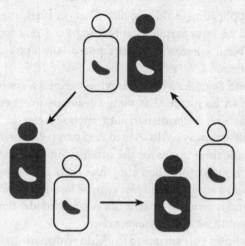

Figure 3: Kidney donation cycle

all three. That kind of exchange is called a *trading cycle*. It too would be a Pareto improvement. Figure 3 shows what this looks like in the case of kidneys. The figure shows three pairs. No pair can make do with the kidney that it has. No two-way exchange is possible. But there is a solution where the pair on the bottom-left offers a kidney to the pair on the bottom-right, which offers one to the pair on the top, which in turn offers one to the pair on the bottom-left. Cycles can theoretically be of any size, involving any number of donors and recipients.

This model made Roth think about developing what he calls 'the potential architecture for a centralized clearinghouse'. The clearing-house helps to identify opportunities for kidney exchanges.[7] You'd just need to know who's compatible with whom, and so on. If you have enough donor–recipient pairs, you can identify opportunities for exchanges and cycles. These cycles can involve three or more pairs. And they would all be Pareto improvements. The architecture provides a solution to the inefficiency that we've discussed. With the proper system for allocating available kidneys, Roth could make trading cycles happen in the real world. And in principle there is no limit to how large they can be.

The architecture of such a system is not totally obvious, however. Roth had to think through all the different ways in which things could go wrong. One problem is that a donor–recipient pair may refuse to participate in whatever trading cycle the system proposes. The pair may find a better one, and decide to participate in that one instead. Suppose you propose a trading cycle involving the Muhammads, the Berkovitzes, and the Jansens. You're scheduling the surgeries as we speak. But now the Jansens find another set of pairs who could be part of another cycle, and the kidney they would get in that transaction is, for whatever reason, preferable to them. You should expect the Jansens to pull out of your cycle, leaving the Muhammads and Berkovitzes stranded. That's not good. The situation would be unstable. It would be *unsafe* for surgeons to proceed, since one or more of the pairs could defect at any time.

Roth realized that the formal model could help solve the problem. Shapley and Scarf had proven that you can always find a set of trading cycles such that no donor–recipient pairs would have any interest in defecting. Shapley and Scarf called them 'top trading cycles'. And you can find a set of top trading cycles no matter how many donor–recipient pairs there are, and whatever preferences they have. It's a neat formal result. But it's also useful. If you just make sure that your architecture proposes top trading cycles, and only such cycles, you can guarantee that nobody will defect. The cycle would be safe, in the relevant sense. Surgeons could proceed.

There's another problem, though. The clearinghouse needs a lot of information about the donor–recipient pairs, their needs and preferences. A clearinghouse without that information won't be able to propose the most desirable cycles. The relevant information is held by patients and their doctors. The only way to secure this information is to ask them. But patients and doctors might worry about saying too much. They might be concerned that information they provide will be used against them, and that they will end up with a less desirable kidney as a result. If that's the case, people will keep their cards close to their chest. And the clearinghouse will not be able to secure the information required to work.

Roth had to solve this problem himself. And he did. He was able to show formally that it's possible to design the clearinghouse in such a way that patients and doctors have nothing to lose by revealing all relevant information. By designing the clearinghouse accordingly, the system is safe in another sense. It is safe for patients and doctors to be completely forthcoming about their needs and preferences. Doing so will never harm them. Because it's in their interest to provide the information required for the clearinghouse to make them part of a trading cycle, they will, and the clearinghouse will work.

Roth and his collaborators also explored the possibility of integrating people who had a kidney but didn't need one. That includes both altruistic and deceased donors. Such 'non-directed' donors made it possible to construct *chains* rather than cycles. A chain is an exchange that starts with a non-directed donor, involves any number of donor–recipient pairs, and terminates with a donation to someone on the waiting list. Figure 4 shows what this looks like. The non-directed donor is over on the right. They offer a kidney to the first pair, which offers a kidney to the second pair, and so on, until the chain ends with a recipient who's not part of a pair. Again, there is no theoretical limit to how long the chain can be.

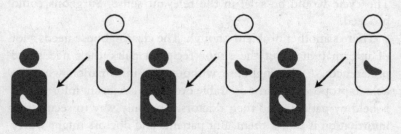

Figure 4: Kidney donation chain

Figure 4, incidentally, describes the chain that Wendy initiated. With her non-directed donation, the clearinghouse identified two more donors and three recipients who could be part of a chain. Although Wendy wasn't born with four kidneys, her donation could help three people in desperate need.

Now Roth and his team had an architecture for a clearinghouse that would take patient needs and preferences as inputs, and generate safe and efficient cycles and chains as outputs.

Having figured out formally how to design a well-operating clearinghouse, it remained only to convince transplant surgeons and other medical professionals to implement it. This bit turned out to be tricky. 'Doctors don't automatically think of economists as fellow members of the helping professions,' Roth notes.[8] I'm sure he's right. Trust in economists could be higher.

They had some success. A collaboration with a Harvard surgeon, who was also the medical director of the New England Organ Bank, helped build something called the New England Program for Kidney Exchange (NEPKE). It was established in 2004. It involved fourteen kidney transplant centres in New England, and it sought to identify as many matches as possible. The NEPKE worked, in the sense that it successfully matched compatible donors and recipients. But even so, the programme only led to two-way exchanges. Many more complex exchanges that could have happened didn't. The main reason was logistics. Even a relatively simple two-way exchange required four separate operating theatres and transplant teams operating in tandem. Many things could go wrong. Trading cycles would be a logistical nightmare. As long as all the surgeries had to be done at the same time, larger cycles and chains were unlikely to happen.

Do transplants have to be done at the same time? They don't. You could, in principle, complete a trading cycle one donation at a time. That would require only two operating theatres acting in tandem: one for the donor and one for the recipient. But there is a problem. With non-simultaneous donations, there's always a chance that one of the donors pulls out of the chain or cycle, thereby ending the cycle or chain. And then a potential recipient could really be out of luck. Suppose the Jones donor offers a kidney to the Smith recipient today, expecting the Smith donor to offer a kidney to the Jones recipient tomorrow, completing the two-way exchange. But tomorrow, the Smith donor reneges. There's not a transplant surgeon in the country who will extract the kidney tomorrow against Smith's wishes. The Smiths are happy: the recipient got a kidney and the donor still has two. But the Joneses are really out of luck. The recipient still needs one, and the donor lost one, meaning they will not be able to participate in any future exchanges. As long as a donor–recipient pair risks being hung out to dry, they are unlikely to participate.

You can probably guess what happened next. Roth asked himself whether it would be possible to tweak the architecture of the clearinghouse to avoid this sort of scenario. He figured out the answer was yes. *Provided* the process starts with a non-directed donor, it is possible to schedule a sequence of donations that avoids the problem. The solution is to start with the non-directed donor and then schedule every donor–recipient pair so that they receive a kidney before they donate one. The chain could still be broken. But nobody would be hung out to dry. A broken chain would leave the last pair better off – not worse off – than they were before. The recipient would have the kidney that they needed, and the donor would still have two. And pairs who would not get a new kidney as part of that trading chain would still have one to donate.

Getting medical centres onboard was harder. NEPKE wasn't yet willing to go ahead with the non-simultaneous transplants, even after the clearinghouse had been tweaked. It can be risky to go first. And the NEPKE was concerned about bad publicity and lawsuits in the event that a chain was broken. A team in Ohio were willing to give it a shot. Something called the Alliance for Paired Donation (APD) was already coordinating exchanges there. It was open to trying exchanges that didn't happen at the same time. The

APD got the ball rolling with the help of an altruistic donor from Michigan. His name was Matt Jones. The chain that started with his donation went on – and on – for several years. It ultimately involved sixteen transplants. It ended when a donor gave a kidney to a person on the waiting list – a person who didn't have anyone who could donate.

After the initial success, and the positive press it generated, the tide turned. Roth calls it 'a revolution'.[9] He writes:

> Kidney exchange has become a standard method of transplant-ation in the United States and is growing around the world. As experience accumulates, the evidence grows that potentially long nonsimultaneous chains are good for kidney patients, and *particularly* good for the hardest-to-match patients. Thousands of transplants have been accomplished that wouldn't otherwise have been possible. In recent years, a majority of these have been through chains.[10]

One benefit of chains is that they have increased the number of available kidneys. Before kidney exchanges were established, an altruistic donor such as Matt could help exactly one person. With kidney exchanges, an altruistic donor can start a chain reaction that helps dozens or more people. When you increase the number of people an altruistic donor can save, you also increase the incentives to donate.[11] If your kidney saves one life, that's good. For many prospective donors, that's good enough. But saving dozens of lives is much, much better. There may well be donors who aren't moved by the prospect of saving one life, but who are moved by the prospect of saving (say) thirty. The exchange has the additional benefit of making more kidneys available for donation. If you, or somebody you know, might be interested in becoming a living donor, like Deb and Wendy, google 'become a living donor' or go to the website in this endnote.[12]

A couple of years later, Shapley and Roth shared the 2012 Nobel

Award 'for the theory of stable allocations and the practice of market design'.[13]

Making good things happen

The kidney exchange is only one example of matching problems that Roth and colleagues have helped solve. In other work, he's asked: 'How can we help new medical doctors find the residency – their first employment opportunity – of their dreams, and also hospitals to recruit the best possible employees?' His solution was another clearinghouse, referred to as 'The Match'.[14] This clearinghouse takes into account the fact that many doctors are partnered with other doctors, and helps them find employment nearby. In this way, it also helps them form families and live happily ever after. He has also explored school choice, asking: 'How can you make sure that schoolchildren end up in the school in which they are most likely to flourish?'[15] The result was a brand-new system for high-school choice in New York City. Roth says it's still 'holding up well'.

Perhaps the most famous example of mechanism design is the *spectrum auction*.[16] A vast number of corporations and organizations want to use some portion of the airwave spectrum. The telecommunications industry is highly dependent on access to the spectrum, for example. The problem is that not everyone can use the same segment of the spectrum at the same time. If they did, the segment would be useless. So there has to be some coordination. There must be a way to allocate the spectrum among alternative users – making sure that only one user employs a given segment at a time. Until the early 1980s, the US used an administrative hearing process. Potential users could petition the government and, after a lengthy process the government would allocate licences to use the spectrum in what seemed to them a sensible way. The process was slow, costly, cumbersome, and opaque. In 1982, the US instead adopted a system of lotteries, in which anyone could apply and licences were allocated randomly. This was much quicker. You could argue that lotteries are fairer too, since everyone has an equal chance of getting a licence. However, licences are valuable. Some companies would participate even though they didn't need a licence themselves, only to sell it for a profit to someone who did. Once the economists got involved, they organized an auction in which licences were given to the highest bidder. The first such auction took place in 1994. Since then, auctions allocating radio frequencies and landing slots at airports have brought vast sums of money into government coffers, without raising taxes on anyone or anything. No less importantly, the auctions are designed to maximize social benefit, and not just government revenue.

Robert Wilson and Paul Milgrom were two of the economists leading this effort, which required both theoretical, formal work, and more practical efforts. The two shared the 2020 Nobel Award. 'Their discoveries are of great benefit to society,' the Prize Committee noted.[17]

Markets that work, and markets that don't

Some markets work well. Some markets don't. When markets function poorly, Roth believes, the explanation may have to do with bad design.[18] The rules that govern the exchange may be ill suited for the purpose. If so, the solution to the problem may well be a better design. Sometimes there is no market at all. Then, the solution may be a brand-new market with appropriate rules. But in order to build well-functioning marketplaces in the real world, we need to know a lot about markets. We need to know when they work, when they don't, and, most importantly, what can be done to improve them.

Market designers have, in fact, learned a great deal about markets in general. Here are some of Roth's insights.[19] The insights are built on the interplay between formal, theoretical work and practical efforts to design exchanges that solve real problems.

One, well-functioning markets are *thick*. That means there is a sufficient number of participants on both sides of the market. If there are too few sellers, or too few buyers, it may be difficult or impossible to find good matches. Without good matches, mutually advantageous exchanges are unlikely to happen. In order to get a workable kidney exchange off the ground, you need a sufficiently large number of donors. You also need a sufficiently large number of recipients. Only then do you have a chance of identifying cycles and chains that help large numbers of people. One way to ensure that the market is thick, Roth points out, is to regulate the times when trades may take place. Exchanges from farmers' markets to stock exchanges have regular hours, ensuring (among other things) that the market remains thick during operation.

Two, well-functioning markets are *uncongested*, meaning that it is possible to complete transactions relatively quickly. If it takes too long to identify and evaluate suitable options, or if it takes too long to close a deal, markets get clogged up in the economic equivalent of a traffic jam. With congestion, participants may find themselves accepting bad deals, or not making any deals at all. In markets where people make decisions about life and death, like the kidney exchanges, congestion courts disaster. To avoid congestion, markets should be organized in such a way that participants quickly can get a sense for what the options are, evaluate which is better, and close the deal.

Three, well-functioning markets are *safe* and *simple*. That means that people should be comfortable participating in the market. It means that participants shouldn't fear truthfully revealing information about themselves, their needs and preferences. It also means that market participants should have no reason to deviate from whatever allocation the market proposes. In the case of the kidney exchanges, ideally, there should be no scenario where a donor or recipient regrets participating in the market. It should always be in their interest to participate, and to truthfully reveal private information about their health status, needs, and preferences.

Insights like these can be beneficial in a wide range of situations. At the time of writing, many countries are struggling to get people vaccinated against Covid-19 and monkeypox. The first problem, of course, is limited supply. Many countries have very limited access to vaccines. If vaccines are unavailable or unaffordable, obviously people will not be vaccinated. But supply is not the only problem. People eligible for vaccination have to be matched with a clinic or other health-care provider able to vaccinate. This means that we're looking at a classic matching problem. Anecdotally, many countries have failed to organize this matching market in a way that's thick, uncongested, safe, and simple. A market designer involved in the process could have improved things considerably, while avoiding congestion and all the rest.

Economics, markets, and values

Market design tells us a great deal about economics. When economists tell you they study markets, they don't mean just stock markets, real-estate markets, and the like. They mean all sorts of things. That includes matching markets. Matching markets are involved when people decide where to send their kids to school, get a date, commit to get married, get a job, join a sorority or fraternity, or find a clinic where they can get a Covid vaccine. These markets do not necessarily involve money, although they sometimes do. Economists might tell you they study humankind in the ordinary business of life. They don't mean business in the sense of commercial enterprise. They mean, effectively, anything that occupies us – anything we're engaged in. Economics has a very broad remit.

Market design also tells us a great deal about economists' attitudes to markets.[20] It is true that economists often favour using markets as a way to distribute things of value. But the fact that they favour markets doesn't mean that they want to handle everything in a commodity market, where everything has a price and where everything ends up in the hands of the highest bidder. Although economists sometimes talk about 'free' markets, this doesn't mean markets that aren't governed by any rules and regulations. *All* markets follow some rules and regulations. The rules may have been supplied by the government. The rules may have been supplied by industry or other private entities. They could have emerged 'spontaneously', meaning without being the result of conscious design. If the existing rules and regulations work, that's great. If they don't, there's a good chance the operation of the market can be improved by means of better design. 'Our work', Roth says, 'gives us new insights into what really makes "free markets" free to work properly.'

Market design demonstrates the value of the entire economist's toolkit, including formal, theoretical modelling. Even the most abstract, formal work can turn out to be directly and immediately relevant to improving people's lives. Shapley and Scarf's story about how to distribute indivisible goods was developed as a purely intellectual exercise, without any specific application in mind. And yet that turned out to be the foundation for the entire kidney exchange. In conjunction with careful study of a real, concrete market, formal modelling enabled thousands of kidney donations to take place. This illustrates how even relatively obscure and highly technical subdisciplines of economics can suddenly be highly relevant. The story is not unlike that of Boolean logic, which started off as a branch of mathematics but ended up being the foundation for all modern computing. Sometimes you just can't know where things are heading.

Market design also sheds light on the role of values in economics. Market design, like much of economics, is very obviously based on values. This is true in at least two ways. First, market designers need to be responsive to the values of the community in which they operate. A matching market won't be perceived as safe and simple to the participants unless it respects their fundamental values. Economists need to pay attention, and at least sometimes incorporate those values in their work. If people consider trade in kidneys repugnant, economists might have to treat those values as a constraint on their proposals.

Second, market design is explicitly aimed at making the world a better place. Market designers are do-gooders. They go about their work in a way that differs from a long history of preachers and reformers who promote moral and intellectual edification. Market designers are not trying to make people more moral. They're not trying to make people smarter or more rational. They take for granted that people will remain fundamentally the same – on the assumption that improving them is either impossible, inappropriate, or undesirable. Instead, they try to build an environment in which people can attain their goals safely and simply. You can think of market design as a modern form of social engineering, if you want. Market design shows that economists don't treat any given market as the final and perfect form. The outcome of market processes is not determined by pure laws of nature. It's not unchangeable. Some markets work; some don't. The ones that don't can be redesigned to work better. Anyway, some people want to rid social science in general, and economics in particular, of all values. But there is no value-free way to try to make the world a better place.

Such a design is not in and of itself going to save the world. It's not the solution to every problem, and it's not guaranteed to work. But it is a useful tool and, when combined with appropriate values, can fix real problems. Like Deb and Wendy, market design can help you save lives. One day, it might save your own.

6

How to Be Happy

In 2015, my family and I faced a dilemma. We were living in the outer suburbs of Washington, DC. We were expecting twins and my employer had just declined my request for paternal leave. The university had recently rebranded itself a 'well-being university'. Its commitment to well-being extended to free yoga lessons on the quad, not parental leave, apparently. Suddenly, I had job offers from my native Sweden, which grants parents of twins a total of 660 days of parental leave to share between them. (That's about twenty-two months, so a lot more than nothing.)

The thing was, we were doing fine in the DC area. Salaries in the US are much higher than in Sweden. Homes are larger, and we happened to live in a particularly beautiful one in a wooded area. Smart and pleasant colleagues made for a stimulating work environment. We had many friends nearby, and loved the vibrant intellectual, cultural, and culinary scene in and around Washington. There was always something to do.

Moving continents with a young family is a big deal. You know the decision will have massively life-altering consequences. But you don't know which. The consequences reach far into the future and are hard to predict. The uncertainties involved gave me a degree of decision paralysis. I expected having outside job offers to feel great. Instead, I felt miserable and exasperated. I started feeling guilty too, anticipating that I would inevitably have to disappoint some current or potential colleagues when I turned down their offer.

One of my doctoral dissertations was on the science of happiness. It seemed natural to try to make the decision on the basis of what I had learned in my research. I had already received my doctoral degree, but this decision was a real test of the science – and my understanding of it.

So, my wife and I constructed lists of the major differences and tried to assess what the science of happiness would say about them. A life in the US would come with more money, a bigger house, more cars, etc. By contrast, a life in Sweden would come with less money, a smaller apartment, and no car. A wealth of research in happiness studies suggests the additional money would yield only modest happiness gains, given our position in the income distribution. A life in the US would also come with much longer commutes – necessarily by car – whereas in Sweden we expected to be able to bike to work. A long commute is known to be a massive downer, whereas exposure to nature, exercise, and fresh air are uppers. Sweden offered more leisure time and parental leave, which would allow for a better work–life balance and a more equitable distribution of the joys and burdens of having three kids. We'd also live closer to the kids' grandparents. In all, the science of happiness suggested that a life in Sweden would, for us, be a happier life for the whole family.

Reviewing the advantages and disadvantages to a life on either side of the Atlantic, then, we decided to make the move. We had no way of knowing whether we'd made the right decision. I joked at the time that if this did not work out, I'd want my time and money back.

In the end, I'd say it was the right call. We have no regrets.

The basic method we used was proposed by Benjamin Franklin back in 1772.[1] Franklin said to take a sheet of paper, divide it into two columns by drawing a line right down the middle, and write 'pro' over the one column and 'con' over the other. (People nowadays call it a T-chart, because it resembles that letter.) List all the reasons *for* whatever decision is preoccupying you in the left column, and all the reasons *against* in the right one. Try to determine how weighty the various reasons are. Finally, check to see which side has more cumulative weight on it. The only difference in our case is that we assigned weights to reasons based on a science of happiness that Franklin could only dream about.

The good news is that everyone can do what we did. You can't use our *answer*, necessarily. We did not try to figure out what's best for everyone. We were certainly not interested in figuring out which country is 'better'. The question was which of two options would be best *for us*. But you can use our method – which is basically just Franklin's with a modern twist. All you need to make a decision is a pen, a piece of paper, and some knowledge of the economics of happiness.

Economists have been applying this sort of thinking for many decades. They've used it to answer questions about how we, as individuals, can lead happier lives. They've also used it to answer questions about how to build a happier world – a world more fit for human flourishing. If you expect economists to be all about money, or to promote the interests of the ruling class, you're in for a surprise. Economists have drawn the conclusion that many of us should work less, make less money, and enjoy more leisure. They have also argued for a more equal society. Some say we should be more like Robin Hood – if not taking from the rich, at least giving to the poor.

As always, economics does not offer a one-size-fits-all solution. But the economics of happiness is customizable, allowing you to adapt it to your circumstances.

The economics of happiness

Hornell Hart was Professor of Sociology at Duke University in North Carolina around the middle of the last century. He had a conviction that being happy was one of 'the basic purposes of mankind'. He also had a question: 'Can recent advances in scientific thinking tells us more and more effectively what to do in order to be happy, and in order to help make our fellow human beings happy?'[2] And he had an answer: he thought it was *yes*. He wrote a whole book, *Chart for Happiness*, to prove it.

Hart was particularly impressed with the way in which fever thermometers and other instruments had been used to diagnose illnesses and promote public health. What the pursuit of happiness lacked, Hart thought, was a sort of thermometer for human happiness. So he developed one. He called it the *Euphorimeter*. It measures happiness on a scale in *Euphor-units*. Hart thought the Euphorimeter would help 'relieve maladjustments, promote the cure of mental suffering, and open the way toward more joyous living'.[3] He proposed using the instrument to track people's happiness over time, and to figure out not just what people *think* makes them happy – but what really does.

Hart's contributions are largely forgotten now. But the project he envisioned lives on. The serious scientific study of happiness has seen a meteoric rise over the course of the last few decades. Although Hart was a sociologist, the science of happiness was always interdisciplinary. It can be traced back to the 1920s and 30s, when educational psychologists started asking questions about whether education improves happiness.[4] The thread was picked up in the 1950s and 60s by epidemiologists, who decided they didn't just want to know who was ill, but also who was happy – and why.

The systematic study of happiness appeared on economists' radar in the 1970s. That's when an economist called Richard A. Easterlin explored how happiness relates to economic growth.[5] Easterlin noted that within a society, at a given point in time, the rich were decidedly happier than the poor. But when a society became richer over time, even in periods of explosive economic growth, the happiness score of that society as a whole barely budged – or at least didn't rise as much as one might have expected. This phenomenon is now known as the *Easterlin paradox*. It has generated a vast literature. The economics of happiness has become a full-fledged subdiscipline of modern economics. Many economists incorporate happiness data in their work. It helps that happiness data are widely available. They're collected both by government agencies and the private sector.

Have we learned anything that points the way towards more joyous living, as Hart thought? We have. And I say that not just because I feel like it worked in my own life.

Most people are happy

It may come as a surprise, but one consistent result is that most people are pretty happy. Hart noticed this phenomenon immediately. As many as 75 per cent of the people he tested scored above zero Euphor-units, meaning that they were more happy than unhappy.[6]

The 2021 *World Happiness Report* shows something similar for countries.[7] The *Report* is a massive undertaking. It tries to take annual snapshots of the happiness across the world. It uses data from the Gallup Corporation, which recruits representative national samples in every country in which it can operate. To assess happiness levels, the report uses a device called Cantril's ladder. The participant is shown a picture of a ladder with eleven rungs. They're told that the highest rung represents the best possible life for them, while the lowest rung represents the worst. They're asked where they currently stand on the ladder. The person's happiness score is the number corresponding to the rung they identify, from 0 at the very bottom to 10 at the top. Out of 149 countries in the survey, 101 countries score above the mid-point.[8] Placid Finland is at the top (with a score of 7.84). The happy countries include the world's most populous one, China (with a score of 5.34). The remaining forty-eight countries score below the mid-point. War-torn Afghanistan is at the bottom (with a score of 2.52).

There's a widespread perception that people in general are miserable. Philosopher Roger Crisp claims there is so much misery that it wouldn't necessarily be bad if humankind suddenly went extinct. He writes: 'Given the amount of suffering on Earth, the value of the continued existence of the planet is an open question.'[9] Crisp offers no systematic evidence about the amount of suffering on Earth. He gets his conclusion by means of a thought experiment. But it's clear he thinks there's a lot of unhappiness. So much that it might be a good thing if we all died.

The science of happiness, by contrast, suggests that there's a lot of happiness in the world. A lot more happiness than unhappiness, for sure. Of course, unhappy people exist – more so in some places than others. And relatively few people score a perfect ten. But the data suggest that the total amount of happiness in the world *vastly* exceeds the total amount of unhappiness.

What does this tell us? I'm not actually arguing with Crisp or his methodology. But I do want to draw a much more optimistic conclusion. The data show that happiness is attainable for most people. And not only that. They show that happiness has already been attained by the vast majority of humans alive today – especially those who live in prosperous areas outside active war zones. Every country in affluent western Europe and North America scores above five in the survey. Better yet: as we will see, the economics of happiness suggests you can be even happier than you already are – by means of a few simple tricks.

Which is the dismal science now?

Can money buy happiness?

You probably expect economists to say that the way to be happier is to make more money. Cash is king, and so on. Is that what they say? The answer is a resounding YES AND NO. Let me explain.

First things first. Yes, money buys happiness. Rich people are happier than poor people. If you're poor and suddenly, magically, become rich, you can expect your happiness to go up – possibly by a lot. There's never really been any serious debate about this among economists. Back in 1974, Easterlin wrote: 'The results are clear and unequivocal. In every single survey, those in the highest status group were happier, on the average, than those in the lowest status groups.'[10] More recent studies agree. In 2008 economists Betsey Stevenson and Justin Wolfers compiled a massive data set and used far more sophisticated statistical techniques. They came to the same conclusion.[11] If you compare a random poor person to a random rich person in some country, the rich one is on average considerably happier than the poor one. Most economists interpret the relationship causally. Provided you're poor to begin with – or at least not already rich – money does in fact buy happiness.

Another thing that all economists agree on is that the amount of happiness you can buy for a dollar goes down as you become richer. As economists would put it, the marginal happiness of money is decreasing. You can think of it graphically. If you draw a graph with income on the horizontal axis and happiness on the vertical one, you'll find that the happiness curve will bend over to the right. It'll be very steep on the left-hand side, where a dollar translates into a great deal of happiness. The curve will get flatter as you move to the right.[12] If you're destitute, a dollar a day can be a matter of life and death. If you're poor, and constantly worry about making ends meet, more money would allow you to pay off some bills and maybe get out of debt – and that would be good for your happiness. If you're rich, a dollar can be a rounding error, with little to no effect.

The big debate among happiness economists concerns whether happiness tops out or not. Some say that it does. They believe there's a point at which the curve becomes completely flat, and more money no longer translates into more happiness. Not even a tiny amount. Such a point is known as a satiation point. Estimates vary, but Nobel laureates Daniel Kahneman and Angus Deaton have floated the number $75,000 for the US.[13] The number is just above the mean household income there. If your family makes more than that in a year, Kahneman and Deaton suggest you're past the satiation point. So they could say that once you're comfortably middle-class, more money does not buy more happiness.

Other economists disagree. They believe that happiness does not top out. At least, they say, there's no evidence that it does. If so, there is no satiation point, and the curve never becomes *completely* flat. Money continues to buy happiness – although less and less per dollar – no matter how rich you are. Stevenson and Wolfers are the most famous proponents of this view.

The debate, then, concerns what the curve looks like way over on the right-hand side. Some say it becomes flat; some say it keeps increasing, though less and less steeply. (Nobody to my knowledge has seriously argued that the happiness curve starts bending down. In case you were wondering.)

There are several reasons why the question has proven intractable. The answer may depend on how happiness is measured. Kahneman and Deaton suggest that measures that tap into people's *feelings* tend to top out, while those measures that tap into people's *evaluations* – like Cantril's ladder – tend not to. There are also more arcane statistical issues involved. I'll spare you the details. We're lucky though. We don't need to worry about this issue here. None of the suggestions below assume that happiness does or does not top out.

Back to the question of fixing the world. How can we use the economics of happiness to make the world a better place, a place more fit for human flourishing?

The most obvious implication is that we should strive to make the world a more equal place if we can. Assume it is true that the marginal happiness of money is decreasing, as everyone thinks. Assume also that you have an extra dollar to give away. Should you give it to a poor person or a rich person? If you want to maximize the total amount of happiness in the world, the economics of happiness suggests you should give it to the poor person. If you're a politician, and you have to choose between an intervention that would benefit the poor and an intervention that would benefit the rich, you would promote happiness by pursuing the former. It may even be justified to redistribute money – Robin Hood-style – by taking from the rich and giving to the poor. This might work, provided the poor person gets happier from gaining a dollar than the rich person gets sad from losing one.

The general argument is ancient. It goes back at least to the classical utilitarians. Jeremy Bentham noted that a king who is a thousand times richer than a labourer is unlikely to be a thousand times happier. He went on: 'The more nearly the actual proportion approaches to equality, the greater will be the total mass of happiness.'[14] If you want to increase 'the total mass of happiness', then, you should take some from the king and give it to the labourer. More recently, a leading behavioural economist was quoted in the *New York Times Magazine* as saying that 'he doesn't see how anybody could study happiness and not find himself leaning left politically', the reason being that 'the data make it all too clear that boosting the living standards of those already comfortable, such as through lower taxes, does little to improve their levels of well-being, whereas raising the living standards of the impoverished makes an enormous difference'.[15] Note that it doesn't matter if the rich have hit their satiation point or not. The argument doesn't assume it. (The argument *does* assume that the intervention does not cause any other harms, which may or may not be true in practice.)

If the job of economists is just to promote the interests of the ruling class, I think we can all agree that they're doing a truly terrible job.

What about our personal lives? Since money buys happiness, does this mean that the way to get happy is to make more money? No, not necessarily.

The answer depends on what you have to sacrifice to get the money. Here's the thing. If you resolve to make more money, you probably can't just will it into existence. (If you can, please give me a call.) You have to *do* something to get the money flowing. You may have to work harder to accelerate the next promotion. You may have to work longer hours, maybe taking on an additional shift. You may have to find a whole new job. Whatever you choose to do, something else has to give. Suppose you decide to work longer hours. Working more may mean less time with your family and kids. It may mean less sleep. It probably means less leisure. Family time, rest, leisure activities – all these things would have (or could have) improved your happiness too. The happiness you could achieve by working more has to be weighed against the happiness you lose when you spend less time with your family, sleep less, and enjoy less leisure.

The stuff you forgo when you work more is what economists call the *opportunity cost* of working. The concept of an opportunity cost is central to modern economics. It should be part of everyone's lexicon. The opportunity cost of something is the next best option – the best thing you forgo when you choose that thing.[16] Economists will tell you that everything has an opportunity cost. No matter what choice you make, there's another choice that you have to reject. If you go to see a movie, there are many other movies that you cannot see at the same time, and a vast number of things you could be doing instead with your time and money. The opportunity cost of seeing a particular movie is the best of all these alternatives. If you want to be rational, you have to pay attention to opportunity costs. It's rational to work more only if the benefits of doing so exceed the benefits of whatever else you could be doing with your time.

If you're poor and bored and have more time on your hands than you can handle, the benefits of accepting a new job are likely to be high and the opportunity costs low. You should take the job, if you can. If you're rich and overworked and wish you could spend more time with your family, the benefits of working more hours are likely to be small and the opportunity cost high. You should probably work less, if that's an option. Even if money buys happiness at all levels of income, it's not necessarily true that you should work more if you want to be happier. Economics might even tell you that you should work less. It may be in your interest to accept the lower income – if doing so allows you to enjoy the benefits of family time, relaxation, and leisure activities.

When economists have looked at what happens to people's happiness when they work more, they've found it's often bad. The effect depends on individual circumstances and personal preferences, as I've said. But often enough, on average, more work comes with less happiness. Economists Lonnie Golden and Barbara Wiens-Tuers, for example, found that working overtime comes with 'increased work stress, fatigue and work–family interference'.[17] When people have to work overtime, the positive effects of making extra money are more than offset by the negative effects. Relatedly, Lucía Macchia and Ashley V. Whillans constructed a data set of 220,000 people in seventy-nine countries.[18] They found that places where people value leisure more than work are happier, at both the country and individual level. That included the Netherlands, Australia, and the UK.

Maybe you ask: 'Where does this leave *me*?' 'What should *I* do?' Well, like Bryan Caplan, I'm here to provide information, not run your life. But the economics of happiness can help. If you're contemplating working longer hours, you can use Franklin's method and list the pros and the cons. You can try to figure out how weighty each reason is by thinking about what the economics of happiness tells us. If you already make a lot of money, the '£££' in the pro-column should not get a lot of weight. If you don't, it should. Then look at the opportunity costs of working more – what you have to sacrifice to do so – and see what the effects on happiness would be. If you already have a lot of spare time, more leisure would probably make a minor difference. If you already feel strapped for time, it might make a big one. And so on.

That's what my family and I did when we decided to leave the job that paid better for one that offered a better work–life balance. I hope it works as well for you as it did for us.

Adaptation, aspiration, and social comparison

So far, we've only talked about one half of Easterlin's paradox. That's the fact that happiness rises with income in a country at a given point in time. Let's return to the other half. That's the claim that the happiness of a nation doesn't rise as much as one would expect over time – even when the country is experiencing explosive growth. Part of the explanation, surely, is that the marginal happiness of money is decreasing. When a country becomes richer and richer, we should expect the increase in happiness to get smaller and smaller. Stevenson and Wolfers find US happiness scores have *declined* over the last half-century, a fact they attribute to rising inequality.

There may well be more to the story, though. Economists have proposed a number of additional explanations. One of these does not exclude the other. In fact, they could all be correct. And each has insights for people who want to be happier and make the world a place more fit for human flourishing.

Adaptation: spend money on things you don't get used to

One possible explanation for the fact that people don't become happier than they do is *adaptation*.[19] That's basically the idea that you get used to things. Imagine that you enter a contest and win a new smartphone. Chances are you'll be pleased with your new device, and everything it can do. For a while. After the rosy first few weeks have passed, the novelty will be gone. You'll continue to find the features of the new phone useful. But the tenor of your life will be determined by other features of how you live – the good, the bad, the tedious. As a result, the boost in happiness you experienced as a result of getting your new phone is likely to subside. When it does, your overall happiness level is likely to return to normal – or close to normal. This is adaptation. It happens both for good things and for bad things.

The extent to which people adapt to good things, and to bad, is sometimes surprising to modern audiences. Somebody who would not have been surprised was Adam Smith. He described a man who loses a leg in an accident and gets a wooden one in its place.[20] At first, the man weeps, laments, and grieves. He imagines his life will never be the same. But soon enough, he realizes that all (or most of the things) that gave him joy before the accident continue to do so. Over time, he comes to regard the wooden leg more as an inconvenience than a disaster.

> A man with a wooden leg suffers, no doubt, and foresees that he must continue to suffer during the remainder of his life, a very considerable inconveniency. He soon comes to view it, however, exactly as every impartial spectator views it; as an inconveniency under which he can enjoy all the ordinary pleasures both of solitude and of society.[21]

In this brief passage, Smith captures not only the fact that people adapt to disability, which they do, but also that people fail to predict that they will, a phenomenon known as *underprediction of adaptation*.

Adaptation helps explain the fact that people don't become as much happier as you'd think when they get richer. More money does allow you to buy more goods and services. That's good for happiness. But the happiness boost we get can be short-lived. When the boost has subsided, we may find ourselves at or close to where we were before we got more money. With adaptation, our happiness when we get richer doesn't rise as steeply as it would without it.

For the person who wants a happiness bang for their buck, adaptation is on the whole bad news. But there's hope. We may not adapt to everything to the same degree. In my experience, there are huge differences. Books are the worst. Like many academics, I love books. I can't resist the urge to buy new books as soon as I come across them. I'm genuinely excited about the ones that I buy. But by the time they arrive in my mailbox, I have often forgotten that I ordered them. After I've opened the box and admired the cover, I put the book on top of a pile of other unread books and forget about it. As long as I can reach the top of the pile next to my bed, I'll continue ordering books. But it's fair to say that the books piling up at home don't give me a lot of happiness. I don't even remember most of them. By contrast, when I was a grad student, I splurged on a pair of pretty good loudspeakers. They've given me immense joy over the years. Whether I'm happy, sad, bored, busy, or whatever, I can find a use for them. And I just don't seem to adapt to the sensation of high-quality sound. The reason may have to do with the fact that public spaces are filled with terrible music streamed through terrible speakers. Either way, I haven't adapted yet.

Suppose we adapt more to some things than to others. This suggests that we should spend our time and money on the latter, if we want to be happy, rather than the former. How do we know which is which? One clue was provided by the economist Tibor Scitovsky back in 1976. He drew a distinction between *pleasure* and *comfort*. Pleasure is a possibly fleeting, enjoyable feeling that we pursue for its own sake. Comfort, by contrast, is a matter of avoiding pain, unpleasantness, and discomfort.[22] Pleasure is 'positive' good, while the search for comfort is an essentially defensive pursuit.

The critical difference, according to Scitovsky, is that we don't adapt to pleasures the way we do to comforts. Pleasures are always enjoyable. Comforts may be enjoyable for a while, but often not for long. In his words: 'Many comforts are satisfying at first, but soon become routine and taken for granted.'[23] I guess I buy books for comfort – not so much for the pleasure of reading. The loudspeakers, by contrast, give me unadulterated pleasure on a daily basis. The difference may help explain why I seem to adapt to the one and not the other. The upshot is that we have to be willing to sacrifice comfort for pleasure if we want to be happy. What might this mean in practice? Ditch the new car and go for a camping trip? Refrain from updating your old phone and buy season tickets to the symphony orchestra? Choose to live in a smaller space and use the money for foreign travel? Overinvestment in comforts, as opposed to pleasures, prevents us from realizing our full happiness potential.

People sometimes advise you to buy experiences – not things.[24] Those people include actual behavioural economists. Three of them write: 'Experiential purchases (money spent on doing) tend to provide more enduring happiness than material purchases (money spent on having).'[25] There's likely more to the story, but the distinction between pleasure and comfort may well be one aspect of it. I suspect positive experiences are relatively more conducive to pleasure, whereas material things often serve to secure comfort.

Pleasure also has another thing going for it, says Scitovsky: it's more easily shared than comfort.[26] A Swedish proverb captures the basic idea: 'Shared joy is double joy.'[27] If I engage in activities that make me happy, and surround myself with things that spark joy, other people may be able to partake too. There are positive externalities, as economists say. My happiness will become their happiness. Comforts, Scitovsky says, don't have quite the same quality. A purchase made to avoid pain and unpleasantness for me will typically not have the same benefits for my neighbour. Think about fences, air-conditioning units, alarm systems, and the like. Some of them may even make my neighbours worse off, if they are eyesores or generate noise. If this sounds familiar, try to engage in activities and invest in things that bring joy to others as well.

Aspiration: keep your aspirations and expectations in check

Barry Bonds was a baseball player with the Pittsburgh Pirates. In 1991, he was offered a raise from $850,000 to $2.3 million. The thing was, he had requested $3.25 million. He was overwhelmed with disappointment. He complained: 'There is nothing Barry Bonds can do to satisfy Pittsburgh. I'm so sad all the time.'[28] This is a funny story because the numbers are so spectacular. Something similar happens to everyone, though. Imagine your feelings if you unexpectedly got a 5 per cent raise. Chances are you'd be pleased, especially since you didn't expect a raise at all. Now imagine your feelings when you get a 5 per cent raise when you expected 10 per cent. There's a good chance you'll be less happy – or even be sad and disappointed.

The general insight is that our happiness reflects not just what happens to us, but what we expected and hoped for. Economists capture this idea in what's referred to as *aspiration-level theory*. This theory says effectively that happiness is a function of outcomes relative to expectations. If the outcome exceeds expectations, you'll be happy. If the outcome fails to reach expectations, you won't. This entails that happiness increases as outcomes improve. All things equal, the better the outcome, the happier you'll be. But this also entails that happiness decreases as aspirations grow. All things equal, the higher your expectations, the less happy you'll be with the outcome.

As an educator, I am often surprised by the reactions that students have when they receive their grades. Some are absolutely furious about an A–, because they expected an A. Others are positively delighted with a C+, because they expected an F. Their reactions reflect not just their exam scores but their expectations as well.

Aspiration-level theory can help explain why happiness levels don't increase more than they do when people get richer. Suppose that people's aspirations rise as they get more money. When you live in a student dorm, you may aspire to have your own apartment, even if small. When you live in a small apartment, you may aspire to live in a bigger one. When you live in a bigger apartment, you may aspire to live in your own property. And so on: the more you have, the more you expect – and maybe the more you think you deserve. If so, the beneficial happiness effect of getting more money will be offset (at least partially) by the harmful effect on happiness of rising aspirations. Behavioural economists call this phenomenon the *aspiration treadmill*. The basic idea is ancient. The Stoic philosopher Seneca diagnosed the problem some 2,000 years ago. He wrote: 'Excessive prosperity does indeed create greed in men, and never are desires so well controlled that they vanish once satisfied.'[29]

Why do aspirations and expectations play such a big role in our happiness, and why do they tend to be so high? One reason may be that it's hard to assess outcomes without them. 'Did I do well on the exam?' 'Am I attractive?' 'Am I a good person?' These are hard questions to answer. It's much easier to answer questions of the form: 'Did I do as well as I thought I would?' 'Am I as attractive as I aspire to be?' 'Do I engage in acts of kindness as often as I think?' If the former questions are harder to answer, we may just substitute the easier ones. Another reason may be evolutionary in nature. Imagine that there was a time, way back in evolutionary history, when some people were satisfied with the bone they were chewing on and the cave they were living in, whereas other people were not. It's not hard to imagine that the dissatisfied types ended up accumulating more resources, which in turn helped them survive and prosper. If so, we're all descendants of the dissatisfied. Think of the fable of the ant and the grasshopper. The ant works all summer to accumulate food for the winter, while the grasshopper does nothing but play music and relax. Come winter, the ant survives whereas the grasshopper perishes. The fable ends there, but suppose it continued. The next generation, with grasshoppers gone, everyone would be an ant. Those of us who have survived this far in evolutionary history are all descendants of ants. We may be conditioned to be dissatisfied.

Setting expectations for yourself is probably a good thing, at least sometimes. Expectations and aspirations may motivate you to work harder and smarter. They may help you accomplish more in life. But excessive expectations can be a problem, as Barry Bonds demonstrated. The ability to rein in excessive expectations and set reasonable goals in life is a critical skill. Researchers talk about it in terms of 'goal regulation'. That's the process of adopting,

disengaging from, and reengaging in personal goals. The researchers will tell you that unreasonable goals are a major barrier to
being happy, and that the ability to get rid of unreasonable goals
can improve your happiness.[30]

Social comparison: try not to compare yourself to other people

There's an old joke about two campers being attacked by a bear.
The one camper kneels down and starts tying his shoes. 'What are
you doing?' asks the other one. 'Do you think you can outrun a
bear?' 'Oh no,' replies the first. 'I don't need to outrun the bear; I
just need to outrun *you!*' The joke captures an important psychological fact. We often think of our performance not in absolute
terms – 'Can I run at 10 mph?' – but rather in relative ones – 'Can I
run faster than the next person?'

The idea of social comparisons is that our happiness reflects how
well we are doing by reference not to some absolute yardstick, but
to how others are doing. Am I making more money than my
brother-in-law? If so, good. Am I making less? If so, not good.
There's evidence that such relative concerns matter a great deal to
many people, at least in some domains.[31]

Sometimes a relative standard makes a lot of sense. If you want
to escape the bear (and don't care about your fellow camper), relative speed is the only thing that counts. If you're going for an
Olympic gold medal, too, the important thing is running faster than
the others – not hitting any one particular speed.

Sometimes the relative standard is decidedly dysfunctional.
When social comparison is dysfunctional, people will often charac-
terize it in terms of 'keeping up with the Joneses'. And it really is
dysfunctional much of the time. For one thing, if everyone is trying
to keep up with the Joneses, they're playing a zero-sum game. No
matter how much they have, there's at most one who can have more
than everybody else. If they weren't all comparing themselves to
their neighbours, they could all be satisfied with what they've got.

Moreover, keeping up with the Joneses risks setting us up in a sort of arms race that cannot be won. Suppose I sacrifice all my spare time and all my money to buy a fancier car than you have. Perhaps I'll succeed, briefly. But suppose further that you do the same. You may also succeed, briefly. In the end, we risk finding ourselves in a situation where we both have made vast sacrifices without gaining an inch on each other in relative terms.

This idea can help explain why happiness levels don't rise faster when a country gets richer. Suppose a rising tide lifts all boats – more or less. Even as all boats gain elevation relative to land, their elevation relative to each other won't change at all. Something similar might be happening with money and happiness. Suppose all of us get richer over time. Even as all of us acquire more money, our relative wealth need not change at all. To the extent that our happiness is determined by whether we make more or less than others, then our happiness won't budge – even though we get materially better and better off.

Why do we find the urge to compare ourselves with others so irresistible? Again, one reason may be that it's hard to make absolute judgements in response to questions such as: 'What's a nice apartment?' 'What's a decent car?' 'What's a good salary?' It's a lot easier to substitute questions about whether my apartment, car, or salary are better or worse than my neighbour's. If we're not careful, we may confuse the answers to the second set of questions with answers to the first. Again, another reason may be evolutionary. Natural selection favours whoever does better in terms of survival and reproduction on a relative scale – not on an absolute scale. In this respect, being subject to natural selection is similar to being chased by a bear.

What gives?

So you want to be happy? Economics will not tell you categorically to try to make more money, although having money might help.

But here are three tips, or strategies, that you can try if you want to be happier. (1) Spend your time and money on things you're unlikely to adapt to: pleasures rather than comforts, experiences rather than things, and so on. (2) Keep your expectations and aspirations in check. (3) Avoid comparing yourself to others unless you must.

There are limits to how happy you can make yourself. First off, your happiness is to some extent constrained by external factors you can't do anything about as an individual. How rich your country is, how much freedom it offers, and so on, will influence your happiness. The possibility that our evolutionary heritage might have conditioned us to be less than fully happy suggests there are some boundaries to how happy we can make ourselves. If you're not as happy as you want to be, or as you think you deserve to be, it's not all your fault!

As always, it's important to keep in mind that the science only reports averages, which may or may not apply to you. What works for you will reflect your values and preferences, and also a number of conditions that may or may not be under your control.

That said, the three insights suggest that happiness is *to some extent* under our control. Happiness is not just something that happens to us, as the English word suggests. (Both 'happiness' and 'happen' derive from the early Scandinavian words for 'luck' or 'chance'.) To the extent that your happiness levels reflect the kind of consumption you engage in, the expectations that you develop, and the comparisons that you make, happiness isn't just a matter of luck or chance. Luck or chance might factor into your happiness, but they're not everything there is to it. To that extent, happiness is under your control – and economics helps you conquer it.

7

How to Be Humble

Astronaut Buzz Aldrin was one of the first two people to set foot on the moon. The spaceflight is known as Apollo 11. It took place in 1969. Thirty-five years after the fact, Aldrin was asked what his biggest concern was at the time. He answered: 'Well, I think we tried very hard not to be overconfident, because when you get overconfident, that's when something snaps up and bites you.'[1]

You don't have to be an astronaut to know what he was talking about. I suspect we all do. As you embark on a new project or journey, you're cautious. You tread lightly. You follow the plan. You carefully monitor the situation for signs that something has gone awry. After a while, you start feeling good about yourself. You're making headway. You're feeling at ease. You're enjoying the fact that things are going swimmingly. Then, suddenly: BOOM! Something goes horribly wrong. You did not see it coming.

When this happens, it's helpful to review the events leading up to the misfortune. You can often, in retrospect, think of signs that something was amiss. But you didn't pay attention. You ignored the signs because you felt things were going so well. You thought the signals couldn't possibly be correct. You thought you had things well in hand. You were overconfident.

'And thus the native hue of resolution,' Hamlet exclaimed, 'is sicklied o'er with the pale cast of thought.' Shakespeare knew what was up.

I've had this experience many times while sailing. I've sailed all my life, but things still go wrong. I've approached rocks and lighthouses that weren't supposed to be there. Once I had to be rescued by the Coast Guard. Accidents are always unexpected, of course, or else we wouldn't call them that. But when I go back and reflect on what happened, I can almost always think of red flags, clearly visible in hindsight. It could be an odd reading on the instrument, a flicker in my visual field, an unexpected light source, or whatever. If I had paid attention, I could have known that something was not right. I dismissed it, because it didn't fit my mental map. I was so sure I knew where I was and what I was doing.

Overconfidence has been called 'the mother of all biases'.[2] Behavioural decision researchers have studied it carefully for half a century now. And they've learned a lot. Much of it is at once hilarious and depressing. In an all-time classic study, 93 per cent of US drivers claimed to be more skilful than the median.[3] Imagine that you line up all American automobile drivers from worst (all the way over on the left) to best (all the way over on the right). If so, 93 out of 100 thought that they belonged on the right-hand side of the line-up. That's mathematically impossible – no matter how good they are. It's as absurd as imagining a long queue where almost everyone is at the head.

Overconfidence is pervasive, resilient, and costly. We find it almost everywhere we look. It's hard to shed. And it's been implicated in mishaps, accidents, and disasters of all kinds. Don Moore wrote the book on overconfidence. According to him:

> Overconfidence has been blamed for the sinking of the *Titanic*, the nuclear accident at Chernobyl, the loss of the space shuttles *Challenger* and *Columbia*, the subprime mortgage crisis of 2008 and the Great Recession that followed, the *Deepwater Horizon* oil spill in the Gulf of Mexico, and more. Overconfidence may contribute to excessive stock market trading, high rates of entrepreneurial failure, legal disputes, political partisanship, and even war.[4]

What makes overconfidence particularly potent is that it's a 'force multiplier', as they say in the military – and not in a good way. A force multiplier is something that gives soldiers an extra edge when it counts. Overconfidence gives extra bite to all the other biases we're subject to. Being wrong or incapable doesn't need to be so bad in and of itself. But being wrong or incapable *and also overconfident* can be deadly. Literally.

The 1980s US TV show *Sledge Hammer!* featured an unstable police officer who never saw a problem he didn't try to fix with brute force.[5] His most famous line was: 'Trust me, I know what I'm doing.' Whenever uttered, things would go horribly wrong. The problem wasn't just that Detective Hammer was incapable of performing tasks such as defusing nuclear bombs. That hardly made him unique. The problem was his confidence that he *could* defuse nuclear bombs. His overconfidence made him think that he knew what he was doing when he did not. It was the gap between competence and confidence that caused all his problems – and the comedy and drama. We all know some Hammers. Worse, we're all Hammers ourselves – at least some of the time.

You'll be relieved to learn, then, that economics can help solve the problem of overconfidence. Behavioural economists have identified three strategies that reduce overconfidence in ourselves and others. These strategies can also be used to build overconfidence-proof teams. First: we can confront our beliefs with evidence that's regular, prompt, and unambiguous. Feedback reminding us how often we're wrong seems to help. That's especially true if the evidence is hard to explain away. Second: we can force ourselves and others to reflect on *reasons we might be wrong*. This is hard. We're much better at producing reasons why we are right. But forcing ourselves to think through the various scenarios in which we turn out to be wrong seems to help us realize that the probabilities are not as remote as they might seem at first. Third: we can change the environment in which decisions are made to make it less conducive to overconfidence.

Epistemic humility is an intellectual virtue. It's grounded in the realization that our knowledge is always provisional and incomplete – and that it might require revision in light of new evidence. Carl Hempel was one of the greatest philosophers of science of the twentieth century. People who knew him tell me he was never prejudiced in favour of a view just because it happened to be his own. That's epistemic humility. It's a good thing. Avoiding overconfidence is a matter of epistemic humility. A lack of epistemic humility is a vice. That's a bad thing. It can cause massive damage both in our private lives and in public policy.

This chapter describes the economic approach to epistemic humility. It offers advice about how to attain it. The ancient Greek philosopher Aristotle thought virtue was the mean between excess and deficiency.[6] Economists agree. Epistemic humility is to be found between over- and underconfidence. You want to avoid overconfidence. But you want to avoid underconfidence too. If you're a member of an actual bomb squad and know how to defuse explosive devices, nothing good will come out of acting as though you don't. Being humble isn't the same as being *meek*. It's fine to be confident when you know what you're doing. You can be humble while avoiding both over- and underconfidence. The goal is to be *calibrated*, as economists say.

Aristotle also believed being virtuous is hard work.[7] Economists agree with this too. You won't get any humbler merely by reading about it. (Sorry.) Striking the right balance between excess and deficiency requires focused attention and consistent practice. Economics tells you what to focus on and how to practise. The advice applies to anyone who occasionally suffers overconfidence. That's all of us. It applies independently of whether you'd like to see more of it in yourself, others, or your team. The advice is supported by a great deal of evidence, as we will see.

The economic approach to confidence is quite distinct from what's available elsewhere. Popular culture offers a wide variety of books, podcasts, and whatnot telling you how to boost your confidence. The assumption seems to be that more confidence will lead to happiness, popularity, and fortune. Economists will tell you that's a mistake. Excessive confidence leads to recklessness, failure, grief, and disappointment. It makes you a Hammer. If you have a child or manage a team, for example, you don't want to boost their confidence indefinitely and across the board.

The point here is to help you find the sweet spot between under- and overconfidence. We want your confidence to be just right, given the task and your level of ability. We want you to know when you can legitimately say 'trust me' and when you cannot.

What is overconfidence?

We need to know what economists think overconfidence is and how they know. First, let's distinguish your beliefs about the chances that some event will happen from its actual probability. Perhaps you buy a lottery ticket and believe that there's a 10 per cent chance you will win a prize today. We call that your *subjective probability*. If you want to know what somebody's subjective probability is, you can just ask them. Subjective probabilities are a feature of a person's belief system. Subjective probabilities can differ across people, even when they concern the same event. Maybe I think there's a 50 per cent chance that you will win today. My subjective probability doesn't need to equal yours. They will often differ, in fact.

Subjective probabilities need to be distinguished from *objective frequencies*. An objective frequency is the fraction of times that the event will happen under the circumstances. Suppose that you bought one of a hundred lottery tickets, and that the winning ticket is chosen at random. The fraction of times you will win under the circumstances is 1/100, that is, 1 per cent. That's the objective frequency. Objective frequencies are a feature of the process that generates the events. We have no direct access to them, meaning that you can't just ask the person who has beliefs about them to figure out what they are. There's a fact to the matter. That fact is independent of people's beliefs. Objective frequencies don't differ across people, when we are talking about the same event.

Calibration concerns the relationship between subjective probabilities and objective frequencies. You are perfectly calibrated when your subjective probabilities match the objective frequencies. In the example above, neither one of us is calibrated. In order to be calibrated, our subjective probabilities need to equal the objective frequency of the relevant event, which is 1/100. A calibrated person who is 90 per cent certain that she's right is in fact right nine times out of ten.

Calibration in belief is often a good thing. Imagine that you hire a structural engineer to tell you the likelihood that your house will collapse. The engineer is 99.99 per cent certain that your house won't collapse. If houses like yours then collapse half the time, you have every reason to be upset and disappointed – not just with the house, but with the engineer as well. A poorly calibrated structural engineer can cause real harm – including the loss of property and human life.

If your subjective probability exceeds the objective frequency, we'll say that you're *overconfident*. If it's lower, you're *underconfident*. The structural engineer is overconfident. So am I every time I set the alarm for 5 a.m., confident that I'll rise and shine at 5 sharp – when, in reality, nine times out of ten I'll hit snooze every ten minutes for an hour at least. Confidence has to do with *beliefs about your beliefs*. In principle, you can be overconfident, perfectly calibrated, or even underconfident.

The most obvious way to assess degrees of overconfidence is to give people a number of true-or-false questions. Ask, first, 'Are the following claims true or false? (a) Sacramento is the capital of California, (b) absinthe is a precious stone,' and so on. Then ask, for each claim: 'How confident are you in your answer?' You invite your participants to report their confidence on a scale from 0 to 100 per cent. That'll give you their subjective probability for each proposition. Then you sort the claims by confidence level. Put all the propositions that the person is 100 per cent certain of in one pile, for example. Then compute the number of those answers that were, in fact, correct. A calibrated person would be correct about every single one of them.

When researchers have done this, they've ended up with results like those in Figure 5.[8] Here you have people's subjective probabilities on the *x*-axis, and the objective frequencies on the *y*-axis. A perfectly calibrated person would have a 'calibration curve' along the diagonal 45° line. For them, subjective probabilities always equal objective frequencies. In reality, things look a little different. Way over on the left, you have all propositions that people have assigned a subjective probability of 50 per cent. These are the things that people feel like they have no idea about. As far as they're concerned, they could just as likely be false as true. For such claims, people are actually right a little more often than half of the time, meaning that they're underconfident. For most propositions, though, people are overconfident. And they get more overconfident the further you move to the right. When people are 100 per cent sure, they're very overconfident indeed. A classic study found that when people were absolutely, positively, 100 per cent certain of something, they were right about 70–80 per cent of the time.[9]

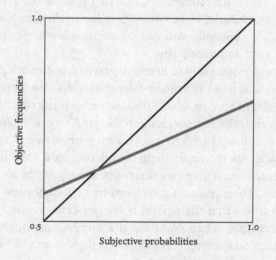

Figure 5: Calibration curves

This immediately tells us something important: *confidence* is a risk factor for overconfidence. The more confident people are, all things being equal, the more overconfident they tend to be. This should not be surprising, if you think about it. We all know people who just scream overconfidence by expressing themselves with total and complete confidence about everything, from who's going to win the Nobel Prize for Literature to how to find the best taco truck in LA. These are the people who go from being experts on constitutional law to experts on epidemiology at the drop of a hat. That kind of confidence is a red flag. It signals overconfidence – and a lack of epistemic humility.

Another risk factor for overconfidence is *difficulty*. The more difficult the task, by and large, the more overconfident the judge. Very knowledgeable people making very easy judgements can sometimes be underconfident. Ask me what city I live in, and I won't be overconfident. But everybody else is overconfident in varying degrees. When the questions are difficult, people are overconfident at almost all levels of subjective belief. For very difficult questions, studies have found calibration curves that are essentially flat. This means that there is no relationship at all between people's confidence in their judgement and its accuracy. Predicting the stock market, for example, is very hard. Indeed, some economists doubt that it can be done at all. In that sort of situation we should expect massive overconfidence. The people you know who are in the habit of expressing themselves with total and complete certainty about very difficult questions are very likely to be overconfident. Perhaps knowing this can make them a little easier to tolerate.

What do we know about overconfidence?

Reams of research suggests that overconfidence is pervasive, resilient, and costly. First, overconfidence is shockingly common.[10] For most people and most judgement tasks, you can expect some degree

of overconfidence. There are exceptions, as we just saw. One example is when the judge is very knowledgeable and the task is easy.
Ask an experienced car mechanic if they can change a car's engine oil
and you're unlikely to get an overconfident answer. But other than
that, it's the norm.

Overconfidence is also *resilient*. It resists many of the actions you
might take to reduce it in yourself or others. The fact that it's so
resilient helps explain why it's so common. It's just hard to get rid
of – even if you try.

Overconfidence is resistant to information. People don't in general
become any less overconfident when they acquire more information,
even when that information is relevant to answering the question. In
one classic study, psychologists at various career stages were asked
questions about the behaviours, attitudes, and interests of a real
patient.[11] When participants received more and more information
about the patient's life, they became more and more confident in
their answers. And yet their accuracy barely increased at all. They
became *more overconfident* as they became more knowledgeable.

In particular, learning the facts about overconfidence doesn't
make a difference.[12] You might think it would help to tell people
about the prevalence of overconfidence; to invite them to consider
that they too might be prone to excessive confidence; and to instruct
them to be careful. But it doesn't. We cannot fix overconfidence by
providing people with more information of this kind. I wish I could
say that simply reading this chapter will help you improve your confidence, but chances are it won't.

Overconfidence also appears to be resistant to expertise. You
might think that experts would be less prone to overconfidence
than non-experts. After all, knowing stuff is part of what makes an
expert an expert. But many studies suggest experts are just as prone
to overconfidence as amateurs and experts-in-training are. Consider
the study about the real patient. The clinical psychologists who
participated – a majority of whom had PhDs – were no more

accurate and no less confident than psychology graduate students and advanced undergraduates. Similarly, Christensen-Szalanski and Bushyhead studied physicians diagnosing possible pneumonia patients.[13] The degree of calibration was low indeed, and the doctors exhibited a large degree of overconfidence. When the doctors claimed to be more than 80 per cent certain that the patient had pneumonia, X-rays confirmed the existence of the disease in only about 20 per cent of the cases. Other studies have found systematic overconfidence among bankers, executives, civil engineers, and others making professional judgements within their area of expertise.

Overconfidence is similarly resistant to incentives. People don't exhibit less overconfidence when they're motivated to be right or to avoid overconfidence. To test whether increased motivation would decrease the degree of overconfidence, Baruch Fischhoff and his colleagues asked subjects to express their confidence in terms of odds, and to place a bet based on those odds.[14] The degree of overconfidence decreased somewhat, but remained high. When subjects said that the odds they were right were 100:1, in order to be well calibrated they should have said 4:1; when they said the odds were 100,000:1, they should have said 9:1. A majority of subjects agreed to gamble for real money. So the experimenters could have made a fair profit if they had actually collected their winnings. In another classic study, two groups of students were given the same set of course-related multiple-choice questions. The test group were told that they were taking their midterm examination, while the control group were told that they were merely practising. The test group, presumably more motivated to do well, scored no higher than the control group, but were significantly more confident. In this case, then, it appears that overconfidence actually *increased* with motivation.

Summing up, overconfidence appears not only inside but also outside the laboratory. It appears when knowledgeable judges make assertions within their field of specialization. And it appears when people are motivated to provide accurate assessments.

Finally, overconfidence is *costly*. Most obviously, overconfidence inspires bad decisions. As Moore pointed out, overconfidence has been implicated in financial crises, accidents, bankruptcies, legal disputes, political partisanship, and even war. To the extent that overconfidence is a contributing factor, its cost in money and lives is vast. Consider the paper 'Trading is Hazardous to Your Wealth', by Brad Barber and Terrance Odean, which shows that active trading is hugely harmful to an investor.[15] The authors diagnose the problem as one of overconfidence. In their view, overconfidence makes people think they're better at predicting stock-market prices than they really are. Their inflated trust in their own abilities causes them to put real money on the line. Because they're not, in fact, very good at predicting the stock market, these investors end up losing money. The people who traded the most made 6.5 percentage points less than what the market delivered. That may not sound like very much. But it can still translate into a lot of money, depending on the size of your portfolio. If you're lucky enough to have invested $1 million, that difference translates into $65,000 in a year. And if you make the same mistake year after year, the consequences will be compounded.

A 2001 paper by the same authors, titled 'Boys Will be Boys', examines gender differences among stock-market investors.[16] Barber and Odean proceed from the assumption that, when it comes to finance, men tend to be more overconfident than women. The authors propose that more confident investors will trade more: trying to time short-term fluctuations in stock prices in order to buy low and sell high. Comparing data from 35,000 households, they found that men trade 45 per cent more than women. And because trading is bad for your wealth, the men did a lot worse than the women. There are lots of Hammers. If these guys are day trading because it's fun – because it's a pastime, hobby, lifestyle, or identity – it's not necessarily irrational. But I hope they appreciate just what an expensive hobby it is. They might save money by getting into Swiss Haute Horlogerie – or offshore sailboat racing.

Part of the story is that overconfidence can breed complacency.[17] Moore cites Scripture: 'Pride goes before destruction, a haughty spirit before a fall.'[18] If you're so sure that you'll ace the exam, win the case, or come first in the competition, you may not feel like you have to prepare very much. But politicians who don't read briefs, lawyers who don't read up on their cases, and athletes who don't train for their races are a lot less likely to succeed than those who do. Complacency is the enemy of success.

Overconfidence can also set you up for disappointment and disengagement, and it makes failure harder to bear. If you believe your success is assured, failure is not only more likely, but will also leave you more disappointed and disillusioned. Anticipating failure, you may be more likely to give up on the effort completely. If you have a teenage child, for example, it would be a mistake to boost their confidence across the board. Excessive confidence in a teenager can lead to all sorts of risky behaviours, some of which can be deadly. A fear of failure may also prevent them from trying in the first place. Developmental psychologists fear that we may cause real harm to our children when we try to pump up their confidence indiscriminately.[19]

Overconfidence can lead to conflict.[20] If you and I disagree about something, our disagreement could be the beginning of a fruitful conversation. A genuine exchange of ideas could benefit both of us, as we explore the nature of our disagreement and the evidence we have for our beliefs. But a truly fruitful conversation presupposes that we both agree that we have something to learn from hearing each other out. It requires some degree of epistemic humility. If you and I disagree, and are also sufficiently overconfident, we might not see any point in talking at all. It may come more naturally to dismiss each other as either incompetent or malicious or both. Such conflict can, in turn, cut into our ability to learn from others.

The fact that excessive confidence can do real harm does not seem to have made much of a mark on the popular literature about the subject. That includes the self-help books which fill several pages of search results on your favourite online marketplace. These books promise a level of confidence that will make you unstoppable, help you achieve all of your goals, create success on demand, and live life on your terms. And all of that is in the title of just one book.[21] It is undeniably true that some people could benefit from more confidence in some specific contexts. But it is a mistake to preach confidence across the board. And high confidence can't deliver all that. It's more likely to cause you harm. A better goal is to be calibrated – to avoid both under- and overconfidence.

Ignore the self-help literature. Listen to the economists instead.

Sources of overconfidence

At this stage you may be sceptical. If behavioural economists are right, most of us are spending most of our lives – and most of our careers – being ridiculously overconfident. Is it even possible for people to be so overconfident for so long? Wouldn't we learn and adapt? Research suggests the answers are yes, and no. Sadly, we don't learn anywhere as much as we think – or should. Overconfidence is due to a sort of perfect storm of cognitive biases. The storm helps explain how overconfidence can be so pervasive and resilient.

First, overconfidence is sometimes the result of selection.[22] US president Harry Truman apparently got so frustrated with economic advisers who would say 'on the one hand . . . on the other . . .' that he exclaimed: 'Give me a one-armed economist!'[23] Truman didn't want epistemically humble advisers. He wanted confident ones. Think about the 'experts' you see on TV. Something similar goes on there. People who get invited to join a panel on a news or current-affairs programme may or may not have formal qualifications. What is required is the ability to say things that make for good TV. Invitations will tend to be issued to the bold, combative, dramatic, and controversial – not the epistemically humble. Whenever experts are selected on the basis of their confidence, they will tend to be overconfident. As we saw above, confidence is a red flag.

Part of the story is that confidence may be confused for competence. Some years ago I developed a skin condition on my face. The dermatologist surprised me by spending most of my visit looking out the window. When I walked out of his office, I remember being impressed. A dermatologist who could diagnose a patient without even looking at him! It only occurred to me afterwards that I had made a mistake. I inferred he must have been fantastically competent from the fact that he acted with fantastic confidence. But they are two different things. I had, at the time, no evidence that he was either more or less competent than any other doctor of his kind. The funny/sad thing about the story is that I was writing about overconfidence at the time, and should have caught myself much sooner. His diagnosis was correct, and the condition was cured. But the episode illustrates how hard it can be *not* to confuse confidence and competence.

Second, we often lack useful feedback. The hope that we will, ultimately, learn from our overconfidence and adapt accordingly assumes a lot. It presupposes that we receive extensive outcome feedback – information that tells us what really happened, if we were right or not, and so on. But proper outcome feedback is often hard to come by. There are many reasons why feedback can be inadequate, ambiguous, expensive, or for some other reason unattainable. Once we make a prediction, we often act on it. By acting on it, we change the expected outcome. Whatever happens after we act on the prediction cannot straightforwardly be used to confirm or disprove the prediction. In some situations, outcome feedback is impossible to come by even in principle. Claims such as 'if the other party were in charge, things would be different now' are *counterfactual*. They say something about what the situation would be like if things were different. Whether a counterfactual claim is true or false cannot be determined by confronting it directly with outcome feedback. Even if we were able to update our confidence in the proper way in light of what happens, we often can't. We simply don't know what happened, or what would have happened.

Third, learning from experience is more difficult than one might think, even in the presence of outcome feedback. One reason why we have trouble learning from experience is that people tend to over-weight evidence that supports their position and ignore evidence that undermines it. This tendency is referred to as *confirmation bias*.[24] Studies suggest people with diametrically opposed initial beliefs are capable of interpreting the same piece of ambiguous information as supportive of their view.[25] People who ignore disconfirming evidence may not realize they were wrong in the past, and may see no need to be more cautious in the future.

Our ability to learn from past mistakes is also compromised by something called *hindsight bias*.[26] This bias is a tendency to exaggerate the predictability of past events. Once something has occurred, we seem to have trouble imagining that things could have turned out differently. We exaggerate in hindsight what we could have predicted in foresight, and we misremember what we predicted so as to exaggerate in hindsight what we actually knew in foresight. Victims of hindsight bias may never learn that past predictions were no good, because they misremember what they predicted. Thus, they will see no need to be less confident in their future predictions.

Evidence shows that both confirmation bias and hindsight bias are stronger when predictions are vague and outcome feedback is ambiguous.[27] Insofar as people have a tendency to misremember predictions and reinterpret outcomes so as to render them more compatible, their task is made that much easier by ambiguity and vagueness. In fact, many of the predictions that we make are both vague and ambiguous. This is true in everyday life, in business, and in politics. When this is so, we should expect sizable hindsight and confirmation biases.

Fourth, our cognitive and metacognitive abilities appear to be intertwined. 'Cognitive ability' refers to the ability to perform some mental task or other. 'Metacognitive ability' refers to the ability to judge our own performance. The point is that people who lack the one also tend to lack the other. In a paper that became an instant classic, Justin Kruger and David Dunning gave participants tests of logical reasoning, English grammar, and the like.[28] They also asked participants to rate their own performance relative to their group of peers. The general finding is that people who were very capable – people who scored very highly on the test – on the mean underestimated their ability a little bit. People who were very incapable – people who scored very badly on the test – radically overestimated their ability. Participants whose test scores in logic and grammar put them in the bottom 25 per cent of their group of peers, on the mean estimated that they were well above average.[29]

The authors went on to explore what happens when participants gain information about other people's performance. Kruger and Dunning let original participants 'grade' other people's tests. This gave them more information about their own performance relative to others. Ideally, the information should lead to improved assessments of one's own performance. High performers did indeed improve. When they gained more information about others' performance, they revised their assessments of their own ability in the right direction (upwards). The low performers, by contrast, did not improve. If anything, they adjusted their assessments of their own performance in the *wrong* direction (also upwards). On the basis of these results, Kruger and Dunning suggest that the least competent are at a double disadvantage, in that their incompetence 'not only causes poor performance but also the inability to recognize that one's performance is poor'.[30] Hence their paper's title: 'Unskilled and Unaware of It'.

These findings have given rise to a substantial secondary literature debating what they *mean*.[31] The phenomenon as such – the pattern in the data – strikes me as robust enough. It certainly meshes with my experience as a college professor. When very strong students come to see me to discuss their grade on a test, usually I can just gesture in the direction of the correct answer and they will immediately get it. When very weak students come to see me, they will continue to protest their low grades even after learning the correct answer. Unlike the strong students, they just don't see the difference between the correct and the incorrect ones. Their inability to pass the test is wrapped up with their inability to recognize their performance as poor. The dual burden is, indeed, heavy. It undercuts any chance of improvement, because it robs the weak students of the recognition that they don't already excel.

These various phenomena – selection effects, a lack of dependable outcome feedback, hindsight and confirmation biases, and the Dunning–Kruger effect – wouldn't be so bad if they cancelled each other out. But they don't. It's easy to think of situations in which they all pull in the same direction when it matters. When this is so, we shouldn't be surprised if people lack epistemic humility – and if it causes harm.

Avoiding overconfidence

The fact that overconfidence is so common and so hard to get rid of may sound depressing. It is. But there's hope. Where pop psychology books just keep promoting confidence, behavioural economists have identified strategies that promote epistemic humility and reduce overconfidence. The first is to confront your predictions with good feedback. The second is to consider reasons that you're wrong. Where do these strategies come from? How do economists know? Key is to explore the exceptions to the rule. If we can identify people who succeed in avoiding overconfidence, we'll be on our way.

John Stuart Mill pointed to a paradox.[32] In principle, everyone knows they're fallible. If we're asked, 'Are you right about everything?' we'll answer in the negative. And yet if we're asked about specific beliefs – 'Are you right about this particular thing?' – many of us will insist that we are. This suggests we're less overconfident about things *in general* than we are about things *in particular*. So the question is: how can we become as humble about particular beliefs as we are in general?

Meteorologists have a bad reputation. Many of us have had the experience of getting drenched when we were promised sunshine. Memories like that are highly salient and emotionally loaded. You may still remember the anger and disappointment during that event when the sun was supposed to shine. The fact that meteorologists' failures are highly available will make them seem more common than they really are. Actual research shows that meteorologists predicting rain are exceptionally calibrated, with minimal overconfidence.[33] The same thing is true for professional bridge players making judgements about so-called 'contracts'.[34] (Amateurs, by contrast, are overconfident, like the rest of us.) What's going on here?

The obvious explanation is that meteorologists and bridge players learn from past mistakes. Two things put them in a better position than the rest of us.[35] First, they make highly repetitive judgements. Meteorologists make the same kind of predictions over and over again. Every day they have to come up with a probability of rain on the basis of a certain set of observations. Bridge players too make repeated judgements of the same kind. What is the probability of a certain contract now? What about now? And now? Second, and this is crucial, meteorologists and bridge players get regular, prompt, and unambiguous feedback. The meteorologists will know whether it rained or not the day after their prediction that it would. The bridge players will know what happened after the previous hand. The feedback is dependable. It's fast. And it's clear. All of this helps them learn from past mistakes, which in turn improves their calibration over time. Laboratory studies have confirmed that overconfidence can be reduced when judges receive feedback that is frequent, prompt, and unambiguous.[36]

These studies suggest two things we can do.

First, we should attempt to make clear, unambiguous, falsifiable judgements. Baruch Fischhoff jokes that if you want to make a living as a forecaster, you should make sure to specify a value, or a time, but never both at the same time. If you insist on predicting that some stock-market index will hit a certain number, make sure not to say when. If you insist on predicting that something will happen at a given moment, make sure not to say what. That way, no matter what happens, you can always claim to have been vindicated – or at least not proven wrong. But this strategy is the opposite of what you want if you aim to be epistemically humble. Make sure to specify what you predict will happen, when you think it will happen, and under what conditions it will fail. Ideally, you'll want to write it down. Only then do you have the sort of unambiguous prediction that you can compare with outcome feedback in a way that doesn't allow confirmation and hindsight biases from kicking in.

Second, we should seek out outcome feedback whenever we can. If you did make a prediction, try to figure out if you were right or wrong. Studies have found that people – including specialists making judgements within their area of expertise – are quite good at explaining away anything that goes wrong. Philip Tetlock has found that people will often insist that they were 'almost right' even when they were clearly wrong.[37] The result, in his view, shows the importance of hindsight and confirmation biases, and prevents experts from learning from their mistakes. For sure, the result underscores the importance of making clear predictions and confronting them with unambiguous feedback.

Another research stream suggests a third thing we can do: consider reasons that we're wrong. If you think it's going to rain tomorrow, ask yourself if there's any reason the sun might shine. If you think the value of your home might rise, ask yourself under what scenario the value might drop. If you think the governing party might lose the next election, ask what might cause it to win. Considering reasons we might be *wrong* does not come naturally. We're much more used to considering reasons why we're *right*. In written work, as well as in casual conversation, we're often expected to back up things we say with evidence. Anticipating requests for positive evidence, we prepare ourselves by thinking up reasons we're right. We ready ourselves to deliver them upon request. This is all normal. But there's a downside. When all the reasons we might be right are top-of-mind, we risk overestimating the probability that we'll be right. When all these reasons are easily available to us, they will seem more likely than they really are.

Asher Koriat and his co-authors showed experimentally that listing contradicting reasons improves people's calibration.[38] The authors found, as expected, that people are better at producing positive rather than negative evidence. But more importantly, the authors also found that forcing people to consider negative evidence improved calibration. Just asking people to list reasons they may be wrong led to more appropriate confidence judgements. (Considering positive evidence did not.) As the authors pointed out, people who care about calibration should spend more time and effort recruiting and weighing evidence.[39] However, time and effort spent producing positive evidence is unlikely to improve your degree of calibration. What you need to do is to recruit and weigh *negative* evidence. That's much harder. But in this study, anyway, it's the only intervention that had any positive effect at all.

Don Moore describes 'consider[ing] the opposite' – asking yourself why you might be wrong – as 'the simplest, most all-purpose debiasing strategy identified by decision researchers'.[40] But he has a new twist on the advice. He suggests considering other perspectives.[41] That's seeking out and pondering the perspective of somebody who disagrees with you. It sounds easy, but it's surprisingly hard. Suppose you believe Russia will start another war in the next five years. Moore proposes you think of somebody whose judgement you trust but who disagrees with you about future Russian wars. He wants you to try to put yourself in their shoes, asking what experiences and other evidence they may draw on, and what line of reasoning might have led them to the contrary conclusion. This will force you to think of reasons you may be wrong. Suppose you believe that this is a good time to invest in airline stock. Moore proposes you think of the person on the other side of that trade. In order for you to buy a stock, there has to be someone else selling. That person might be an amateur investor, just like you. But, more likely, that person is a professional – somebody who trades stock for a living, who has an appropriate education and access to all sorts of proprietary information, and so on. Again, you want to reflect on what might have caused this person to decide now would be a good time to sell. Doing so will force you to consider reasons you may be wrong.

Seeking out and pondering the perspective of someone who disagrees with you means getting along with people who reject your assumptions, conclusions, and modes of reasoning. You'll want to identify such people. (Nutjobs on the other side don't count.) You'll need to try seeing the world as they do. You'll have to engage them in respectful, mutually beneficial conversation. You may even wish to cultivate a friendship with such people. Again, this can be uncomfortable – even difficult. We're a lot more used to seeking out people who agree with us. But if you're interested in improving your calibration, it's a good thing to do. As Moore says: 'Others' disagreement is . . . a gift of great value, but it is not always easy to appreciate it.'[42]

Building overconfidence-proof teams

So far we've talked about things we can do to promote epistemic humility and avoid overconfidence on an individual level. But often we're no less interested in social aspects of overconfidence. Is there anything we can do to build a culture that's more conducive to epistemic humility? Can we build overconfidence-proof teams? There is, and we can.

Let me start with the 'circle of competence' – an idea from the legendary investor Warren Buffett. A 'Chairman's Letter' to shareholders from 1996 spelled out the basic idea.[43] Your circle of competence is the space of things you know well. It may include things you know about, and things you know how to do. Everyone has a circle of competence. All of us know something. None of us knows everything. Our circles are likely to overlap. There are things that both you and I know how to do. We can both tie our shoelaces, perhaps, or visualize a circle. But the overlap is only partial. There are things you know that I don't, and the other way around. Anyway, Buffett's point is not that our circles are too small. The size itself is not a problem. The point is that we need to know where the boundaries are. He writes:

> I would say that the most important thing in business, and investments, which I regard as the same thing, from our standpoint, is being able to accurately define your circle of competence. It isn't a question of having the biggest circle of competence. I've got friends who are competent in a whole lot bigger area than I am, but they stray outside of it.[44]

It's not the size that matters. It's the boundaries.

Buffett describes one of his business managers, a Russian immigrant, who knew *nothing* about stocks and such.[45] She knew cash, and she knew furniture. She built a spectacularly successful furniture business. The secret to her success was knowing her circle of competence – and staying within it. Buffett cites Tom Watson Sr, founder of IBM: 'I'm no genius. I'm smart in spots but I stay around those spots.'[46] That's the spirit.

The connection with overconfidence is obvious. As long as you stay within your circle of competence, your degree of overconfidence is bounded. You're bound to be reasonably calibrated. The moment you stray outside of your circle of competence, though, the threat of overconfidence becomes more acute. This is especially true if you're unclear on where the boundaries are and still *think* you're inside your circle. If so, expect the degree of overconfidence to balloon.

Knowing our circles of competence is useful to us as individuals. But it's no less useful to an employer, manager, supervisor, or the like. If you have some say over what other people do, and when and how they do it, then you need to be attentive to their circle of competence. As long as you let people do what they do best, you don't need to worry about overconfidence quite so much. If you let them – or, worse, encourage them – to stray too far outside of their circle, you're inviting overconfidence. This is especially true, of course, if they *think* they remain inside of it – maybe because you made them, or allowed them, to think so.

So that's the first thing to keep in mind: know your circle of competence.

The second thing to keep in mind is to avoid selecting for overconfidence. It sounds obvious, but it's not. If you're an employer, manager, investor, or what have you, you will have some degree of influence over whom you work with, whom you listen to, and whom you trust. As I said in the previous section, it's easy to confuse confidence with competence. If you hire the most confident job seekers, you are virtually guaranteed to be surrounded by overconfident employees. If you promote the most self-assured co-worker, you're likely to end up with overconfident leadership. If you listen to the guy who speaks the loudest and with the greatest conviction, you are likely to get overconfident advice. I say 'guy' because that person is not unlikely to be male. If you favour him, you're likely to disfavour much better calibrated female colleagues. In the long run, you'll all be worse off for it.

The third thing is to encourage people to make clear and unambiguous predictions, and to provide quality feedback. Most organizations are more or less data-driven now, but it's still worth keeping in mind. Obviously, the data can't just sit there. You'll need to link prediction with outcome, and honestly assess any discrepancy.

The fourth thing is to develop a culture in which people feel comfortable expressing a reasonable degree of calibration. That means fostering an environment where people feel comfortable admitting they don't know things. In some contexts, such an admission is considered shameful, and may be met with scorn and ridicule. Such environments incentivize people to pretend that they know things when they don't, and invite overconfidence. Instead, we need to reinforce expressions of ignorance or uncertainty. We need to express our appreciation of people who are willing *not* to act confidently.

When I first started teaching at university level, I was around twenty-five, and younger than some of the students in the class. I was desperate not to come across as ignorant and unable to answer the students' questions. Over the years, however, I've realized that it does little harm to confess that I don't know the answer to every question. In fact, some students seem to appreciate frank admissions of ignorance. It's often quite sufficient to say, 'I'll look it up', and get back to the topic. Sometimes I'll turn the question back on the person asking it: 'What do *you* think?' It turns out that when people ask a question, very often they already have some idea of an answer, and are grateful for the opportunity to articulate it. Admitting ignorance and uncertainty, it seems to me, can actually garner more respect than not.

So here's something you can do, especially if you have a leading position somewhere: be a good example! Admit that you don't know what you don't know. Admit uncertainty when you're not sure. Show that there's no shame in confessing ignorance by asking others for their honest opinion. And when other people admit their own ignorance, make sure to respond with appreciation rather than scorn or ridicule. Thank them for being honest – and maybe confess you don't know either.

Developing a culture in which people feel comfortable expressing a reasonable degree of calibration also means fostering an environment where people feel comfortable admitting they were wrong. Again, in some contexts it's considered shameful to be wrong, and embarrassing to have to admit that you were. Such environments encourage people to avoid admitting that they were wrong in the past. In the worst case, such environments cause us to double down on what we (at some level) already know was wrong. Such environments invite overconfidence too. Instead, we need to reinforce admissions that we were wrong. We need to express our appreciation to people who are willing to confess that they made mistakes.

So again: be a good example. Admit you were wrong when you were. And when people confess their own mistakes, make sure to express your appreciation. Avoid the urge to make fun of them.

Developing an overconfidence-proof team also involves asking people for reasons. When people make various claims – especially when very confident – ask what reason the speaker has for thinking so. But, even more importantly, ask what reasons might speak against it.

This, in turn, requires building a culture where people dare to ask difficult questions – even, or especially, of superiors. If you punish people for challenging you, you certainly won't get the difficult questions that you need to be less overconfident.

And when things go wrong, which they inevitably will, try to make sure to learn the right lessons from the failure. Ask: 'What happened, exactly?' Or else: 'What sequence of events led to the bad thing that happened?' Then follow up with: 'How could we have prevented the bad thing from happening?' And finally, ask: 'What can we do differently to make sure it doesn't happen again?' Having this conversation will force you and your team to discuss all the errors that were made, in the spirit of getting more calibrated and making fewer mistakes.

Discussion

The great Austrian economist Joseph Schumpeter is famous for using the phrase 'creative destruction' as a way of capturing the potential in modern capitalism for both destruction and innovation. Schumpeter, who ended up teaching at Harvard, claimed that he had set himself three goals in life. He intended to be the greatest economist in the world, the best horseman in Austria, and the greatest lover in Vienna. By the end of his life he added, mournfully, that he had achieved only two of the three. (He didn't say which.) Given all the work on overconfidence, its causes and consequences, you might think that economists would be the very model of epistemic humility. You'll be shocked to learn they're not.

Economists in fact may be more overconfident than the average person, especially when they appear as experts in matters of public policy.[47] That's a bad thing. Overconfident economists are likely to oversell and underdeliver, which sets them up for failure. Failure invites ridicule, which makes all of us look bad – especially when it's deserved. As economist Ken Binmore writes, 'have we not got ourselves into enough trouble already by claiming vastly more than we can deliver? I am certainly tired at having fun poked at me.'[48]

Economists would likely be more effective in the long run if they moderated their confidence. As Robbins pointed out: 'Economists have nothing to lose by understating rather than overstating the extent of their certainty. Indeed, it is only when this is done that the overwhelming power to convince of what remains can be expected to have free play.'[49] Anyway, persistent overconfidence is what we should expect, based on existing research.

In this chapter, I've offered some advice that you can use to become more epistemically humble and to build overconfidence-proof teams. It should be obvious how this is economics, but if not, just think about its implications for business and investing. It should also be obvious how the advice explored here differs from advice on offer elsewhere. The economic approach is quite distinctive. The advice is immediately actionable: you can start implementing it today. And it's based on half a century of data. None of it guarantees that your team will be perfectly calibrated. As we have seen, overconfidence is hard to avoid. But still: behavioural economists have identified strategies supported by evidence. You could do a lot worse than implementing them in your own personal and professional life.

8

How to Get Rich

When my father died unexpectedly in 2021, I was put in charge of managing his estate. He was an exceptionally smart man, and accomplished too. He was an air-force fighter pilot and flight instructor, aerospace engineer, and ultimately a test pilot and chief engineer for the JAS 39 Gripen, a new-generation multi-role fighter jet. But when I learned what his investment strategy had been, I was aghast. He had invested a large share of his savings in exactly three stocks. He had picked the three (for all I can tell) based on the feeling he had in his gut at the time. It obviously hadn't occurred to him to ask anyone for advice. He could have asked an investment professional. Maybe, in the absolutely worst case, he could have asked his son, the PhD economist.

Economists sometimes respond poorly if you ask them for investment advice at cocktail parties, on aeroplanes, and so forth. Economists think of themselves, first and foremost, as social scientists. They resent being confused with investment professionals – or, God forbid, professors of finance. (The latter tend to be employed by business schools, not departments of economics, and are considered a totally different species.) The disdain is unfortunate. It might discourage others from asking for advice.

Do you have to be an economist to do well financially? Of course not. Can economics help? Absolutely! Economists have much to teach about financial behaviour. Their advice applies if you want to get rich, as the chapter title says. But it also applies if you want to build up a modest nest egg, or just get out of debt. It applies even if your goal is to put some money aside so that you can give it to somebody who needs it more than you do. The advice is theoretically grounded and immediately actionable. It's stuff you can start working on today.

Here, I will focus on four straightforward pieces of advice: (1) Save when you can. (2) Invest in index funds, not individual assets. (3) Borrow judiciously. And finally: (4) Improve your skills. The advice might strike the professional economist as so obvious that it's not even worth spelling out. But, as the example of my father shows, even very smart and accomplished professionals could make use of it. Research confirms the impression that many people find these principles unfamiliar or even counterintuitive. And that includes the professionally and academically accomplished.

Economists' investment advice is grounded in two central pieces of machinery: the theory of rational choice under risk, and the theory of efficient markets. Economists have employed surveys and experiments to study financial literacy – basically, the skills required to make wise choices about money. The results are somewhat alarming. Surveys show that most of us, including highly educated people, lack the financial literacy required to complete elementary tasks, such as choosing a credit card or getting a mortgage, wisely. Finally, economists have a story to tell about why people fail to act in accordance with their advice. The story comes from behavioural economics, the strand of modern economics that incorporates insights from psychology. The story suggests that much of the stuff people hear about investment strategies is worse than useless and actively harmful. It may be more likely to trip you up than to guide you along. That includes, sadly, stuff you may have heard in business school or read in the financial press.

There's no reason economists should resent talking about investment strategies. Real people have much to learn – and economists have much to teach.

A note of caution. When I offer advice about how to get rich, what I hope to provide are guidelines that will give regular folk, given where they're at, as good a shot as any. If you're not a regular person – if you're Tiger Woods or an investment professional – the advice might not apply to you. As economists say, this is advice that applies 'on the margin'. It's aimed to help you progress from where you're at, rather than where you're not. I'm not saying following my advice is the only way to make more money. (It obviously isn't.) But, most importantly, it is designed to give you the best *chance* of getting rich. None of it is guaranteed to succeed. *Such advice does not exist.* People who offer get-rich-quick schemes are trying to take you for a ride. Following the advice here may even leave you poorer. Its purpose is simply to give you the best possible expectation – in the sense that there's no alternative advice which gives you better chances.

Finally, this chapter is not about *explaining* poverty, or *blaming* it on anyone. The point is not that poverty is due to bad choices at the individual level, or that poverty should be blamed on individual people and their decisions. It isn't, and it shouldn't. We've already seen how economists want to deal with poverty. The point of this chapter is to explore, specifically, what individuals can do from where they're at – 'on the margin' – to get out of debt and build wealth, if they want to.

Save when you can

In a previous life, I had a colleague who was ready to retire. I'll call him Robin. Robin had had a long career as an academic, with a research programme and a teaching record. Now it was time to retire. There was just one problem: Robin had no savings, and so couldn't afford to. Back when he took the position, he had opted out of the employer-sponsored pension scheme. The scheme was highly beneficial, given that Robin's employer would match his contributions. But Robin felt as though he could not afford to opt in. He didn't make enough as a junior academic, and figured he'd start saving later. Now he was suddenly past retirement age, and felt like he had no choice but to keep working. Some of us feared he'd have to stick around until we carried him out of his office on a stretcher.

The most obvious piece of advice is to save when you can, whether you're building wealth or getting out of debt. Many Americans are like Robin. They don't save at all, even when they could. In a 2021 survey, 25 per cent of respondents said they had no emergency savings whatsoever.[1] More than half (51 per cent) said they have less than three months' worth of emergency savings. Younger Americans are in particularly bad shape, as you'd expect. As many as 57 per cent of millennials would be unable to cover three months of expenses in an emergency.

Having minimal savings makes you vulnerable. The loss of a job, a natural disaster, or an adverse health event could be enough to push you into bankruptcy. I've known solidly middle-class families who've felt compelled to enter bankruptcy after relatively minor setbacks such as an unfortunate real-estate deal, a sudden divorce, or similar. If you don't have a cushion to fall back on, it could happen to you too.

Not everyone is in a position to save. If you're struggling to pay the bills today, saving for the future just may not be on the cards. If you have credit-card debt, it's wise to pay it off before you start saving. Whatever interest you'd earn on your savings is likely to be outweighed by the interest rates you have to pay the credit-card company. Not everyone needs to save. If you're independently wealthy, it might not matter to you if you save or not.

But many people could and should save for the future and don't. Robin was gainfully employed his entire career, and certainly could have found a way to squirrel away 5 per cent of his salary. (With the employer's contribution, that amounted to 10 per cent.) Part of the problem is that many of us start off with low salaries and low savings. Then we respond to rising salaries by increasing our expenditure to a commensurate degree. When you start a new job or gain promotion, you're often tempted to get a bigger apartment or a fancier car, or adopt more expensive habits – thereby eliminating your chances of saving for the future.

Many people could probably trim their expenditure a little. Even minor economies could make a huge difference over time. To figure out what would happen, you need nothing but high-school-level maths and some basic economic principles.[2] Let's suppose you make 100 units of money every year and that you manage to save 5 per cent. That means that every year, you can put five units of money in your bank account.

Imagine, first, that there's no interest. In five years, you'll have 25 units of money in your account – enough to cover three months' expenses in an emergency. After twenty years, you'll have a year's salary squirrelled away. After forty years, two years' salary. By then, you may be approaching retirement, when the money will come in handy.

In the real world, though, you can invest your money in such a way that you collect interest. Suppose, again for the sake of the argument, that you can earn 10 per cent per year by investing in an index fund (see below). This is roughly in line with historical data, although the future may be less bright.[3]

Year 1. You squirrel away 5 units on 1 January. By 31 December, you've accumulated 0.5 in interest. But you still have the 5, so your balance is 5.5.

Year 2. You have another 5 to save, so your total at the beginning of the year is 10.5. By the end of the year, you've earned 10 per cent interest on the total, meaning 1.05. Your balance becomes 11.55.

Year 3. You have 5 more to save. That's 16.55 at the beginning of the year, and 16.55+1.655≈18.21 at the end.

Figure 6 will give you a good idea of where this is going. After twenty years, you'll have 281 units of money in your account. That's almost three years' salary right there. After forty years, if you can keep it up, you'll have 2,434. That's more than twenty-four years' salary! If you start saving at twenty-five and retire at sixty-five, you'll

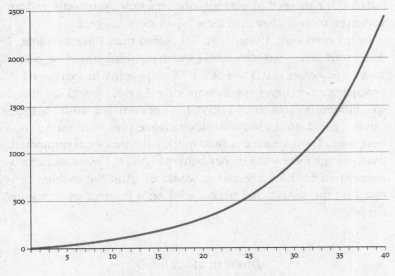

Figure 6: Total savings by year

have enough money to maintain your standard of living until you're about eighty-nine years old.

Note the difference between saving for twenty years and saving for forty years. If you plan to retire at sixty-five, that's the difference between starting saving at twenty-five vs. forty-five. If you start at twenty-five, you'll have almost nine times as much money in your account upon retirement.

The numbers here are made up. I'm not suggesting you'd see these exact returns if you followed my advice. The outcome depends on a range of factors outside of your control – and outside of mine. You could, if you're unlucky, do as I say but end up with much less money upon retirement. Inflation could eat much of your gains. You could also end up with more. In these examples, I have assumed that your salary and savings rate (5 per cent) remain constant throughout your career. If you are promoted, get yearly raises to keep pace with inflation, or succeed in saving more over time, you could end up with even more money than these calculations suggest.

In my own case, I was more like Robin than I like to admit. I didn't start saving seriously until I was in my third job out of graduate school. Before that, I was one of those people who increased my expenditure whenever my income rose. I wish I could say that I spontaneously came to my senses, but not even that would be true. I didn't get started until a bank employee pressured me to. But once I did, I was amazed at how quickly the money accumulated. Even though I knew the theory behind Figure 6, I was emotionally unprepared for how effective it would be. And the cushion provided by the savings has been useful on a number of occasions already.

Invest in index funds

What do you do with your savings, once you have them? If you ask economists, they'll tell you to invest in *index funds*. What you should not do is what my dad did, which is invest in individual assets. When you invest in a fund, you don't own individual assets, such as Google stock. You instead own a share of a (possibly very large) collection of stocks or other assets. An index fund is a collection of stocks or other assets linked to an index. The index may be Standard & Poor's 500, the Dow Jones Industrial Average, or some such. An index fund is constructed so that it tracks the index: it goes up when the index goes up, and down when it goes down.

There's a whole range of jokes about how economists can't agree on anything. 'If all the economists in the world were laid end to end, they would still not reach a conclusion.' 'If you put ten economists in a room, you'll get eleven opinions.' 'Economics is the only field in which two people can share a Nobel Prize for saying the complete opposite.' But when the IGM Forum at the University of Chicago asked leading economists about index funds, every single one of those who responded agreed that they're the best choice.[4] No exceptions.

Keep in mind what this means, though. When economists say that index funds are the best choice, they don't mean to say that the outcome is necessarily good. If the index goes down, the fund will lose value. Nor are they saying that the outcome is necessarily better than every individual asset. After the fact, you can always identify at least one stock that did better than the index as a whole. What they mean is that *over time*, there's no other investment that gives you a better expectation of riches. There is no alternative investment that gives you licence to expect to do better.

There is an exception, which is if you happen to have inside information – information that's relevant to the price of a stock that's not available to other market participants. Trading on inside information can be very profitable indeed, but it's also illegal. I wouldn't encourage you to try it.

What is it about index funds that makes economists like them so much? There are at least three things.

First, compared to other funds, they're *cheap*. The professionals who manage funds of all kinds are typically paid some percentage of the assets that they manage. You pay them whether the fund goes up or down. Index funds are cheap to administer. The reason is that the manager of an index fund doesn't do very much apart from identifying a collection of stocks that will make the fund behave like whatever index it is tied to. Other than rebalancing the fund from time to time, the manager can sit by passively and let the fund do its thing. By contrast, an actively managed fund is one where managers are continuously buying and selling in the interest of beating the market. Actively managing a fund requires more work. It just costs more.

The price difference between passive and active funds is huge. The cost of managing a fund is expressed in *expense ratios*. That's the share of all assets that are spent on administration. It comes out of your money. You can think of it as the price you pay for the benefit of investing in the fund. At the time of writing, index funds with my financial institution have an expense ratio hovering around 0.05 per cent. If I invest $1,000 with them, I pay $0.50 every year. The most expensive actively managed fund with the same institution has an expense ratio of 1.27 per cent. That might not sound like much. But if I invest $1,000 with them, I pay $12.70 every year. The two numbers differ by a factor of 25! That difference can translate into a lot of money over the course of a lifespan – especially if you do well and your assets keep growing. Index funds are a great deal, compared to other funds.

These numbers will be different where you are, at the time when you're reading this. If you go to the website of a bank or financial institution, you should be able to pull up a list of all the funds they offer. You should also be able to order them by expense ratio, from lower to higher. That way you can see what numbers apply to you, right now. If you have money to invest, just look at the three to five funds at the top. Chances are, you can safely ignore the rest.

Second, index funds allow you to *diversify*. This means not putting all your eggs in one basket. It may be worth reflecting, for a second, on why you *shouldn't* put all your eggs in one basket. Imagine that you put all your eggs in individualized little baskets. You may be *more* likely to drop one, if you do. But dropping one basket with one egg in it isn't a big deal when you have so many more which you have not dropped. Meanwhile, you'd be very unlikely to drop all the baskets with all the eggs. That's good, because breaking all your eggs would be very bad. Similar principles apply to investments. If you invest in a fund consisting of many different stocks, it is very likely that one of them will underperform the market. That's not a big deal. Meanwhile, it is extremely unlikely that all of them will do so. When you invest in an index fund, you don't need to worry about what individual stocks are up to. The entire fund, by construction, will never underperform the market index it's linked to. (Neither will it overperform it, of course.)

Investing, in individual stocks especially, is an inherently risky activity. But index funds are safe by comparison. They're a much, much safer bet than individual stocks. And by and large they're much safer than actively managed funds too. Investing in index funds gives you more safety, in this sense, at a lower price. That's pretty good.

Third, index funds are likely to perform as well as any other investment. This last bit might sound surprising. How could an index fund ever be expected to perform as well as an actively managed one? Isn't it obvious that smart, active managers can beat the market if you pay them to? No. This is where the theory of efficient markets comes in.

Economist Deirdre McCloskey explains it best. 'Take it as an axiom of human behavior that people pick up $500 bills left on the sidewalk,' she writes.[5] If you found that kind of money on your way home today, you'd pick it up. I know I would. Maybe we'd try to return the bill to its rightful owner; maybe we'd keep it. Either way, we wouldn't leave it on the ground. McCloskey calls the principle the *Axiom of Modest Greed*. As she points out, it's not controversial. If you doubt it, I invite you to put it to the test in your neighbourhood – or even better, please, in mine.

The axiom has one particularly interesting implication. It's this: 'Today there exists no sidewalk in the neighborhood of your house on which a $500 bill remains.' Call it the *Theorem of Modest Greed*. How could McCloskey know this? Well, she says, if there had been a $500 bill lying there at some point in time before now, the Axiom of Modest Greed says that someone would already have picked it up. So, by contradiction, there isn't a $500 bill for you to pick up right now.

The point generalizes. Suppose some fellow approaches you with a get-rich-quick scheme of some sort. 'Give me your money and I will return it one hundred-fold,' he may say. What he is telling you is that there are many $500 bills on some sidewalk, that he knows where they are, and that if you only give him your money first, he'll go fetch them for you. The man is lying. There is no pile of $500 bills anywhere for him to pick up. If there were, somebody would have picked them up already. If nothing else, the fellow could just as easily have taken them himself, without involving you in his scheme. You can safely assume the man is a fraud.

The point generalizes even further. Suppose some individual or institution approaches you with an offer. 'Give us your money and we will pay you handsomely,' it may say, as it invites you to invest in niche stocks, the latest blockchain crypto invention, or NFTs. What they're telling you is that they know where the free money is, and, if only they can get your money first, they'll secure it. If they really did know where the free money was, they could just as easily have invested their own. But they want to invest yours. What does that tell you?

The upshot is that no fund or other vehicle can dependably and predictably outperform the market in any significant way, at least not in the long term. *After* the fact, you can always identify individual stocks or funds that outperformed the market and did better than the index. But *before* the fact, you can't dependably identify which one it's going to be. After the fact, you can identify who won playing slot machines too. Before the fact, you can't. Same thing. Markets are, by and large, efficient. There are a lot of smart people out there looking for free money. If there were any, they would have picked it up. Thinking that you can amounts to believing there's free money just sitting around for the taking.

There is somebody who's guaranteed to make money when you invest in a fund. It's not you. It's the manager of the fund. As we know, they get paid a fraction of your assets no matter what the performance. In poker, there's a saying: 'Every table has a sucker. If you don't know who that is, it's you.' Something very similar is going on in the markets. There are a lot of smart people looking for opportunities. The opportunities in question will often be a matter of finding people to fleece. If you don't know who's being fleeced, you can assume it's you.

The point generalizes to economists too. Economists get a lot of flak for being unable to predict things like commodity prices and stock-market crashes. But suppose an economist were able to predict the price of corn. The economist could quickly make a fortune. McCloskey writes: 'With a little borrowing on the equity of his home or his reputation for sobriety, he can proceed to pick up $500 thousand, then $500 million, then more. Nothing to it.' But the economist doesn't, even when sober. He can't. If you meet economists who claim to be able to predict stuff like that, they're likely deluded or deceptive. Feel free to ask what McCloskey calls the American Question: '*If you're so smart, why ain't you rich?*'

Once you've put some money in an index fund, it's important that you leave it alone until you need it. A sure way to *lose* money is to invest when the market is doing OK, then panic and sell off your assets in a downturn. Sit tight, even if it hurts. Do the ostrich thing and don't even look at your financial statements. An article published in the *Journal of Finance* in 2000 compared individual investors who left their money alone to those who traded actively in order to time the rise and fall of individual stocks.[6] During a period when the market as a whole rose by almost 17.9 per cent, the investors who traded the most made 11.4 per cent. The people who traded actively were hugely overconfident. They were nowhere near as good at predicting market swings as they thought. They were swiftly punished by the markets. The title of the paper? 'Trading is Hazardous to Your Wealth'.

The one remaining question is whether to invest in stocks or bonds. There are index funds for both. From our perspective, there are two main differences. Historically, stocks have appreciated more than bonds. But stocks fluctuate more, meaning they make for a riskier bet. To a great extent, the choice comes down to personal preference. Can you tolerate bigger swings in the interest of making more money over time? If so, stocks may be for you. Would you find a rapid drop intolerable, and maybe feel like selling it all off? If so, bonds may be for you. In general, the more risk tolerant you are, the more you'll want stocks; the less risk tolerant you are, the more you'll want bonds.

But your time horizon matters too. If you're saving for the longer term – decades or more – then stocks may be the better choice. Fluctuations in the near term don't matter, since you won't cash in anyway. If you're saving for the shorter term, fluctuations matter a lot more. You don't want to risk having to cash in halfway through a downturn. Bonds may be the choice for you. Suppose you're saving for retirement. Chances are you'll want more stocks than bonds when young, but that you'll want to switch to more bonds than stocks as you near retirement. You can do that yourself, by rebalancing your portfolio every five or ten years. Or else you can invest in a low-cost retirement fund that does it for you. There are funds specifically for your age bracket that will take care of it for you.

The case for investing in index funds assumes that your goal is to have a shot at building wealth. There are other reasons to invest in the stock market, bitcoin, stamps, fine wines, or whatever captures your fancy. For some people it's a game, a hobby, or a lifestyle. Judging by some people's Twitter biographies, certain kinds of investment approach an identity. If that's you, and you can afford it, the argument here does not apply. Go ahead and trade to your heart's content. There are many hobbies and pastimes that are weirder and more expensive. The sport of offshore yacht racing is sometimes described as akin to standing fully dressed in a cold shower while tearing up $100 bills. And that's by the people who enjoy it!

Borrow judiciously

If saving money is so good, it may seem that borrowing money must be bad. But that would be too quick a judgement. Economists think there are very good reasons to borrow – if you do it judiciously.

There's a lot of evidence to suggest that people in general borrow too much. About one-quarter of Americans have more credit-card debt than emergency savings.[7] And the total amount of debt carried by Americans is going up. It reached record-breaking levels after the pandemic struck, as the labour market struggled and prices rose. In September 2021, total household debt reached $15.24 trillion.[8] That's more than 15 and then twelve zeros, which is a number so large most of us have trouble grasping it. Credit-card debt alone increased by $1.1 trillion from late 2019 to late 2021. Meanwhile, at the time of writing, consumer spending keeps going up.[9]

This level of debt will get a lot of people into trouble. The biggest concern is that a sudden loss of income, or an emergency expenditure, will make you unable to service the debt. When you borrow money, you commit to paying it back, with interest, in instalments on a certain schedule. As long as you stick to the schedule, you're fine. But if you fall behind – even through no fault of your own – things can escalate quickly. The lender can impose additional fees and may jack up your interest rate. In this situation some people feel compelled to borrow money from a second lender, offering even worse rates, to pay off the first one. The cycle can easily lead to very bad outcomes, including personal bankruptcy. Somewhere between 500,000 and 2 million people declare bankruptcy every year in the US alone.[10] The 25 per cent with more credit-card debt than emergency savings would be in a particularly tight spot if they lost their job or other source of income.

Some people are loath to borrow at all. They eschew charging stuff to a credit card – or using any one of the services encouraging you to buy now and pay later. These people instead insist on saving first and consuming later. A prominent politician where I live is famous for citing Scripture: 'The rich rule over the poor, and the borrower is slave to the lender.'[11] Being indebted makes you subject to somebody else's whims, the argument goes, so borrowing makes you unfree. People who never accrue any debt are, indeed, free in this way. That's a good reason to avoid debt.

But borrowing money can give you a great deal of freedom too.

This is why economists think there are situations in which we *should* borrow – with care.

Sometimes you need money in order to make money. In the Bible, the Parable of the Talents makes this point: 'Whoever has will be given more, and they will have an abundance. Whoever does not have, even what they have will be taken from them.' Maybe you need an education to get your dream job. Maybe you need a car to commute to it. Maybe you need to buy tools to be able to do your craft, or supplies to do your art. Maybe you need a new shirt or suit to look presentable. Maybe you need a babysitter to be able to work at all. Maybe you need some wiggle room to be able to focus on the future. If you need money to make money, borrowing is great. Assuming the income gained exceeds the cost of servicing the loan, it'd likely be smart to borrow. Maybe very smart.

Borrowing also allows you to spend when you need, and pay when you can. Many people need money in time for the holidays, but won't have any until after their wages come through a week or two later. In such a situation it can make sense to borrow, even at relatively high interest rates. Many people need money early in their career, when the kids are young, salaries low, and expenditure high. Many of them can expect to have more money later in life, when the kids are out of college, salaries are higher, and expenditure once again more modest. In such a situation too it can make sense to borrow, even over a long period of time.

Economists talk about *consumption smoothing*. That refers to maintaining a somewhat constant standard of living over time, even under changing conditions. You can think of consumption smoothing as a matter of redistribution. Consumption smoothing takes resources from yourself in a stage of life when you're relatively rich to yourself in a stage of life when you're relatively poor. Many people are relatively poor when they're in the process of forming a family – early in their career, when salaries are low, and expenditure associated with buying a first home and family car, etc. are high. You may be relatively rich before the kids arrive, when you and your partner are dinkies – 'Double Income No Kids' – and later in life when you're enjoying retirement after a long career.

There are, therefore, many reasons that borrowing may be smart. It may even make sense to borrow and save at the same time. If the interest you pay on your mortgage is less than the returns on your index fund, it makes sense to carry debt in order to invest. Increasing your mortgage in order to keep some money in your savings account can also give you liquidity – money to spend in a pinch, allowing you to avoid charging unexpected expenditure to a credit card. Again, you shouldn't borrow more than you can service. You need to take into account the possibility of losing your income – maybe as a result of an economic downturn, or extended sickness or disability – and of sudden expenditure – maybe as a result of an uninsured 'Act of God'.

Whether it makes sense to borrow or not in a given situation will depend on the interest rate. Interest is the price you pay for borrowing money. Interest rates vary dramatically, depending on where you live, who you are, and what you're borrowing for. At the time of writing, the interest on my mortgage is 1.25 per cent, on my line of credit 3.50 per cent, and on my credit card 15.50 per cent. Borrowing money from a credit-card company is more than ten times as expensive, in terms of interest, as mortgaging your house. If you don't carry any debt, it doesn't matter; if you do, it matters hugely. But these interest rates are all completely dwarfed by the interest charged by payday loan establishments, whose interest rates (on a yearly basis) can add up to more than 600 per cent.[12]

If you borrow money, all things being equal, you want to pay as little interest as possible. Typically this means getting a mortgage if you can, a line of credit if necessary, and a credit card if you absolutely must. Payday loan establishments are best avoided, except possibly in an emergency as a bridge to a more sustainable solution. If you have borrowed money from multiple sources, see if you can reduce the total amount of interest that you pay. Transfer debt from credit cards to lines of credit, and from lines of credit to a mortgage (if you can).

The problem with debt is that it's a lot easier to accumulate than to pay off. If you're contemplating borrowing money to cover some expenditure, it may help to think about the future in the manner of Bryan Caplan. Suppose you're considering borrowing money for a new purse and paying it back over thirty-six months. How long will the purse spark joy? If the answer is that the purse will spark joy every month from here until eternity, then borrowing might make sense. (This assumes that the joy it sparks exceeds the pain of making the monthly payments.) If the answer is that the sparks will diminish and may disappear entirely, things look rather different. Suppose you adapt to your new purchase in such a way that the purse will spark more joy than the payments hurt for no more than three months. If so, you're looking at three months of net joy, followed by thirty-three months of net suffering. That may make the purchase seem a lot less appealing.

Whenever you're unsure whether a purchase is worth it, consider saving up first and making the purchase later. If you save for thirty-six months before making the purchase, you may find that the purse is out of fashion and completely uninteresting to you. If so, you can skip the purchase and just keep the money.

There's another reason to postpone consumption, if you can. Behavioural economist George Loewenstein has studied the pleasures (and pains) of anticipation. He argues that postponing consumption can *increase* its contribution to a person's well-being. His studies reveal that people often prefer to delay pleasurable experiences, such as a kiss from a movie star of their choice. A significant part of the joy we derive from a positive event is what Loewenstein calls 'savouring'. That's the pleasant feeling we get inside from anticipating good things. We can, therefore, increase the total amount of utility we get from good things by pushing them into the future. The flip side of this coin is that a significant part of the unpleasantness we derive from negative experiences is 'dread'. That's the unpleasant feeling we get from anticipating bad events. Consequently, people often prefer to accelerate unpleasant experiences, such as an electric shock. We can, therefore, decrease the total amount of disutility we get from bad thing by dragging them into the present. This suggests surprise birthday parties are a mistake, because they eliminate all savouring on the part of the object of the celebrations. But more importantly, it suggests that we have reason to repress the urge for instant satisfaction and push things we look forward to into the more or less remote future. Saving first and consuming later not only allows you to save on interest, but also gives you something to look forward to. That counts for a lot.

Improve your skills

A&W Restaurants is an American fast-food chain. The chain is famous not only for its burgers, but also for being at the centre of one of the most famous marketing flops of all time. In the 1980s, A&W decided to take on McDonald's by improving on its centrepiece burger, the Quarter Pounder. As the name suggests, it contains one-quarter of a pound of beef. In a bid for market share, A&W decided to offer the same thing, but make it with more and fresher meat. Their one-thirder contained a full one-third of a pound of beef. That's one-sixth of a pound (or 33 per cent) more beef than McDonald's used. It's a sizable upgrade. And it was sold at the same price.

The effort was a total and complete failure. A post-mortem investigation revealed why. A majority of focus-group participants thought the one-thirder was a bad deal because it contained less meat. They thought ⅓ was less than ¼! Three is less than four, so . . . As the owner of A&W concluded, perhaps overly diplomatically: 'the American consumer may not fully understand or value the third-pound promise'.[13]

People's inability to understand fractions when ordering a burger may not matter much to people who don't themselves own A&W. Many people (and vast numbers of cows) would even be better off if burgers contained less meat. But the story illustrates something important. Many people don't have the skills required to make smart choices in their financial environment, whether for their own benefit or for the benefit of their community. Even worse, they don't realize it. The majority who thought the one-thirder was a bad deal were apparently quite sure of themselves. And if people can't deal with simple fractions, what are the chances that they can assess credit-card offers with annual percentage rates, fixed fees, and compound interest? Not great.

A final piece of advice is to develop the skills required to make smart decisions about money. The ability to process information and make informed decisions about financial matters is called *financial literacy*. For many people, financial literacy can literally be a matter of life or death. There's no practice mode. By the time we're old enough to have our own money to spend, real money is at stake. And for many big decisions, we have limited opportunities to learn. Buying a house is something you're unlikely to do more than a few times over the course of a lifetime. Saving for retirement is effectively something you do only once. You can change savings strategies during your active years. But by the time you retire and learn what you did right and wrong, it's too late for a restart. Some people begin in easy mode, in the sense that they can afford to make mistakes – allowing them to acquire financial literacy through trial and error. Others start in hard mode, already balancing on the edge of the precipice.

Financial literacy is something economists have studied for years.[14] They've learned a lot about the nature of the problem, and what can be done to fix it. Studies have shown that people's financial literacy in general is quite bad, and also far from as good as people think. People with low financial literacy are much worse off, financially, than others. The good news is that financial literacy is a skill you can acquire. And when people do acquire it, they make more and worry less.

First off, how can you measure something like financial literacy? Economists Annamaria Lusardi and Olivia S. Mitchell have developed a test based on three simple questions.[15] Try it for yourself:

1. Suppose you had $100 in a savings account and the interest rate was 2 per cent per year. After five years, how much do you think you would have in the account if you left the money to grow: (a) more than $102, (b) exactly $102, or (c) less than $102?

2. Imagine that the interest rate on your savings account was 1 per cent per year and inflation was 2 per cent per year. After one year, would you be able to buy: (a) more than, (b) exactly the same as, or (c) less than today, with the money in this account?

3. Do you think that the following statement is true or false? 'Buying a single company stock usually provides a safer return than a stock mutual fund.' (a) True, (b) false.

Each question also had 'do not know' and 'refuse to answer' options. If you want to confirm your understanding of these questions, you'll find the answer in the endnotes.[16]

The headline finding is that regular folk are surprisingly financially illiterate. In one study by Lusardi and Mitchell, randomly selected Americans over fifty fell into three roughly equally large groups. One-third (34.3 per cent) got all three answers right. One-third (35.8 per cent) got two answers right. The rest (26.1 per cent) got one or no answers right. Only about half (52.3 per cent) of all the people responding to the questions knew the answer to the third one. It apparently didn't help that everyone in this study, because of their age, had had decades of experience with financial decision making, and also had lived through multiple stock-market crashes and periods of inflation. If *you* were able to answer the third question, maybe because you got the answer earlier in the chapter, you're already in a better position than about half of older Americans.

The problem is not unique to America, if you're wondering. The evidence suggests that it is quite common, even in rich countries. Germany is known as one of the more financially literate countries.

But, even there, only a little more than half (53.2 per cent) got all three answers right.

While people in general score quite low, there's a lot of variation within a country. Financial literacy varies with age. It's lowest among the young, who don't yet have a great deal of experience with financial decision making, and among the old. By contrast, middle-aged people have relatively high financial literacy scores. There's a gender gap that's large and persistent. In Germany 59.6 per cent of men answered all three questions correctly. The corresponding number for women was only 47.5 per cent. In the US the numbers were 38.3 for men and 22.5 for women. In Switzerland they were 62.0 for men and 39.3 for women. Financial literacy also varies with ethnicity. In the US context, African Americans and Hispanics score particularly low. As you'd expect, the more educated have higher financial literacy. Among Americans with a post-graduate degree, 63.8 per cent knew the correct answers to all three questions. Among Americans who never completed high school the number was 12.6 per cent. That said, having a lot of education does not immunize you completely. Even among the Americans with a post-graduate degree, more than one-third were still unable to get all three answers right.

Although people's financial literacy is generally low, they don't realize it. As we saw above, people who are unable to compare simple fractions are generally ignorant of that fact. Economists have assessed people's confidence in their abilities in the financial area alongside their actual financial literacy. Confidence in one's financial literacy is measured, for example, with a question like this: 'On a scale from 1 to 7, where 1 means very low and 7 means very high, how would you assess your overall financial knowledge?' The results show a certain mismatch between ability and confidence. In one US 2009 study, 70 per cent gave themselves a score of 4 or higher. That is, they rated themselves on or above the mid-point on the scale. And yet, only 30 per cent could answer the questions correctly. Again, it's not just in the US. Similar findings have been made elsewhere. People seem to be dramatically overconfident in this arena as well.[17]

The degree of overconfidence varies. Unsurprisingly, there's a gender gap here too. Women are a lot more likely to answer 'don't know' to questions about financial literacy. In the US, 50 per cent of women said 'don't know' in response to at least one of the questions. The corresponding figure for men was 34.3 per cent. The pattern holds across countries. It suggests that women are maybe less overconfident than men. Overconfidence also appears to increase with age. As people's financial literacy falls during older adulthood, confidence in their financial abilities actually *increases*. Lusardi and Mitchell think this may be why older people are particularly prone to financial scams.[18] If you're an older adult, consider getting competent advice in financial matters even if – especially if – you don't think you need it.

The three questions were selected because they tap into fundamental concepts at the root of savings-and-investment decisions. The low scores suggest many people, maybe two-thirds, don't have the most basic skills required to save and invest. The term 'functional illiteracy' is used to denote a lack of skills necessary for one's own and the community's development. Using this terminology, we can say that most people are functionally financially illiterate. And the situation is made even worse by the fact they don't know it.

Economists are also interested in whether, or to what extent, financial literacy comes with financial success. A vast array of studies have found exactly what you'd expect: the two things go together.[19] No matter which generation you look at, financial wellness is considerably lower among people with low financial literacy.[20] People with low financial literacy report having more trouble making ends meet, having more difficulties coming up with $2,000 in an emergency, being so indebted that they cannot address other financial priorities, and spending more time thinking about and dealing with money problems. The differences are particularly pronounced in Generation Y. They were between twenty-four and thirty-nine years of age when the survey was done. Gen Y'ers with low financial literacy report spending almost three times as much time worrying about money (fourteen hours per week) than their more financially literate counterparts (five hours per week).

Encouragingly, financial literacy can be taught – cheaply and effectively. To test whether financial education can improve people's financial literacy and financial wellness, economists have run a series of randomized controlled trials. Tim Kaiser and his co-authors recently performed a meta-study, which takes all these studies into account.[21] They considered seventy-six financial-education programmes, in thirty-three countries and six continents, with a grand total of 160,000 participants. Their meta-study showed that financial education improves financial literacy. That's maybe not so surprising. Importantly, though, the study also showed that financial education changed financial behaviour down the line. And because financial education can be delivered relatively cheaply, in schools and workplaces, on the internet and over television, it's highly cost-effective. That is, it delivers far more benefit to the participants than it costs to implement. This is important, because a meta-study of randomized controlled trials is widely considered the best evidence we could possibly have.

Similar results appear under less controlled conditions in the real world. When high schools require financial-education classes before graduation, good things happen.[22] Graduates end up with less debt, better credit scores, lower default rates, better loans, and other benifits. There's also evidence of positive external effects. When students are offered financial education, it improves teachers' and parents' financial literacy and financial behaviours.[23] Financial education can be a benefit to the whole community. It should not be surprising, therefore, that the OECD's Programme for International Student Assessment (PISA) has taken an interest in financial literacy. As Lusardi and Mitchell remark: 'PISA has taken the position that financial literacy should be recognized as a skill essential for participation in today's economy.'[24]

So, to improve your chances of getting rich (or out of debt), you should improve your financial literacy. Your ability to process economic information and to make wise financial decisions can have huge downstream consequences. It can benefit you, and your community too. The advice applies even if you've got a lot of experience making financial decisions already, maybe because you're an older adult. The advice also applies even if you're highly educated. Take medical doctors: Lusardi believes medical doctors may be some of the 'worst offenders'.[25] Rich and confident, but not very sophisticated about money, they are vulnerable to being taken advantage of. Finally, again, get competent economic advice if and when you can use it – even if you already know a lot. Like my dad should have.

Why aren't we rich already?

Poverty wasn't caused by individuals failing to heed the advice in this chapter, and it cannot be blamed on the poor themselves. But many of us (including yours truly) would like to have more money. Why don't we? There are several explanations, all of which could be true to some degree.

Poor financial literacy is obviously part of the answer. Most of us lack the skills we need to process economic information and make wise financial choices – and we don't know it. Meanwhile, the financial environment is getting more and more demanding.[26] First, the number of financial products available to the small investor is rapidly growing. There was a time when saving money required you to go to a bricks-and-mortar location with a handful of options. With online banking and whatnot, regular people can access a huge number of financial institutions, offering a vast range of options. Second, changes in national pension systems put more responsibility on the workers themselves. It used to be that you could depend on state benefits and, if you had one, your employer-sponsored pension plan. These days, workers have to take responsibility for their own retirement savings to a much higher degree. These developments can be beneficial for some people who know what they want and what they're doing. But they put very high demands indeed on the bandwidth and financial literacy of the small investor. And our financial skills are simply not keeping up. Think about the baby boomers, and how different the financial environment is now from when they entered the workforce. With all these changes, we have to run faster and faster just to keep up with developments.

But poor financial literacy is only part of it.

Another part of the answer is the fact that there are people out there who want your money as badly as you do. There are scams, of course. There are also perfectly legal ways to get you to part with your money. We should not be surprised that banks and other financial institutions are doing what they can to make you fork it over. They advertise aggressively, and they're good at it. Some financial institutions use a scheme along the following lines. Write ten newsletters making ten different predictions about the stock market. Wait a while, until by chance alone one or more predictions come true. Then advertise your proficiency at predicting the stock market, using as evidence the one newsletter that turned out to be accurate. It is not unusual for banks and such to cite the fact that some niche fund made fantastic returns last year as evidence of their proficiency – without mentioning that they have 200 other funds that did not do quite so well. It's the same scheme. It's taking advantage of the limited financial literacy among potential clients. Doing so is (mostly) legal.

Yet another part of the answer has to do with the way in which our brains are wired. The ways in which our psychology messes with our economic behaviour is the domain of behavioural economics.

Behavioural economists have shown that we are both impatient and impulsive. *Impatience* means that we discount stuff that happens later, relative to stuff that happens now. If you have the choice between a fun experience sooner and the same fun experience later, you'll often choose to have fun now. (One exception is when you're savouring the good, as I explained earlier.) Impatience is widely considered to be rational. Some people just want to have fun now, even at the cost of less fun later. *Impulsivity* means that we fall prey to instant gratification, even when we're otherwise patient. Impulsivity is widely thought to be irrational, because it can override our rational pursuit of more distant goods. Both impatience and impulsivity work against us when we try to save. Saving is, by definition, a matter of giving something up *now* in exchange for something good later. The impatient and the impulsive might not be able to handle it. It's not like it's impossible to overcome impatience and impulsivity, but it might require work and willpower.

Behavioural economists have also studied the power of stories. Humans love stories. The book *Narrative Economics*, by Nobel laureate Robert J. Shiller, argues that narratives are a principal driver of human behaviour and economic events.[27] We've all heard stories of people who made it big by launching a successful start-up business, investing in the latest crypto invention, or whatever it may be. Such stories are compelling, especially if they include a history of hardship and struggle. They stick. Stories are great; I love reading fiction. I use them in my writing too, as you've noticed.

But telling and retelling good stories has a downside. If you doubt it, just ask a wolf. Wolves pose a trivial danger to humans. The number of verified fatal attacks by wolves on humans is vanishingly low. And yet fear of wolves runs deep. Part of the explanation is that there are so many stories about big, bad wolves eating little girls' grandmothers in the forest and chasing wayward princesses through the snow. As a result of all these stories, the idea of wolves attacking humans is highly salient to us. If you enjoy stories such as *Little Red Riding Hood* and *Frozen*, the possibility of a wolf eating you might be the first thing that comes to mind when you think of one. Moreover, and this is key: how salient an event is to our mind affects how likely we judge it to be. Something that is easily available to us – something that comes to mind effortlessly – will be considered more likely to happen than something that does not. The result is something called *availability bias*.[28] When the image of a big, bad wolf attacking vulnerable humans is easily and vividly available, we will tend to overestimate the probability of that sort of thing happening in the real world.

What does availability bias have to do with investing? Stories about successful investment strategies are legion. You read them in the financial press and business magazines, under headings such as 'How I got rich'. You also hear them in business school, where they are referred to as 'cases'. The stories are often focused on one individual investor: the person who made tons of money betting using some more or less idiosyncratic strategy – purchasing a particular kind of asset, launching a successful start-up, or messing around with bitcoin. I can't recall ever reading a story about somebody who made money investing in index funds. That would be boring by comparison.

There are two problems with this kind of writing and pedagogy, even when the stories are true. First, the cases you hear about are obviously not representative. The stories are selected because they're good stories – fun to read or to discuss in class. They're a lot like the successful newsletters or niche funds mentioned above. You'll never hear of all the people who did the same thing as the people in your stories but weren't similarly successful. For all we know, the success of the people in the stories may be due to good luck. Learning about the strategy they used might be as instructive as learning the numbers somebody used to win the lotteries.

Second, good stories about idiosyncratic investment strategies will make them more salient to us. And when they're more easily and vividly available to our minds, we'll tend to overestimate the chances of that sort of thing happening to us. This, in turn, may trick us into trying some idiosyncratic strategy ourselves, when doing so would be a mistake. In all: the stories you read about in the financial press and the cases you discuss in business school may be worse than useless – they may trip you up. There's a good chance you'd be better off ignoring them completely.

Why is our cognitive apparatus so poorly suited to dealing with the current financial environment? There's an obvious explanation. Our brains evolved to be more or less what they are now a long time ago – way before there were stock markets, NFTs, and online scammers. To the extent that they're adapted to the environment, they're adapted to an environment that simply doesn't exist any more.

People who want to save, or get out of debt, therefore face a triple threat: lower-than-ideal financial literacy, scammers and marketers, and a cognitive apparatus not designed to deal with the waters they have to navigate. Again, it's not as though we can't use our brains to deal with the current environment. Brains are, in fact, highly adaptive. But it takes work and effort. And that starts with the realization that we can't make choices on autopilot. We need to take charge of our financial behaviour, and develop the resources to do it right.

Having it all

Economists should be pleased when asked for investment advice. It means somebody trusts them. And economics indeed has useful, immediately actionable advice that can help most people. It's not guaranteed to make you rich, or even free from debt. Nothing is. Get-rich-quick schemes are all fraudulent. The advice is designed to give us the best shot, given where we're at, and that's not nothing. The advice applies whether you're already in the black or have found yourself deeply in the red. It applies whether you want more money for yourself and your family, or if you want more to give away to the needy. You don't have to be selfish to want to build wealth.

Some people object to economists trying to help people make better financial decisions. The objection is that such advice is useless, or even harmful, in that it doesn't solve the problem of poverty. 'Stop telling poor people to try to save,' someone might say. 'Fix the problem of poverty instead.'

To the economist, the objection looks like a failure to think on the margin. Of course, we should try to fix the problem of poverty. As you know from the chapter on poverty, economists have much to say about how to go about that. There's no contradiction between trying to fix the bigger problem of poverty and empowering people to make better choices in their own lives. The latter is not an effort to explain poverty, as I've said before, or to blame the poor for their predicament. We should simultaneously reduce poverty and help people make better choices. It's simply a mistake to think we have to choose one or the other. Economics can do both.

9

How to Build Community

On a late-summer afternoon of 1938, two eleven-year-old girls waded into the water in Stora Rör harbour on the Baltic island of Öland. They were awaiting their mother, who was returning by ferry from a hospital visit on the mainland. Unbeknownst to the girls, the harbour had been recently dredged. Where there used to be shallow sands, the water was now cold, dark, and deep. The girls couldn't swim. They drowned mere feet from safety – in full view of a powerless little sister on the beach.[1]

The community was shaken. It resolved that no such tragedy should ever happen again. To make sure every child would learn to swim, the community decided to offer swimming lessons to anyone interested. The Stora Rör Swimming Association, founded that same year, is still going strong. It's enrolled thousands of children, adolescents, and adults. My grandmother, a physical-education teacher by training, was one of its first instructors. My father, myself, and my children all learned how to swim there. I hope and trust my grandchildren will too, should I have any.

It's impossible to know if the association has saved lives. It may well have. The community has been spared, although kids play in and fall into the water all the time. Nationwide, drowning is the leading cause of death for Swedish kids between one and six years of age.

We do know that the association has had many other beneficial effects. It has offered healthy, active outdoor summer activities for generations of kids. Learning to swim is fun and useful, even if it doesn't save your life. The activities of the association remain open to all. Fees are nominal. Children come from families of farmers

187

and refugees, artists and writers, university professors and CEOs of major corporations, locals and tourists. Some participants travel considerable distances by car, bike, or bus to join in. Unlike many other athletic organizations, the goal is not to teach a small percentage of children to swim very fast, but to teach 100 per cent of the children to be competent swimmers. (Parents who get too agitated on the pier are told, politely, to sit down and shut up.)

The benefits extend beyond the participants themselves. Local young adults can work as swimming teachers. They get money, training, and early work experience. The cold seawater may even build character. The association has generated massive quantities of goodwill and social capital in the community. Lifelong friendships have been forged in the water, or on the shoreline, as children, their parents, and relatives spend hours and hours on the same beach for weeks on end. Meanwhile, the association has become a trusted community partner. The city that owns the beach and its facilities turns to the association for information about what improvements and services are needed. This allows the association to act as an intermediary between citizens and government, among other things helping funnel tax money into the projects most valuable to the community. Finally, the association boosts property values. The local property market is hot, and estate agents have been known to advertise the Swimming Association and its activities as a unique selling point of the village, alongside its many other virtues.

The association itself is entirely self-funded. It receives no taxpayer money at all. To keep fees low and activities accessible, it needs a dependable source of revenue. For better or worse, Sweden doesn't have a tradition of charitable giving like that found in the US or UK. Direct donations are entirely insufficient. Instead, the association gets a good chunk of its revenue from an annual charity auction. Members donate home-baked goods, home-made jams and marmalades, original art – or whatever they happen to be good at making. The donated goods are then auctioned off to other members. It is an open-bid auction, meaning that all bids immediately become common knowledge.

The auction generates hilarious amounts of revenue because members compete to bid the most absurd amounts. A modest, although delicious, home-baked cake can easily fetch the equivalent of £100 or more. The auction works, not only in the sense that it raises the requisite funds with minimal transaction costs but also in the sense that it extracts the funds from those people who can most afford to give. Members who are strapped for cash don't need to bid at all. Others can fork out as much as they want in exchange for cinnamon buns, the satisfaction of having won a bidding war with their neighbours, and a reputation for gracious generosity.

In economic terms, the Stora Rör Swimming Association is an *institution*. It's a set of rules, or 'prescriptions', that humans use to structure all sorts of repeated interactions.[2] These rules can be formalized in a governing document. The constitution of the association says that you have to pay dues if you want to remain a member in good standing, for example. But the rules that define the institution don't need to be written down. They don't even need to be formulated in words. 'Attend the charity auction and bid on things if you can afford it.' 'Volunteer to serve on the board when it's your turn.' 'Treat swimming teachers with respect.' 'Sit down and shut up while your children are in the water.' These are all unwritten rules. They may never have been formulated quite like this before. Still, they're widely – if not universally – followed. And, from an economic perspective, these rules taken together define what sort of thing the Swimming Association *is*.

Economist Elinor Ostrom studied institutions throughout her career. She wanted to know what institutions do, how and why they work, how they appear and evolve over time, how we can build and improve them, and, finally, how to share that knowledge with the rest of us.[3] Lin Ostrom (as her friends called her) believed in the power of economics to 'bring out the best in humans'. The way to do it, she thought, was to help them build community – developing the rich network of relationships that form the fabric of a society. In the process, Ostrom constructed a vision of the good society, consisting of overlapping and nested institutions of different size, delivering solutions for people at the proper scale. She called it *polycentricity*. And she thought economists had a legitimate role to play in realizing that vision. She rejected the traditional binary of market and state. She did not believe in *laissez-faire* economics, which advocates standing by while waiting for things to sort themselves out. Nor did she believe in command-and-control solutions, which favour fixing problems by means of central planning and social engineering. Instead, Ostrom believed the economist should properly act as a *catalyst of self-governance*.[4] That means helping people build institutions that work for them, given where they are.

Ostrom's research earned her the Nobel Memorial Prize in 2009. She was the first woman economics laureate. Her 1990 book *Governing the Commons* is a citation classic, with more than 47,000 citations at the time of writing.[5] An excellent introduction to her life and work is Vlad Tarko's *Elinor Ostrom: An Intellectual Biography*.

The Stora Rör Swimming Association is a perfect example of the sort of institution that occupied Ostrom her entire adult life. The association emerged as a solution to a problem identified by the people most affected by it. It's modest in size and scope. It's as large as it needs to be to fix the problem, but not much larger than that. It's run in a manner consistent with the values of the community. It's taken a form that the original members did not design and could not have predicted, but which reflects knowledge of local conditions and available resources. It blurs the distinction between individual and collective, as it appears on a scale different from both. It also blurs the distinction between market and state, as it's not taking advantage of either market or government solutions. Above all, it operates with the consent of the governed. People willingly – enthusiastically, even – agree to be bound by association rules in order to take advantage of its benefits. People consent because the benefits vastly exceed the costs – and the burdens and joys are distributed fairly across the community.

Perhaps you find the story about the Stora Rör Swimming

Association entirely unremarkable. You may feel an urge to point out that organizations of this kind exist all over the world, and not just on windswept Baltic islands. And you'd be right. That's the point! Institutions like this exist everywhere people live together in communities. They appear in rich countries and in poor, in peacetime and in war. Sometimes they're legally chartered, sometimes entirely informal. Sometimes they're smaller, involving merely a handful of people or households. Sometimes they're larger, even approaching the size of a country or federation. They exist because they solve problems facing people living together in communities. The problem doesn't have to be children drowning, although it obviously can be. It can also be a matter of providing potable water, keeping the environment clean, fairly dividing up a limited resource, preventing war and violence – or anything at all that people care about.

Even more importantly, where people living together face problems that have not yet been solved, there's a good chance that the solution could take the form of an institution.

If you don't read about modest institutions like the Stora Rör Swimming Association very often, it's not because they're not numerous enough. It's because they're less dysfunctional than national politics.[6] Local institutions don't always work, of course. Sometimes they fail in a manner spectacular enough to garner national attention. But, more frequently, they deliver the goods. Local institutions are the pillars of the community. If we want to build a society that works, we need to build and support our local institutions. If we want to help, though, we first need to understand how they work and why – and under what conditions they flourish. That's what Elinor Ostrom can teach us.

What's the problem?

Baltic cod is specially adapted to the brackish conditions of the Baltic Sea. Traditionally it's been one of the most important fish resources in the region.[7] When my dad took me cod fishing as a child, we'd barely have time to lower the lure to the proper depth before something would bite. Half an afternoon of fishing would give us enough cod to fill the freezer. Now the Baltic cod is mostly gone. The stock has collapsed. There are multiple causes, as you'd expect. Factors are as varied as environmental degradation, parasites, and seals. But a large part of the story is overfishing. The Baltic is surrounded by nine countries. Nothing prevented fishermen from these countries from fishing away as though there was no tomorrow, and that's what they did. The harvest far exceeded sustainable levels, especially given the declining conditions. Surviving fish are few in number and of poor quality. Even though an entire industry depended on the cod stock for its survival, its members destroyed it.

When Vikings settled in Iceland around the end of the ninth century, the place was lush with forests, mostly birch.[8] Over the next hundred years, the Vikings cut down some 97 per cent of the trees. The settlers wanted firewood and building materials, and land for grazing. The Vikings must have known that it would be bad to lose the forests. But they cut them down anyway. There was nothing and nobody to stop them. By now, a mere 0.5 per cent of Iceland is covered with forest. The lack of trees has led to extensive desertification, erosion, dust storms, and loss of arable land. If you visit, you'll find much of the island looks like a lunar landscape – dramatic, beautiful, and devoid of trees. Bringing forests back is a lot harder than cutting them down. Iceland is still struggling.

Depletion of common resources – be it fish stocks, forests, or whatnot – appears to have happened wherever humans live together in society. The Viking example shows that it's not unique to the capitalist mode of production, in case you were wondering. There's evidence humans have hunted prey to extinction for thousands (maybe even millions) of years.[9] But how can this happen, when people know that depletion and extinction are bad?

To understand what institutions do, we need to understand what problem they're meant to solve. Ostrom herself described the problem in terms borrowed from game theory.[10] That's the branch of economics that studies strategic interaction at the most abstract level. It provides a pithy description of the fundamental challenge facing communities around the world.

You may have heard the story of the *prisoner's dilemma*.[11] Two thieves, let's call them Bill and Bull, have been arrested on suspicion of two separate crimes, one major and one minor. The District Attorney (DA) has sufficient evidence to convict the two on the minor charge, but not on the major one. If Bill and Bull *cooperate* (C) with each other and stay mum, they will be convicted on the minor charge but not on the major one. They will both serve two years in jail. After separating the prisoners, the DA offers each of them a reduced sentence if they *defect* (D), and testify against the other for the major crime. If one prisoner defects but the other one cooperates, the defector walks free whereas the cooperator serves twenty years in jail. If both defect, both get convicted on the major charge but (as a reward for testifying) only serve ten years each. They have to make their decision independently of one another. They have no way of knowing what the other one will do. The two thieves don't care about anything except going to jail for as short a time as possible.

Bill and Bull's predicament is technically a game. It can be analysed with the tools of game theory. Simple games like this one can helpfully be represented in tabular form, as in Table 1.

	C	D
C	3,3	0,5
D	5,0	1,1

Table 1: Prisoner's dilemma in its original form

Each row represents an action taken by Bill (Player 1). Each column represents an action taken by Bull (Player 2). Because each player has two alternative courses of action, there are four possible outcomes. The numbers in those four cells represent the payoffs to Bill and Bull, respectively, separated by commas. Payoffs are given in utilities, which are just numbers that represent how good or bad an outcome is to a player. If the two cooperate (C) and avoid a lengthy prison sentence, Bill and Bull each get a payoff of three. That's pretty good. If both defect (D) and get a long sentence (but with a reduction), Bill and Bull each get a payoff of one. That's pretty bad. Now suppose that Bill defects while Bull cooperates. Then Bill walks and gets a payoff of five. That's very good! Bull gets the long sentence (with no reduction) and gets a payoff of zero. That's very bad! Same thing, but the other way around, if Bill cooperates while Bull defects.

What's going to happen? Look at the situation from Bill's perspective first. If Bull cooperates, Bill has the choice to cooperate for a payoff of three or defect for a payoff of five. Five is better than three, so he'll defect. If Bull defects, Bill has the choice to cooperate for a payoff of zero or defect for a payoff of three. Three is better than zero, so he'll defect. This means that Bill will defect no matter what Bull does! Defecting is a *dominant strategy* for him, meaning it's better no matter what. The same analysis obtains from Bull's perspective. Defecting is a dominant strategy for him too. Both players will defect. Both will get a payoff of one. The game is called a 'dilemma', but in a way there's no dilemma. Rationality requires that they defect. *And that's true even though both of them know that mutual cooperation would have been better for both.*

A Nash equilibrium, as you know, is a situation in which no one player can improve their outcome by choosing another strategy, given what the other player does. In this case, there's only one Nash equilibrium. The unique equilibrium is the situation in which both players defect. (In the table, that situation is represented by the shaded cell on the bottom-right.) The game shows that a Nash equilibrium doesn't need to be particularly good for anyone. One thing that game theory teaches us is that the outcome of a strategic interaction can be bad for everyone – even when everyone involved is rational and well informed. Individual incentives can pull us very far away from the social good.

Some purported 'solutions' might come to mind. What if Bill and Bull could chat ahead of time? They could talk things through and pinky promise to cooperate. The problem is that such a promise would ultimately carry no weight. No matter what Bill and Bull have promised each other, there comes a time when they have to decide whether to cooperate or to defect. As long as they're playing the same game as before, the same analysis applies and both will defect. Empty promises like that are *cheap talk*, as game theorists say. Cheap talk is inconsequential.

What if Bill and Bull play the same game over and over again? Imagine that the two stupidly keep committing the same pair of crimes and keep getting confronted by the same DA. You may think that the threat of defection in later rounds might inspire them to cooperate in the earlier ones. That's true, but only under certain conditions. Suppose Bill and Bull play the same game some definite number of times, say 57. What will happen? Consider the last round first. The 57th time Bill and Bull get caught, there's no threat of future defection, so both will defect. The 56th time, both of them know that the other will defect the following time, so there's no hope of inspiring cooperation in round 57 by cooperating in round 56. Both will defect in round 56 too. Same thing for round 55. By *backward induction*, as this mode of thinking is called, we can tell that Bill and Bull will defect from the get-go. Sustained cooperation is possible only if the game is repeated indefinitely, and also if the two players care enough about the remote future – which may be unlikely, given their career choice. And even so, there are no guarantees. Sustained mutual defection can be a Nash equilibrium even under these conditions.

The only dependable way to avoid the terrible outcome in the

	C	D
C	3,3	0,−9
D	−9,0	−9,−9

Table 2: Prisoner's dilemma in its modified form

prisoner's dilemma is not to play that game – that is, to change the nature of the game. How might Bill and Bull do that? There are many ways. But here's one. Suppose Bill and Bull went to see the local gangster boss before committing the crimes. We can call him Mean Mike. Bill and Bull could say: 'Hey, Mike: if either one of us ever defects, we'll pay you to throw us to the dogs.' This sounds like a good deal to Mike, so he'll accept. And this is no cheap talk: Mike is both able and willing to throw Bill and/or Bull to the dogs if he can make a quick buck. The next time Bill and Bull are caught, they're playing a very different game (see Table 2). Cooperation leads to the same outcome as before. But defection now means getting thrown to the dogs, for a payoff of minus nine. In this new game, Bill prefers to cooperate no matter what Bull does. And Bull prefers to cooperate no matter what Bill does. Cooperation has become the dominant strategy for both players. There's a unique Nash equilibrium still. But now the equilibrium is mutual cooperation (the shaded cell in the table). That's the best possible outcome. Individual incentives are suddenly in line with the social good.

It may seem weird that it could be in Bill and Bull's interest to ask Mike to throw them to the dogs if they defect, and to pay him to do so to boot. But it is! Understanding why requires you to 'solve for the equilibrium', as economists say. When Bill and Bull bring Mike into the picture, they change the nature of the interaction. That changes the Nash equilibrium. The new Nash equilibrium is the best possible outcome for both. In this new equilibrium, nobody gets thrown to the dogs. Getting thrown to the dogs is bad, but because it's 'off the equilibrium path', as economists put it, it doesn't matter. All's well that ends well.

Ostrom believed there were not one but two central insights in this story.

One: individual incentives are sometimes poorly aligned with the social good. In such situations, rational and well-informed individuals will not dependably reach the best possible outcome. The problem can be intractable enough. You can't fix it merely by giving people more information about whatever predicament they're in. It won't help to emphasize that there's a better outcome than the one they've settled on. You can scream it from the rooftops, but as long as the game is what it is, you won't change anyone's behaviour. You also can't fix the problem by building character, nor by instructing people to be more rational. Superficially, it may seem as though the community is doomed to failure. But this depressing bit is only half of the story. The other half is more uplifting.

Two: people have some degree of control over what game they're playing. If they don't like the outcome of the game they're actually in, they don't have to play it. They can choose to play another one. The other game can have other Nash equilibria, meaning that it leads to very different outcomes. Because the outcome can be better for all, switching games may be in everybody's interest. The switch will often involve setting boundaries. But when the outcome of the new game is better than that of the original one, people have every reason to respect these boundaries. The solution can garner everyone's consent. The community is not, in fact, doomed to failure. And it doesn't need a benevolent despot, military junta, or politburo to avoid disaster. It can succeed on its own.

Game theory does two things for us here. It explains why people sometimes end up with bad outcomes, in spite of them acting rationally and self-interestedly. And it upholds the hope that the very same people may figure out a way to avoid the crappy outcome.

Many real-life interactions are a lot like the prisoner's dilemma. Consider the so-called *tragedy of the commons*.[12] Here's the story. A commons – a piece of open land for public use – is surrounded by herders. The herders are dependent on the commons for grazing. Each herder is motivated to add animals to his herd. But the commons has limited capacity. If too many animals graze there, the commons will be ruined for all. The problem is that each herder has an incentive to add animals to his herd no matter what the others do. If the others refrain from growing their herds (cooperate), our herder still wants to grow his (defect). If the others grow theirs (defect), our herder would feel silly not to grow his too (defect). When everyone is motivated to grow their herds (defect) no matter what, everyone will, and the commons will be ruined. *And this is true even if they all know that it would be better not to.*

The commons is what's known as a *common-pool resource*. That's a good with two features, in Ostrom's analysis.[13] It's not *excludable*, meaning it's difficult or impossible to prevent people from using it if they like. At the same time it's *subtractable*, meaning that whenever one person is using or consuming a unit of the good, another person can't use or consume the same unit at the same time. The problem with common-pool resources is that they can be depleted, but even so it may not be possible to prevent people from depleting them. The Baltic cod is a common-pool resource. So are groundwater, irrigation systems, rainforests, farmland, and many other things that humans depend on for their survival. All these goods are at least potentially subject to a tragedy of the commons. Every fisherman is motivated to fish as much as they can. But when everyone does, the stock of fish is depleted and everybody hurts. 'Much of the world is dependent on resources that are subject to the possibility of a tragedy of the commons,' Ostrom wrote.[14] The result is overharvesting.

A related kind of resource is a *public good*: a good that's not excludable, and also not subtractable. It's still difficult or impossible to prevent someone from using it. But the fact that one person is enjoying the good doesn't prevent another person from enjoying it too. The light from a lighthouse is a classic example. If you build a lighthouse to help you navigate at night, you can't prevent me from using the same lighthouse in the same way. But then, the fact that I'm using it doesn't prevent you from using it too. Public goods are common. Fresh air, flood protection, public health, and public safety are all valuable public goods. Public goods don't run the risk of being depleted in the same way as common-pool resources do. But when people who haven't contributed to the public good cannot be prevented from using it, people will provide less than the community would want. The result is underprovision.

You can think of both problems in terms of free-riding.[15] When goods are not excludable and people have no obvious reason to provide, we should expect widespread free-riding. Perhaps nobody cares enough to preserve the common-pool resource or provide the public good. Perhaps only a small number do. Either way, the community will suffer the consequences of overharvesting and underprovision. Because of free-riding, the commons will be ruined, the irrigation system depleted, the number of lighthouses insufficient, public safety sketchy, the air quality bad, and so on.

Ostrom believed people living in society routinely face challenges akin to the prisoner's dilemma. Sometimes they're common-resource problems, like the case of the Baltic cod. Sometimes they're public-goods problems. Ostrom also believed that many of the big problems facing humankind – from deforestation and over-fishing, to environmental degradation and a lack of potable water, to violence and war – were the result of interactions where individual incentives are poorly aligned with the common good.

But – and this is the central point – Ostrom also believed that many of these problems could be solved by means of institutions. Institutions work because they transform the actual game people play into one where individual incentives align with the common good. Institutions constrain individual action. But because they ultimately deliver the goods, people can agree to be constrained. Institutions can garner the consent of the governed.

Ostrom's design principles

In the early 1970s, an inshore fishery in Alanya, Turkey, was on the brink of collapse.[16] As Ostrom told the story, unlimited use of the fishery had led to confrontations among the roughly 100 fishermen who operated in the area. The confrontations had sometimes turned violent. Meanwhile, competition for the best fishing spots had increased production costs. And the fishermen faced a great deal of uncertainty. They couldn't easily predict where they'd be able to fish or how much they'd be able to catch. The fishermen faced a classic common-pool resource problem. Fish and fishing spots are non-excludable. No single fisherman could prevent others from using the good fishing spots to harvest the fish. And yet both fishing spots and the stock of fish are subtractable. They can run out.

Members of a local cooperative decided to start experimenting with ways to solve these problems. It took them a decade of trial and error, but in the end they settled on a system that fixed the problems. The area was divided up into fishing locations. These locations were suitably large and spaced out so that they could all be used at the same time without conflict. Every September, the right to use these fishing locations was distributed randomly across eligible fishermen. After the first day of fishing, the fishermen started rotating. From September to January, the fishermen moved one slot east every day. From January through May, they moved back west one slot every day.

Unlike the fishermen around the Baltic, the Turkish fishermen got their system to work. The system is technically an institution. By limiting each fisherman to one allocated spot every day, the institution all but removed uncertainly, confrontation, and conflict. It also helped increase yield, though in a sustainable way. The system was cheap and easy to administer. It required little effort to monitor and enforce. Fishermen have a strong incentive to stick to their allotted location. If anyone for whatever reason did not, they would immediately be noticed and reported by whoever was supposed to have that location to themselves that day. But transgressions were rare, because it was so obviously in the interest of each fisherman to abide by the rules. The problem wasn't solved by the free market, exactly. Nor was it solved by the government. It was solved by the community of fishermen themselves. They were the ones who identified the problem, who designed the solution, and who monitored and (if necessary) enforced its rules. The solution worked by the mutual consent of the governed.

The story about the Alanya fishery had a happy ending. Not every common-pool resource does. To Ostrom, this was a key observation. Some communities remain 'remorsefully trapped into destroying their own resources', while others 'have broken out of the trap inherent in the commons dilemma'.[17] The observation led her to reflect on what the differences were. Which internal and external factors predict whether a community will remain shackled by the commons dilemma, she asked, and which will succeed in breaking out of it?

Ostrom did not believe in quick fixes and one-size-fits-all solutions.[18] Any successful solution, she believed, must fit the specific social and ecological setting. It must be responsive to local knowledge, tradition, and values. The scheme that worked in Alanya won't necessarily work elsewhere.

Although economics cannot deliver a one-size-fits-all solution, economics can tell us a great deal about the preconditions for success. 'By "successful"', Ostrom wrote, 'I mean institutions that enable individuals to achieve productive outcomes in situations where temptations to free-ride and shirk are ever present.'[19] She articulated her fundamental insights in the form of eight *design principles*. The principles are not laws of nature. No one principle or set of principles will guarantee success. Nor did she mean to suggest that communities that developed successful institutions necessarily had articulated these principles or been guided by them. But institutions consistent with these principles, Ostrom believed, were more likely to deliver the goods in a sustainable and acceptable manner.

Economists need to remain humble about their ability to develop solutions and deliver fixes from the outside, as it were. The best thing they can do is to help people help themselves. The proper role of the economist is to help the community develop institutions that fix the problems they're facing, and to fix those problems in a way that's responsive to local knowledge, tradition, and values. The design principles allow them to do this. By helping people establish the preconditions for successful, long-lasting institutions, economists can help people help themselves.

How would Ostrom know what works? Her design principles are based on very extensive empirical material, in addition to the more analytical game-theoretic approach.[20] Ostrom did original field research, studying things such as the management of groundwater basins in the 1960s and policing in large US metropolitan areas. This research was done on location, sometimes in the back of police cars and on inner-city streets. She and her team performed a long series of laboratory experiments, which allowed her to independently vary different parameters in a controlled setting. She did her own large-scale studies, e.g. on irrigation systems in Nepal and forest management across the world. Finally, she built a database of case studies from a variety of fields: anthropology, sociology, history, ecology, political science, forestry, etc. As of 1989, the database contained almost 5,000 entries.[21] The theoretical framework gave her a way to classify these studies and structure the database, which then allowed her to make inferences about what worked and what did not.

On the basis of this vast quantity of empirical material, Ostrom looked for conditions that are present where institutions emerge and survive for long periods of time, and that are absent where they don't. These eight design principles, or 'success factors', are listed below.[22]

1. Clearly defined boundaries

The first design principle says that the problem needs to be clearly delineated. It needs to be clear which specific resource the institution is supposed to govern, and how to distinguish it from the broader social and ecological system of which it is part. The fishermen in Alanya had to identify the boundaries of the fishery they were trying to manage. It also must be clear who the potential users of the resource are. The fishermen needed to identify who, exactly, should have the right to be allocated a fishing spot. If either one of these conditions fail, problems will emerge. Fishermen who are not bound by the rules of the institution may show up and start fishing in a location allocated to another fisherman, for example. Then we can expect uncertainty, conflict, and confrontation to return.

Relatedly, the size of the institution needs to be matched to the size of the problem. A common-pool resource that is concentrated in a small geographical location and that has a small number of potential users is best managed by a small institution. A resource that's extended over a large geographical area and that has a large number of potential users needs a large institution. The Stora Rör Swimming Association works, in part, because it deals with a well-defined, limited problem – but also because the organization is no smaller and no bigger than it needs to be. If it were any smaller, it wouldn't be able to do its job; if it were larger, it would run into problems that are entirely unnecessary.

2. Congruence between rules and local conditions

The second design principle says that the rules need to be tailored to local conditions. Studying irrigation systems across the world, Ostrom discovered that there were sizable variations. The differences reflected disparities in time, place, technology, resources, and more. The rules that worked in Alanya were designed to reflect the distribution of fishing locations and migration patterns of the local fish. Rules that fail to match local conditions are unlikely to succeed, no matter how well they have worked elsewhere. Again, no set of rules will work everywhere.

Different types of rules, moreover, have to be congruent with each other. Some rules govern who gets to appropriate a common-pool resource. Other rules govern who has to provide. These rules, taken together, determine the distribution of benefits and costs across the community. In general, costs need to be roughly proportional to benefits. If some members of the community are expected to shoulder a large part of the costs without receiving some commensurate part of the benefits, they're unlikely to consent to the arrangement.

3. Collective-choice arrangements

The third design principle says that people who are affected by institution rules should be allowed to participate in making and modifying them. Giving insiders a voice serves multiple purposes. For one thing, the people affected by the rules are often the people who know the most about local circumstances. That includes knowledge about the physical environment; knowledge about the people, their values, preferences, traditions, and culture. It also includes their experience of previous and existing arrangements – what's worked and what hasn't. Allowing users and providers of the good to participate in the rule-making process means that the deliberations will be shaped by the knowledge that is dispersed in the population. Which specific irrigation solution is most likely to work in a given place, for example, is not obvious. Insider information is clearly useful.

Giving insiders a voice in rule-making might also make them more invested in the institution, and more favourably disposed to following its rules. But there is no guarantee. Individual incentives still need to be aligned with the common good. That's what the next couple of principles are about.

4. Monitoring

The fourth design principle says that there must be some degree of monitoring. Someone needs to pay attention to the condition of the common-pool resource or public good, and to the performance of users and providers of the good. The monitors can be other users or providers. In Alanya, a person fishing outside his allotted fishing spot would immediately be noticed by the person who had the right to fish there that day. Monitoring in this case is effected by the fishermen themselves as a part of their regular activities. Monitors can also be third parties. Outside monitors need to be appointed by, or in some other way accountable to, the users and providers of the resource. Monitoring doesn't need to be 100 per cent effective. But if the state of the resource is not tracked, it is hard to maintain it at suitable levels. And if transgressions by users and providers are not systematically observed, then they have no reason not to free-ride after all.

Mere monitoring is still not enough. There also have to be some sort of negative consequences for free-riders and other violators.

5. Graduated sanctions

The fifth design principle says that there must be *sanctions* in place. Sanctions are penalties imposed in response to transgressions. Sanctions may take multiple forms. They may involve returning ill-gotten gains, including resources harvested in violation of institution rules. Their imposition will likely involve a loss of reputation in the community, as monitors will inform others of the infraction. Sanctions could involve monetary or other fines as restitution. For particularly serious infractions, sanctions could take the form of banishment from the community. Sanctions should be *graduated*. This means that they are mild at first. An initial infraction may be met with a simple reminder of the rules. For repeat offenders, however, the sanctions escalate. Sanctions will motivate the offender to get back on the straight and narrow. They will also remind others of the potentially serious consequences of transgressions. Sanctions, like monitoring, don't need to be 100 per cent effective, but some sanctions are required if we want individual incentives to be aligned with the common good, and people to follow the rules.

'Who guards the guardians?' you may ask. Since it may be costly to monitor and impose sanctions on others, you may fear that nobody will be motivated to do so. And yet this appears to be less of a problem in practice than in theory. Ostrom pointed out that real communities succeed in solving it. This fact suggests that sanctioning offenders is less costly and/or more beneficial to users and providers than you might think. When each member is invested in the stability and longevity of an institution, they have a stake in making sure sanctions are imposed in the proper way.

6. Conflict-resolution mechanisms

The sixth design principle says that the institution must provide some way to adjudicate disagreements and conflicts. Users and providers must have access to some arena in which they can air and resolve their disagreements. The procedure should be low in cost, both in time and in other resources. Some conflicts are unavoidable. No rule is completely free from ambiguities. Even honest and well-intentioned members of the community may differ on what a rule requires. Some may exploit ambiguities for their own benefit. And people sometimes make mistakes. A suitable arena for settling disagreements can prevent them from escalating, consuming resources, and maybe even causing the institution to unravel.

7. *Minimal recognition of rights to organize*

The seventh design principle says that governmental authorities must recognize, or at least not challenge, the right of users and providers to build their own institutions. Sometimes government officials believe that they, and only they, have the right to determine who shall provide and who shall use. For example, officials may think that it's their job – and nobody else's – to decide who should have the right to harvest a common-pool resource. When that is true, it is difficult to sustain local institutions that manage the very same resource. An institution built and managed by the users themselves is likely to flourish only where the government stays at arm's length. Suppose the Turkish government had stepped in and organized its own system for allocating fishing rights in Alanya, for example. Then any fisherman unhappy with the system could have petitioned the government to interfere in the allocation of rights and duties, causing an otherwise functional institution to collapse.

8. *Nested enterprises*

The eighth and final design principle says that governance should be organized in multiple, nested layers of institutions. You could in principle imagine having one massive institution that tries to appropriate, provide, monitor, enforce, and solve all problems within its jurisdiction. Such an institution would look a lot like a traditional state. None of the successful cases that Ostrom had studied are like that, though. Successful communities build multiple stable and long-lasting institutions of different sizes, operating at different levels, to manage the resources and goods in the social and ecological system of which they are part *at that level*. The result is a system of overlapping and nested institutions, each of whose size is matched to the size of the problem.

Although Stora Rör is a small village, it has several associations and other institutions designed to manage resources (such as the harbour and private roads), provide services (such as maintain tennis and padel courts), organize activities (such as community festivals), and more. These institutions operate in more or less the same geographical area, have overlapping memberships, and interact in all sorts of ways. The point is that rather than having one massive organization that does everything that needs to be done in the community, people have organized themselves in a series of overlapping and nested organizations, each of which is appropriate for its task. Again, none of this is unusual. If Ostrom was right, it's the norm.

Again, these design principles don't guarantee success. Such a system of principles does not exist. Ostrom's principles raise the probability of success. They give us pointers about what the Baltic cod fishermen could have done to prevent the cod stock from collapsing. The fishermen would have had to identify both the boundaries of the Baltic cod and who had the right to harvest the stock (design principle 1). They would also have had to develop their own operational rules governing how and where the cod could be harvested, and in what quantities (design principle 3). These rules would have had to be appropriate for local conditions, given the relevant social, economic, and ecological constraints (design principle 2). The fishermen would have had to consider the possibility that conditions might vary from one part of the Baltic to another, and if appropriate build a series of nested institutions to deal with them (design principle 8). Fishermen, or somebody appointed by them, would have had to monitor compliance with these rules (design principle 4). If necessary, they would also have had to apply some set of gradually escalating sanctions on those who violated the rules (design principle 5). They would have had to develop an arena in which complaints could be adjudicated smoothly and swiftly (design principle 6). Meanwhile, the project presupposes that the governments of the countries surrounding the Baltic leave the fishermen be – and wouldn't ruin their efforts with gratuitous interventions (design principle 7).

Ostrom's polycentric vision

Ostrom didn't just provide a series of design principles – she offered a vision of a good society. The idea that the size of the institution must be matched to the size of the problem inspired a view of society consisting of a richly textured patchwork of institutions.[23] Ostrom used the term *polycentric* to denote a society without a single central governing authority, as in a monocentric society. In a polycentric society, decisions about the provision, management, and distribution of resources are handled by many different institutions. These institutions will come in different sizes, and they will operate at different levels. These institutions will be *formally independent*, in the sense that they make their own decisions about the resources under their control. And they will often be *functionally independent*, in the sense that they operate independently from one another.

What's so great about a polycentric society? Ostrom's research on a number of different governance systems told her there were several advantages.[24] A polycentric society is better able to use local and distributed knowledge, because it authorizes the users of each common-pool resource to make the rules that govern how that particular resource is to be used. A polycentric society is more adaptive. It allows experimentation with alternative forms of governance. It also permits one community to learn from others involved in parallel trial-and-error learning processes. And a polycentric society is more resilient. It offers a certain degree of redundancy in organizational forms, just like a well-built aeroplane offers redundancy in its number of engines, pilots, and batteries. If one institution fails at one level, there may be another overlapping or nested institution available – on the same or another level – to pick up the slack. By distributing decision making across a wide range of autonomous centres, you reduce the probability of total and complete failure.

This polycentric vision is quite different from what you find elsewhere.

One common vision suggests privatizing everything and depending on the market to sort things out. Only this way, the thinking goes, can we make sure the resource will be used profitably and responsibly. The suggestion, effectively, is to solve common-resource problems by eliminating the common part – that is, by putting the resource in the hands of private actors. As a general solution, Ostrom thought that was a bad idea.[25] Many common-pool resources cannot easily be divided up and privatized. These are situations in which common-resource problems tend to be particularly acute. The stock of fish in an ocean is an example. A forest is another. Well-managed forests are the source of multiple products, the site of multiple productive operations, and the home of multiple users. There may not be a good way to divide them up into parcels that permit all those users to continue their operations. Privatization can also lead to inefficiencies. It increases the need for markets that allocate the produce and for insurance schemes that distribute the risks – all of which are associated with transaction costs and risk of market failure.

Another common vision suggests centralizing ownership and control of common resources and letting the state sort it out. The idea is to remove control from local people and communities and place it in the hands of a central government with major coercive powers. Only in this way, the thinking goes, can we trust that the resources will be managed responsibly and sustainably and for the benefit of all. Ostrom had little faith in centralization as a general solution.[26] To administer common resources efficiently and fairly, a central government – at some remove from the actual community – would still need a great deal of accurate information that it doesn't, and maybe cannot, access. That includes information about the resource in question, but also about people's needs, goals, preferences, and so on. A central government would need monitoring capabilities too. It would need a reliable system for administering consistent sanctions. It would need to make sure the incentives of everyone involved are properly aligned with the common good.

And it would need to do all this without incurring prohibitive administration costs.

Both these visions, in a way, reflect a pessimistic view of human society. They share the assumption that human communities are largely unable to manage common resources together. Both arguments presuppose that human beings, when left to their own devices, will destroy and deplete. The privatization argument says the only way to avoid destruction and depletion is to make sure there aren't any common resources to ruin. The centralization argument says the common resources need to be taken out of people's hands and managed by a benevolent state. Both agree that people, in this way, need to be saved from themselves.

Ostrom's vision is far less dismal. She considered a certain degree of optimism one of the central take-home messages of her work. Ostrom wrote: 'The most important lesson for public policy analysis derived from my intellectual journey . . . is that humans have a more complex motivational structure and more capability to solve social dilemmas than posited.'[27] Ostrom was not naive about people's ability to manage their joint resources. She was well aware that many communities simply fail to protect and preserve fish stocks, forests, and whatnot. But she remained optimistic. Her research uncovered many examples of communities that succeeded. It helped us see the conditions under which success is more likely. It taught us how to pave the way for successful governance – 'beyond markets and states', as the title of her Nobel lecture put it.

Economics, expertise, and values

Ostrom showed us how to build community, manage resources, solve problems, and more. She wasn't naive about people's ability to solve their own problems. She recognized that people often fail. She also was not naive about an economist's ability to help. She happily admitted that economics provides no sure-fire ways to achieve all the outcomes that we value. 'For some readers, this is a depressing lesson,' she wrote. 'They are looking for "the" answer of how best to solve common dilemmas and other policy problems.' But then she adds that aerospace engineers and software designers don't have sure-fire ways to make aeroplanes fly and computers work. If you will only accept an aeroplane that is guaranteed to fly, or a computer that's guaranteed not to crash, that's on you – not an imperfect science.

Ostrom's work is fascinating, not the least because it tells us so much about what economics is – and can be. There's no question that Ostrom was doing economics. The entire project is deeply inflected by the game-theoretic analysis with which we began. Game theory gave us a crisp and clear picture of the problem. It focused our attention on the nature of interactions – that is, situations in which individual incentives and the common good can pull apart and bad things can happen. Game theory also gave us a principled answer to the question of what a solution could look like. Economic theory provided a framework for classifying the vast and rich empirical material from a variety of disciplines, in a way that allowed Ostrom to articulate the eight design principles. On this basis, Ostrom produced a unique analysis – and a compelling vision of a good society, beyond markets and states.

Ostrom's work illustrates the way in which economists treat – and can treat – the individual. Some people fear that economics promotes a vision of society in which individuals are asocial atoms, bound together by nothing but market relations. Ostrom's vision is nothing like that. Her analysis is individualist in one sense. She explains institutions ultimately in terms of individuals – their goals and purposes, and so on.[28] Institutions exist only because they are developed and upheld by individual people pursuing their interests, as they see them, to the best of their ability. But the individuals in Ostrom's analysis are no asocial atoms, and society is not just the sum of the individual parts. Individuals are part of a dense network of market and non-market relations. Their behaviours, beliefs, and attitudes reflect the fact that they live in a richly textured, polycentric society. In a polycentric society, people are dependent on each other in all sorts of ways. And it's ultimately the network of social institutions that gets people out of the social dilemmas that imprison narrowly rational, short-sighted, and selfish agents.

Ostrom's work also illustrates the role that values and ideology play – and can play – in economics. Economists are often accused of being ideological and/or of promoting their own parochial values. There's no doubt that Ostrom had values that she wanted to realize, and that they inspired her design principles and her vision of a polycentric society. But this is unremarkable. Anyone concerned with making the world a better place, as economists are, will have to start out with some notion of what a good society might look like. The question we should ask isn't whether do-gooders have values. Of course they do. Questions we should ask instead include whether the values are transparent, whether they are defensible, and whether they play a reasonable role in the analysis.

Ostrom's use of values is both explicit and responsible, it seems to me. She's clear about what her values are. Here's what she wrote:

> A core goal of public policy should be to facilitate the developments that bring out the best in humans. We need to ask how polycentric institutions help or hinder the innovativeness, learning, adapting, trustworthiness, levels of cooperation of participants, and the achievement of more effective, equitable, and sustainable outcomes at multiple scales.[29]

The values of effectiveness, equity, and sustainability were all central to Ostrom's analysis – as a means to bring out the best in humans. No less importantly, she underscored repeatedly and emphatically that the economist should be guided by people's own values. She likened the role of the economist to that of a facilitator, or midwife, helping communities identify their problems and construct their own solutions – in a manner responsive to their own values. Her work wasn't value-free – it couldn't possibly be – but it was designed to respect the values of the people involved as far as possible. As Tarko writes, Ostrom's focus on consent and self-governance allows us to remain agnostic, to a great extent, about which values should be given priority. He continues: 'Rather than trying to impose our own personal values upon everyone, the focus, instead, is on enabling people's capacities to build communities that best fit *their* priorities.'[30]

10

Conclusion

Economics has been about making the world a better place, more fit for human flourishing, since day one. The reason it exists is that moral philosophers recoiled against widespread misery and suffering, and thought a scientific economics could help relieve it. When economics was attacked as 'the dismal science', and maybe even the work of the Devil himself, back in the nineteenth century, economists were already busy opposing slavery and injustice. The discipline has come a long way since then, but the ambition to help people lead better lives and improve the world is still alive and well.

Economics delivers the next best thing after silver bullets and magic wands: actionable, evidence-based solutions that can, on the margin, improve human lives, people's communities, and the world that we live in. The advice is distinctive, in the sense that it differs from what's on offer elsewhere. It's non-obvious, in the sense that it's not always what you'd expect. Economics helps us face big challenges and small annoyances. It paves the way for eliminating poverty. It gives advice about how to raise well-adjusted children and (no less importantly for everyone involved) remain sane in the process. It tells us how to deal with climate change and pollution. It tells us how to encourage pro-social behaviours and promote human rights. It provides us with algorithms that save lives and give people what they need. It tells us how to be happy, humble, and rich – possibly even at the same time. And it tells us how to build sustainable and resilient communities within the boundaries set by the planet on which we live. The advice is designed to benefit us, our communities, and the world as a whole.

My thesis is that economics can help us save the world in the manner that a toolkit can help you construct a house. What I mean is that you're better off with the toolkit than without. I'm not saying economics can fix every problem. I'm not saying its solutions are guaranteed to work. I'm not saying its solutions shouldn't be complemented with insights from other disciplines and domains. I'm not saying it can't be abused. I'm not saying economics, in its current form, is perfect. I'm not defending the econom*ists*, or the economics profession. What I am saying is that economics, on the margin, makes a positive contribution to our efforts to build a better world.

Economics is a lot like modern medicine. Modern medicine is amazing. And yet! No matter how good it is, medicine can't fix every problem that ails humanity. No surgery or medication is guaranteed to work. Medicine is an art as well as a science, and doesn't fix problems magically and on its own. It can be misused and abused. Some medical doctors are awful human beings. Some have done real harm. Some of the things even good doctors do are pointless or redundant. And seeing a medical doctor is not the only way to promote your health. A running coach, for example, might help you get into shape and avoid injury. None of this, though, is a reason to dismiss medicine as a discipline. Nor is it a reason not to seek out medical help when you need it. With medicine, as with economics, we don't want to make the perfect the enemy of the good. If you refuse to see a doctor unless they offer remedies that are guaranteed to work, that sounds like a *you* problem, as the kids say.

I should add that it's not as though I've described *all the ways* in which economics can help. What I've covered is only a selection, drawn from a much wider pool. What I've covered isn't even a representative selection, whatever that might mean. But I hope you trust me when I say that I haven't focused on minor, fringe figures. The economists we've met in the preceding chapters are, by and large, extremely well-respected members of the profession. They're firmly part of the mainstream. They hold positions in top departments and at reputable institutions. Their work appears in top-flight journals. And the economists have won some of the most prestigious prizes and awards – up to and including the Nobel Memorial Prize.

Along the way, I've tried to give you an idea of how the house of economics is constructed. I've described the evidence that economists collect, and the tools that they use. That's laboratory experiments. It's field experiments. It's big data. It's information gleaned from databases of all kinds. It's abstract theories and models. It's econometrics – statistics repurposed for economic purposes. I haven't tried to describe the full empirical basis for the advice I've described. (You'll find that among the references.) But I've tried to give you an idea of how economists come up with their ideas, how they determine if they're true or not, and what gives them reason to think their advice is good and will work.

One important tool that I have referred to several times is the 'economic way of thinking'. That comprises a set of rules of thumb, or heuristics. The rules of thumb don't tell us anything about the world. They tell us how to approach it – or the study of it. Ideas such as thinking on the margin and solving for the equilibrium might not sound like much to write home about. But it takes training (or discipline) to apply them consistently. And when you do, you come up with answers that might not have occurred to you otherwise. This distinctive mode of analysis helps explain why economic solutions are often different from what's on offer elsewhere.

A third goal has been to indicate why we shouldn't be seduced by anti-economics. Just like a discussion about climate-change science would be incomplete if it failed to mention climate-change sceptics, a discussion about economics as a science can't entirely avoid the topic of economics sceptics. As I pointed out in the introduction, economics has always been trailed by critics who argue that we'd be better off if the entire enterprise was blasted into the sun. I'm sure there are individual theories, practices, models, measures, and solutions that are objectionable in the ways that anti-economists suggest. I'm also confident that there are individual economists who are both morally and intellectually deficient. To the extent that economics can be improved, it's a moral duty to do so. But anti-economic writers aren't just attacking specific ideas or individuals. They're attacking the entire enterprise. They generalize, and advance on a broad front against the entire discipline. And the picture that emerges from these generalizations is simply not recognizable as a description of actual economic theory and practice.

A reasonable question to ask is: what would be better, and who would benefit, if we discarded economics *en bloc* – not because we had access to a better theory, but because we decided the existing stuff wasn't good enough. Consider, for example, the economics about how to get rich – to focus on what might be seen as the most vulgar part of the enterprise. Would things be better if we didn't have access to the theory of rational choice, which tells us what's the best course of action given our goals and values? Would things be better if we didn't have the theory of efficient markets, which tells us to be sceptical of anyone promising consistently greater returns than the stock market? Would things be better if we didn't have systematic research on financial literacy and the obstacles that it poses? Would things be better if we didn't have the pedagogical tools developed in order to help people boost their financial literacy? Would things be better if we didn't have randomized controlled trials to show that those tools help people graduate from high school, get jobs, work their way out of poverty, and build wealth? I think not. Obviously, all tools can be misused and abused. But again, that's no reason to think we're better off without them.

Whence the scepticism?

If economics is so useful, why aren't all of its proposals implemented already? It's a good question. If economics is as useful as

I've made it out to be, it behoves us to understand the obstacles to realizing its gains – and to remove those obstacles.

First off, it should be said again that economics could be better. For one thing, the economics profession could be more diverse.[1] At least part of the story is systematic discrimination against under-represented groups. Discrimination hurts both the individuals and the profession. There's no knowing how many otherwise talented and innovative students and early-career academics choose another career as a result of ill treatment.

Economists could also be much better at communicating what economics is and why one should study it. There's evidence that a simple email message to incoming students can improve enrolment and retention.[2] The most effective message is an invitation to enrol in an economics course, alongside 'information showcasing the diversity of research and researchers within economics'. To the extent that ignorance of economics is a factor (and I'll return to this below), better communication could make a big difference.

Economics could be less insular. Bibliographic data show that political scientists and sociologists cite economists far more often than economists cite political scientists and sociologists.[3] The asymmetry may be due to the fact that economists think they're so much better than other social scientists. Economists are not all as cocky as Schumpeter (chapter 7). But many of them could use a measure of humility, since they have so much to be humble about.

Above all, economics could use more engagement with philosophy. Philosophy includes the philosophy of science, which reflects on the use of scientific theories, models, measures, and methodology. That includes exploring both the power of scientific tools and their limitations. Explicit attention to the philosophy of science could make economists better scientists. No less importantly, it could give them a better idea of what a scientific economics *cannot* do. But philosophy also includes moral philosophy, which deals most explicitly with normative matters. What's welfare? What's a good society? What are justice and fairness, and how should these values factor into our efforts to make the world a better place? Many of the more serious critiques of economics boil down to a critique not of the relevant science, but of the values that inform the enterprise. The critique of GDP as a measure of economic welfare and development, for example, often proceeds from the claim that it doesn't measure what *really matters*. That's a fair critique. But note that what matters is a question of values. Similarly, economists are often criticized for giving more attention to the size of the economy – efficiency, economic growth, and so on – than to questions of how goods and services are distributed. That's also a fair critique. But it is at root an argument that economists place insufficient weight on the value of equality or similar. These sorts of problems are solved not by improving the purely scientific methodology – at least not by that alone. These problems are solved by honest engagement with philosophical reflection on the nature of a good life and a good society, and by an effort to incorporate better values into our scientific theory and practice. And, to the extent that economics is animated by values, it will require engagement with other stakeholders. That's especially the public who (through taxes) fund some of the work, and who will be the target of any public policy.

The fact that economics and the economic profession are imperfect is undeniable. But it's not a reason to dismiss the entire enterprise. First, note that the researchers uncovering the various ways in which economics is suboptimal are often economists too, using the tools of their trade. But, more to the point, the flaws don't add up to an argument that economics ought to be eliminated from the face of the earth. You don't throw out your toolkit because it's not as good as it could be.

If you ask economists why people don't like them much, historically there have been two recurring answers. One is that people don't like to hear that they can't have everything they want. Economics teaches there's scarcity, and that we have to make tradeoffs. Regarding our personal lives, the economist might say we have to choose between splurging today and having money in the bank tomorrow. Regarding the public sphere, the economist might say that we have to choose between making massive infrastructure projects and paying down the national debt.

The other answer is that people don't like to hear the economic system cannot be reorganized at will. Economics emphasizes that the economy is a complex system with many interdependent parts. A change in one part of the system may have far-reaching – and sometimes undesirable – consequences for other parts. The economist, then, might say that even well-intended reforms may be misguided and have sharply negative consequences. And this is true even if the economist agrees with the aims of the reform. In such a situation, as Hayek noted, 'it is perhaps inevitable that [the economist] should become the object of dislike and suspicion'.[4]

To my mind, though, people are suspicious of economics mainly because they know so little about what it *is*, what it *does*, and what it is *for*. There are many reasons why ordinary people don't – indeed, can't – know what economics is and economists are up to. Here are four.

First, real economics is famously inaccessible. It's articulated in a language that's highly technical and often mathematical, and requires an economics degree to take it in. Even if the research were readable, it often appears in journals that are locked to the public, or else costs a dollar a page even in electronic format. There are successful popular books: *Freakonomics* and *The Undercover Economist*, among others, do a great job of capturing the nature and joy of economic thinking.[5] And yet, they only scratch the surface. Economists as a community are doing a terrible job of explaining themselves.

Second, real economists are easily confused with wannabes and imposters. People who present themselves as economists in the media often aren't anything of the sort. Some of them are just charlatans and cranks. It is obvious why they should want to wear the mantle of science. Journalists and producers allow them because it makes for good television. Some of the pretenders are from the world of business. These are people who may have a business degree and business experience, but who have no background in economics at all. And the ones who are real economists are often hired guns: people employed by special interests, such as banks or think-tanks. Their job is not in the first instance to present a dispassionate assessment of the state of economics or the economy. Their job is to convey convincingly what their employer wants you to believe. If you have formed your view of economics on the basis of your impression of people who appear as economists in the media, it is only natural to be suspicious. You may have been actively misled. Unless you are yourself an economist, how are you supposed to know? Economists have allowed non-economists to hijack the brand.

More insidiously, perhaps, there are *bona fide* economists who oscillate between a more scientific mode and a more ideological one. When the switch is not clearly flagged, we should not be surprised if a reader or listener concludes it's *all* ideology. If you want to assess their contributions, you first have to separate the scientific content from the rest. Doing so requires a good enough handle on what the actual economics says. Cambridge economist Joan Robinson thought this was a good enough reason to study economics:

> To make good use of an economic theory we must first sort out the relations of the propagandist and the scientific elements in it . . .
> The purpose of studying economics is not to acquire a set of ready-made answers to economic questions, but to learn how to avoid being deceived by economists.[6]

Third, even if you studied economics at college, you may not have gotten a very good idea of what real economics is. You probably read generalized textbook treatments, which give little idea of the power and joy (and complexity) of real economics. You were probably also exposed to what's sometimes called *economism*: overly simplistic models applied to thorny real-world problems. More advanced and interesting models typically complicate the picture painted at the beginning of a course of study. But they're only taught in upper-level or even post-graduate courses. A student who doesn't stick with it until they get to that point may get an entirely incorrect picture of what economics is about. And while textbook treatments change over time, they don't change as fast as the profession does. There are exceptions (see the Further Reading section that follows this chapter). But economics textbooks are often stuffier than the reality.

Fourth, and above all, economics has changed. So much has happened in the last two decades. It is not an exaggeration to say that twenty-first-century economics is radically different from twentieth-century economics. Economists talk about an *empirical turn*, in which data and evidence play a relatively more important role than they used to – and pure theory plays a relatively less important one.[7] Part of this development is the establishment of experimental economics, which is based on evidence gathered in the economics laboratory. Experimental economics was still controversial in the 1990s, but this is no longer true. The same is true of behavioural economics, which integrates economics with psychology. When I went to graduate school, behavioural economics wasn't even considered economics. (I studied it in a department of social and decision sciences.) Behavioural economics is now firmly part of the mainstream.[8] Happiness economics, which studies who's contented and why, is based on large-scale surveys about feelings like happiness. It used to arouse great amusement in economist circles in the early 2000s, but is now largely uncontroversial. Economists nowadays also ask a broader set of questions and consider a wider set of answers. All of this has made economics far more interesting and relevant to human concerns. But if you're not immersed in the world of economics, you have no way of knowing just how radically things have shifted.

Ignorance about economics and what it can accomplish is not a new phenomenon. Lionel Robbins noticed widespread confusion and misinformation in 1932. Dispelling it was the whole point of his book. Here's what he said:

Confusion still persists in many quarters, and false ideas are prevalent with regard to the pre-occupations of the economist and the
nature and the extent of his competence. As a result, the reputation
of Economics suffers, and full advantage is not taken of the knowledge it confers.[9]

The fact that ignorance, confusion, and misinformation are not
new does not make them any less consequential. The ignorance
and confusion have left economics with an undeservedly bad reputation and, more seriously, undercut efforts to use economic
knowledge to improve the world. We're all worse off as a result.

Final words

We have two tasks before us. One is to make good use of social science in general, and economics in particular, to build a better world,
more fit for human flourishing, whenever it is possible to do so.
There are obstacles. They range from simple ignorance to fact
resistance and straight-up science denial. The other is to make economics better, more useful, and more appropriate to address human
concerns. (There's no contradiction involved in saying economics is
good but could be better.) Among other things, this means providing economics with appropriate values: ideas about what problems
are worthy of attention, what solutions are morally acceptable, and
what visions of the good life and great society should guide economists' efforts. There are obstacles here too. They range from inertia
to a lack of sophistication in our thinking about values, the good
life, and the great society. But let's not be defeatist about it. A better
world is within reach. Economics can help us get there.

Further Reading

This may or may not be the first economics book you've read. Either way, I hope it's not your last. A book like this one can only scratch the surface. If it does nothing except inspire you to read more, it will have achieved its purpose.

If you're interested in the specific topics I've covered here, please look up the references and go straight to the source. There's a lot more to each and every story than I've been able to convey. I hope and trust you'll find the full story every bit as fascinating as I do. (Above all, don't judge anyone I've mentioned merely on the basis of my description of their research. If a question or objection occurs to you after reading this book, there's a good chance it's answered in the original work.)

If you want to know more about economics in general, there are serious textbooks written by thoughtful people who know their stuff. An excellent starting point is *The Economy* by the CORE project.[1] It's available for free online, and comes with a range of ancillary materials. If you've got money to spend, two recent textbooks are *Economics* by Acemoglu, Laibson, and List, and *Principles of Economics* by Stevenson and Wolfers.[2] If you're interested in behavioural economics and its applications (including the nudge agenda), modesty won't prevent me from mentioning my own textbook, *A Course in Behavioral Economics* (now in its third edition).[3]

There is also a thoughtful literature that takes a wider perspective, reflecting on the power and potential (and problems) of economics. Diane Coyle is a prolific author and excellent writer. She has a series of books offering an insider's view on what economics is and what it does.[3] Philosopher and historian of economics

James R. Otteson explores the nature of economics from the point of view of recurring economic fallacies.[4]

The history of economics is fascinating in its own right. It also offers a unique window into the minds of historical and contemporary economists, and a better understanding of what the discipline is up to. *The History of Economic Thought*, by Medema and Samuels, will give you a selection of original texts.[5]

The philosophy of economics provides philosophical reflection, frequently lacking, on the theory and practice of economics. I might as well confess that I think of this book as philosophy of economics, because it is *about* economics – its powers, promises, and pitfalls. The textbook *Philosophy of Economics*, by Julian Reiss, will quickly get you up to speed, even if you've had no previous exposure to philosophy or economics. The recent *Routledge Handbook of Philosophy of Economics*, edited by Reiss and Conrad Heilmann, contains short pieces on a range of current topics.[6]

Finally, I just have to mention *Mezzanine*, by Zoë Hitzig – a delightful, economics-inspired collection of poetry.[7]

Glossary

Analytical egalitarianism	The working hypothesis that people are fundamentally the same.
Calibration	The relationship between subjective probabilities and objective frequencies.
Econometrics	Statistics for economists.
Economics	The study of individual choice under *scarcity*, and the consequences of those choices for society as a whole.
Efficiency	See *Pareto optimality*.
Epistemic humility	An intellectual virtue grounded in the realization that our knowledge is always provisional and incomplete – and that it might require revision in light of new evidence.
Experimental economics	An *economics* that relies centrally on *laboratory* and *field experiments*.
Externality	The effect (positive or negative) of an action or transaction on some third party.
Field experiment	A study that explores how people respond to changes in the environment in which they live and work.

Field study	A study that observes people in the environment in which they live and work.
Financial literacy	The ability to process information and make informed decisions about financial matters.
Game theory	The economic theory of strategic interaction.
Good	As a noun: anything that you have *preferences* over.
Happiness	A positive and desirable affective mental state.
Heuristic	A rule of thumb.
Incentive	A feature of some action or option that makes a person want more of it.
Institution	A set of rules that structure repeated interactions.
Laboratory experiment	A study that explores how people make decisions under controlled conditions.
Macroeconomics	The *economics* of big things (unemployment rates, inflation rates, money supply, etc.).
Marginal utility	The *utility* you get from the last unit of some *good*.
Market	A site, whether physical or virtual, where exchanges can take place.
Matching market	A *market* in which both parties to a transaction have to approve it before it can take place.
Methodological individualism	The notion that all explanations of group-level phenomena must ultimately be in terms of the

behaviours and attitudes of the individuals in the group.

Microeconomics
The *economics* of small things (esp. individual choices, beliefs, and *preferences*) and their effects on society as a whole.

Nash equilibrium
A situation in which no one player can improve their situation by changing their behaviour, given what everybody else is doing.

Opportunity cost
The most preferred option you must forgo when you choose something else.

Overconfidence
An excessive confidence in one's own knowledge and abilities.

Pareto improvement
A change that makes at least one person better off without making anybody else worse off in the process.

Pareto optimality
A situation in which nobody can be made better off without making somebody else worse off in the process.

Pigouvian tax
A tax on activities that generate negative *externalities*, to remedy a situation in which *markets* deliver inefficient results.

Preference
A desire or want for one thing over another.

Preference ordering
Goods organized in order of *preference*.

Randomized controlled trial
A study in which people are randomly divided into a group that gets the intervention (the test

	group) and a group that doesn't (the control group).
Rational-choice theory	A theory of individual behaviour that starts from the assumption that people are fundamentally rational.
Rationality	The ability to choose the best means to given ends.
Scarcity	1. A situation in which there is less of a *good* than people want.
	2. The *feeling* that there's less than enough to go round.
Social norm	An informal rule that governs behaviour in groups and societies.
Solving for the equilibrium	Thinking through the consequences of people adapting to each other's behaviour.
Survey	A study that asks people about their feelings, attitudes, and behaviours.
Thinking on the margin	Analysing decisions in terms of marginal effects.
Time discounting	The practice of letting future events and experiences count for less in one's deliberations simply because they're in the future.
Tradeoff	Compromise between two features that are desirable but mutually exclusive.
Utility	A measure of *preference* satisfaction.
Value	A commitment concerning what's good or bad, just or unjust, fair or unfair, beautiful or ugly, or similar.
Welfare / well-being	What you have when your life is going well; what makes for a life well lived.

Acknowledgements

This book is far more of a group project than the cover would suggest. I compensate for not being a genius by not being alone.

The project wouldn't exist even in concept if it weren't for my agent, Jaime P. Marshall. He was my publisher a decade ago. We had so much fun working together that we resolved to do it again. He encouraged me to dream big. He saw what my project was before I did. And he worked with me on the proposal until it sang (his word). He applied thoughtful advice, energetic encouragement, gentle pressure, patient reminders, and emotional support as necessary and appropriate. And he made the entire process every bit as enjoyable as it could possibly be. Every author should be so lucky.

The brilliant Martina O'Sullivan, Celia Buzuk, Jamie Birkett, and the entire team at Penguin offered the best conceivable home for the manuscript. Their enthusiasm and appreciation throughout meant a lot. They got it. Their literary ability helped me see what would make for a good book; their market knowledge helped me see what would fly. They gave me big-picture suggestions and detailed comments. They gave me the deadlines that I required, and the extension that I needed. The champagne helped too.

My writing coach, Teresa Masterson, helped realize the vision. She understood not only what the project could be but also how to get there. She helped me overcome obstacles of multiple kinds. She made me unlearn decades' worth of academic writing 'skills'. She made me see how to tell the story in a way that people who are not me or my friends would want to read – while remaining true to the material. Without her, there's a good chance I would have just given up.

Trevor Horwood copy-edited the manuscript with care and sensitivity to the nature of the project. He eliminated rough edges, leaving the text more polished, consistent, and effective. Ellie Smith deftly saw the book through to production. Together, they helped me eliminate many potential sources of embarrassment.

Others played an important role without being directly involved with the work. I am especially grateful to the teachers whose generosity and love of learning inspired me to pursue philosophy and economics in the first place. That includes some of the path-breaking figures whose work I discuss in this book. Cristina Bicchieri, Baruch Fischhoff, George Loewenstein, and Alvin Roth were all teachers of mine in Pittsburgh during a formative period of my intellectual development.

I want to thank my students too. This book project took shape while developing a new undergraduate course in philosophy of economics at Stockholm University. I am grateful to the students for allowing me to experiment with pedagogical innovations on them. I hope I didn't cause too much damage.

A couple of friends volunteered to read the entire manuscript in a premature state. I appreciate their sacrifice. The fresh eyes of Siska De Baerdemaeker, Ella Flintberg, Johannes Haushofer, Louise Hedlund, and Caroline Uggla were hugely beneficial.

Above all, I'm grateful to my family – my most consistent source of inspiration and support. This book was written during less-than-ideal conditions, during a raging pandemic and in the aftermath of the sudden and unexpected death of my father. Crafting this book, alongside everything else that must be done in a household of five, was very much a group effort. This book is dedicated to my wife, Elizabeth, for being such a terrific partner in love and in life. I'm grateful to our children, for simultaneously encouraging me to live in the moment and to consider the more remote future. This saving-the-world business is for them and their generation. My mother, Elisabet, a political journalist, first inspired in me an interest in economics and politics. She remains a constant source of encouragement and support – moral and logistical.

Apologies to all whose contributions have gone unmentioned.

There is one way in which I am truly alone. It's in the responsibility for the errors, infelicities, embarrassments, malapropisms, superfluities, redundancies, and pleonasms that remain.

Notes

Introduction

1 See Ryan Bourne, *Economics in One Virus: An Introduction to Economic Reasoning Through COVID-19* (Washington, DC: Cato Institute, 2021).

2 www.nationalgeographic.com/animals/article/coronavirus-linked-to-chinese-wet-markets

3 www.nytimes.com/interactive/2020/03/22/world/coronavirus-spread.html

4 www.ecdc.europa.eu/en/publications-data/covid-19-guidelines-non-pharmaceutical-interventions

5 Arthur C. Pigou, *The Economics of Welfare*, 4th edn (London: Macmillan, 1935), 5.

6 Auguste Comte, *A General View of Positivism*, 2nd edn, trans. J. H. Bridges (London: Trübner and Co., 1865), 19.

7 Pigou, *The Economics of Welfare*, 5.

8 Friedrich A. Hayek, 'The Trend of Economic Thinking', *Economica*, no. 40 (1933): 122.

9 Karl Marx, *The German Ideology: Including Theses on Feuerbach and Introduction to The Critique of Political Economy* (Amherst: Prometheus Books, 1998), 571.

10 Alfred Marshall, *Principles of Economics: An Introductory Volume*, 8th edn (London: Macmillan, 1920), 1, 3.

11 Lionel Robbins, *An Essay on the Nature and Significance of Economic Science* (London: Macmillan, 1932), 15.

12 www.pgpf.org/chart-archive/0053_defense-comparison

13 Robbins, *An Essay*, 27.

14 For the reader who wants to know more about the evidence underlying the advice, each chapter contains references to recent books and

survey articles that will give you a far better idea. Because I want to discuss where these ideas came from, and not just what economists believe right now, some of the references will be to classic contributions to the literature. The fact that they're dated is intentional. Each chapter also contains references to at least one recent book or survey article with the more up-to-date material. All these can be found in the Bibliography that follows these notes.

15 Paul T. Heyne, Peter J. Boettke, and David L. Prychitko, *The Economic Way of Thinking*, 11th edn (Upper Saddle River: Prentice Hall, 2006), ch. 1.

16 William Oliver Coleman, *Economics and Its Enemies: Two Centuries of Anti-Economics* (London: Palgrave Macmillan, 2002); Don Ross, 'Economic Theory, Anti-Economics, and Political Ideology', in *Philosophy of Economics*, ed. Uskali Mäki (Amsterdam: North-Holland, 2012), 241–85.

1. How to Eliminate Poverty

1 www.nytimes.com/1988/11/13/books/l-the-rich-are-different-907188. html

2 Alan O. Ebenstein, *Friedrich Hayek: A Biography* (New York: Palgrave, 2001), 291–2.

3 The 'Nobel Memorial Prize for Economics' refers to The Sveriges Riksbank Prize in Economic Sciences in Memory of Alfred Nobel. The prize is awarded by the Royal Swedish Academy of Sciences in Stockholm, Sweden, according to the same principles as the original Nobel Prizes.

4 Friedrich A. Hayek, *Law, Legislation, and Liberty, Vol. 3: The Political Order of a Free People* (Chicago: University of Chicago Press, 1979), 55.

5 Abhijit V. Banerjee and Esther Duflo, *Poor Economics: A Radical Rethinking of the Way to Fight Global Poverty* (New York: PublicAffairs, 2011); Abhijit V. Banerjee and Esther Duflo, *Good Economics for Hard Times: Better Answers to Our Biggest Problems* (New York: Allen Lane, 2019).

6 Banerjee and Duflo, *Good Economics for Hard Times*, 288–90.

7 Ibid., 288–9.

8 Banerjee and Duflo, *Poor Economics*, ix.

9 Banerjee and Duflo, *Good Economics for Hard Times*, 326.

10 David S. Jones and Scott H. Podolsky, 'The History and Fate of the Gold Standard', *The Lancet* 385, no. 9977 (2015): 1502–3.

11 Petter Lundborg, Erik Plug, and Astrid Würtz Rasmussen, 'Can Women Have Children and a Career? IV Evidence from IVF Treatments', *American Economic Review* 107, no. 6 (2017): 1635.

12 Johannes Haushofer and Jeremy Shapiro, 'The Short-Term Impact of Unconditional Cash Transfers to the Poor: Experimental Evidence from Kenya', *Quarterly Journal of Economics* 131, no. 4 (2016): 1973–2042.

13 Ibid., 2026.

14 Banerjee and Duflo, *Good Economics for Hard Times*, 326.

15 Sendhil Mullainathan and Eldar Shafir, *Scarcity: The New Science of Having Less and How It Defines Our Lives* (New York: Henry Holt and Co., 2013).

16 Ibid., 169.

17 Ibid., 4.

18 Ibid., 7.

19 Ibid., 13.

20 Laurel Aynne Cook and Raika Sadeghein, 'Effects of Perceived Scarcity on Financial Decision Making', *Journal of Public Policy & Marketing* 37, no. 1 (2018): 68–87.

21 Ibid., 76.

22 Colin F. Camerer et al., 'Evaluating Replicability of Laboratory Experiments in Economics', *Science* 351, no. 6280 (2016): 1433–6.

23 Michael O'Donnell et al., 'Empirical Audit and Review and an Assessment of Evidentiary Value in Research on the Psychological Consequences of Scarcity', *Proceedings of the National Academy of Sciences* 118, no. 44 (2021): e2103313118.

24 Mullainathan and Shafir, *Scarcity*, 15.

25 Cook and Sadeghein, 'Effects of Perceived Scarcity on Financial Decision Making', 76–9.

26 Mullainathan and Shafir, *Scarcity*, 13.

27 Ibid., 231.

28 Ibid., 176–7.

29 Ibid., 171.

30 Thomas Carlyle, *Occasional Discourse on the [N-Word] Question* (London: Thomas Bosworth, 1853), 9.

31 'dismal, *n.* and *adj.*' OED Online. March 2021. Oxford University Press. www.oed.com/view/Entry/54731 (accessed 5 March, 2021).

32 John Stuart Mill, *Utilitarianism*, 7th edn (London: Longmans, Green and Co., 1879), ch. II.

33 Jeremy Bentham, *An Introduction to the Principles of Morals and Legislation*, new edn (Oxford: Clarendon Press, 1823), 5.

34 Mill, *Utilitarianism*, ch. III.

35 John Stuart Mill, *The Subjection of Women* (London: Longmans, Green, Reader, and Dyer, 1869), chs. I–II.

36 Jeremy Bentham, 'Principles of the Civil Code', in *The Works of Jeremy Bentham*, vol. 1, ed. John Bowring (New York: Russell & Russell, 1838), 345.

37 Jose Harris, 'Mill, John Stuart (1806–1873)', *Oxford Dictionary of National Biography*, 5 January 2012, https://doi.org/10.1093/ref:odnb/18711

38 David M. Levy and Sandra J. Peart, *The Street Porter and the Philosopher: Conversations on Analytical Egalitarianism* (Ann Arbor: University of Michigan Press, 2009).

39 Adam Smith, *An Inquiry into the Nature and Causes of the Wealth of Nations*, 5th edn, ed. Edwin Cannan (Chicago: University of Chicago Press, 1976), 19–20.

40 John Stuart Mill, 'The Negro Question', *Fraser's Magazine for Town and Country* 41 (1850): 29.

41 David M. Levy and Sandra J. Peart, 'The Secret History of the Dismal Science. Part I. Economics, Religion and Race in the 19th Century', *EconLib* (blog) 22 January 2001, www.econlib.org/library/Columns/LevyPeartdismal.html

42 Richard J. Herrnstein and Charles Murray, *The Bell Curve: Intelligence and Class Structure in American Life* (New York: Free Press, 1996).

43 Ibid., 91.

44 Ibid., xxii–xxiii.

45 Ibid., 25, 10.

2. How to Raise Happy Children and Remain Sane

1 An amusing blog post on this literature was written by Ava Neyer, 'I Read All the Baby Sleep Books', *Huffington Post* (blog), 6 December 2017, www.huffpost.com/entry/i-read-all-the-baby-sleep-advice-books_b_3143253

2 Michael Gradisar et al., 'Behavioral Interventions for Infant Sleep Problems: A Randomized Controlled Trial', *Pediatrics* 137, no. 6 (2016).

3 Emily Oster, *Expecting Better: Why the Conventional Pregnancy Wisdom is Wrong – and What You Really Need to Know* (London: Penguin, 2014); Emily Oster, *Cribsheet: A Data-Driven Guide to Better, More Relaxed Parenting, from Birth to Preschool* (New York: Penguin, 2020).

4 Oster, *Cribsheet*, xiii–xxv.

5 Oster, *Expecting Better*, 77.

6 Ibid., 85.

7 Oster, *Cribsheet*, 118–19.

8 www.bbc.com/news/magazine-22751415

9 Bryan Douglas Caplan and Zach Weinersmith, *Open Borders: The Science and Ethics of Immigration* (New York: First Second, 2019).

10 Bryan Caplan, *Selfish Reasons to Have More Kids: Why Being a Great Parent is Less Work and More Fun Than You Think* (New York: Basic Books, 2012).

11 Ibid., 5.

12 Ibid., 84–6.

13 Ibid., 5.

14 Ibid., 88–9.

15 Ibid., 4–5.

16 Ibid., 14.

17 Ibid., ch. 4.

18 Ibid., 6–7.

19 Ibid., 4.

20 www.usda.gov/media/blog/2017/01/13/cost-raising-child

21 Oster, *Cribsheet*, xix.

22 www.ft.com/content/50007754-ca35-11dd-93e5-000077b07658

23 Friedrich A. Hayek, *Studies in Philosophy, Politics and Economics* (London: Routledge & Kegan Paul, 1967), 27–9.

3. How to Fix Climate Change

1 https://clcouncil.org/economists-statement/

2 https://clcouncil.org/our-story/

3 https://clcouncil.org/faqs/

4 Desmond Kirwan, 'We Need to Change the Way We Talk About Climate Change', *Behavioral Scientist*, 11 October 2021.

5 Julius J. Andersson, 'Carbon Taxes and CO_2 Emissions: Sweden as a Case Study', *American Economic Journal: Economic Policy* 11, no. 4 (2019): 1–30.

6 Ibid., 1.

7 Ariel Rubinstein, *Economic Fables* (Cambridge: Open Book Publishers, 2012), 78.

4. How to Change Bad Behaviour

1 https://washdata.org/monitoring/inequalities/open-defecation

2 www.unicef.org/protection/child-marriage

3 www.who.int/news-room/fact-sheets/detail/female-genital-mutilation

4 Cristina Bicchieri, *The Grammar of Society: The Nature and Dynamics of Social Norms* (Cambridge: Cambridge University Press, 2005); Cristina Bicchieri, *Norms in the Wild: How to Diagnose, Measure, and Change Social Norms* (Oxford: Oxford University Press, 2017).

5 https://penntoday.upenn.edu/features/penn-project-aims-to-stop-open-defecation-by-changing-social-norms

6 https://thepenngazette.com/the-philosopher-queen-of-unicef/

7 www.coursera.org/learn/norms

8 Cristina Bicchieri, 'Norms, Conventions, and the Power of Expectations', in *Philosophy of Social Science: A New Introduction*, ed. Nancy
   Cartwright and Eleonora Montuschi (Oxford: Oxford University Press,
   2014), 226.

9 Damon Centola et al., 'Experimental Evidence for Tipping Points in
   Social Convention', *Science* 360, no. 6393 (2018): 1116–19.

10 Bicchieri, *Norms in the Wild*, ch. 3.

11 Ibid., 114–18.

12 www.mitti.se/nyheter/en-fjardedel-farre-pboter-i-innerstan--pa-sju-ar-
   6.27.33517.b2c4f90c9e

13 See the definition 'economy, *n.*' OED Online, www.oed.com/view/
   Entry/59393 (accessed 19 March 2021).

5. How to Give People What They Need

1 www.kidneyfund.org/kidney-donation-and-transplant/transplant-
   waiting-list/

2 If you haven't recorded an organ donation decision yet, do it now! The
   law is different in different countries. If you live in the UK, this link will
   tell you what to do: www.organdonation.nhs.uk/uk-laws/

3 That idea is not to be confused with the Pareto Principle, which is
   named after the same guy. The Pareto Principle is the idea that 20 per
   cent of employees produce 80 per cent of the value, that 20 per cent of
   people cause 80 per cent of the problems, etc. etc.

4 Alvin E. Roth, *Who Gets What – and Why: The New Economics of Matchmaking and Market Design* (Boston: Houghton Mifflin Harcourt, 2015).

5 Ibid., 32ff.

6 Ibid., 196.

7 Ibid., 34.

8 Ibid., 36.

9 Ibid., 45.

10 Ibid., 51.

11 Ibid., 41.

12 www.organdonation.nhs.uk/become-a-living-donor/

13 www.nobelprize.org/prizes/economic-sciences/2012/summary/

14 Roth, *Who Gets What*, ch. 8.

15 Ibid., ch. 9.

16 Francesco Guala, 'Building Economic Machines: The FCC Auctions', *Studies in History and Philosophy of Science Part A* 32, no. 3 (2001): 453–77.

17 www.nobelprize.org/prizes/economic-sciences/2020/press-release/

18 Roth, *Who Gets What*, 27.

19 Ibid., 8ff.

20 Ibid., ch. 12.

6. How to Be Happy

1 Benjamin Franklin, *The Private Correspondence of Benjamin Franklin*, vol. 1, ed. William Temple Franklin, 2nd edn (London: Henry Colburn, 1817), 19–20.

2 Hornell Hart, *Chart for Happiness* (New York: Macmillan, 1940), 16.

3 Ibid., v.

4 Erik Angner, 'The Evolution of Eupathics: The Historical Roots of Subjective Measures of Wellbeing', *International Journal of Wellbeing* 1, no. 1 (2011): 4–41.

5 Richard A. Easterlin, 'Does Economic Growth Improve the Human Lot? Some Empirical Evidence', in *Nations and Households in Economic Growth: Essays in Honor of Moses Abramovitz*, ed. Paul A. David and Melvin W. Reder (New York: Academic Press, 1974): 89–125.

6 Hart, *Chart for Happiness*, 19.

7 John Helliwell et al., eds., *World Happiness Report 2021* (New York: Sustainable Development Solutions Network, 2021).

8 Ibid., 20–22, fig. 2.1.

9 www.newstatesman.com/international/2021/08/would-extinction-be-so-bad

10 Easterlin, 'Does Economic Growth Improve the Human Lot?', 100.

11 Betsey Stevenson and Justin Wolfers, 'Economic Growth and Subject-ive Well-Being: Reassessing the Easterlin Paradox', *Brookings Papers on Economic Activity*, Spring 2008, 2.

12 Confusingly, income is sometimes plotted on a so-called 'log scale'. If so, the relationship I described might look like a straight line.

13 Daniel Kahneman and Angus Deaton, 'High Income Improves Evalu-ation of Life But Not Emotional Well-Being', *Proceedings of the National Academy of Sciences*, 107, no. 38 (2010): 4.

14 Bentham, 'Principles of the Civil Code', 305.

15 Jon Gertner, 'The Futile Pursuit of Happiness', *New York Times Maga-zine*, 7 September, 2003, 86.

16 Erik Angner, *A Course in Behavioral Economics*, 3rd edn (London: Red Globe Press, 2021), sec. 3.2.

17 Lonnie Golden and Barbara Wiens-Tuers, 'To Your Happiness? Extra Hours of Labor Supply and Worker Well-Being', *Journal of Socio-Economics* 35, no. 2 (2006): 382.

18 Lucía Macchia and Ashley V. Whillans, 'Leisure Beliefs and the Subjec-tive Well-Being of Nations', *Journal of Positive Psychology* 16, no. 2 (2021): 198–206.

19 Shane Frederick and George Loewenstein, 'Hedonic Adaptation', in *Well-Being: The Foundations of Hedonic Psychology*, ed. Daniel Kahne-man, Ed Diener, and Norbert Schwarz (New York: Russell Sage Foundation, 1999), 302–29.

20 Adam Smith, *The Theory of Moral Sentiments*, 6th edn, ed. Knud Haakonssen (Cambridge: Cambridge University Press, 2002), 172.

21 Ibid.

22 Tibor Scitovsky, *The Joyless Economy: The Psychology of Human Satisfac-tion*, revised edn (New York: Oxford University Press, 1992), 59.

23 Ibid., 137.

24 www.theatlantic.com/business/archive/2014/10/buy-experiences/381132/

25 Amit Kumar, Matthew A. Killingsworth, and Thomas Gilovich, 'Wait-ing for Merlot: Anticipatory Consumption of Experiential and Material Purchases', *Psychological Science* 25, no. 10 (2014): 1924–31.

26 Scitovsky, *The Joyless Economy*, 143–4.

27 The proverb continues: 'Shared sorrow is half the sorrow.'

28 Cited in David G. Myers, *The Pursuit of Happiness: Who is Happy – and Why* (New York: William Morrow, 1992), 57.

29 Lucius Annaeus Seneca, *Dialogues and Essays*, trans. John Davie, ed. Tobias Reinhardt (Oxford: Oxford University Press, 2008), 189.

30 Carsten Wrosch et al., 'Adaptive Self-Regulation of Unattainable Goals: Goal Disengagement, Goal Reengagement, and Subjective Well-Being', *Personality and Social Psychology Bulletin* 29, no. 12 (2003): 1494–1508.

31 Christopher K. Hsee et al., 'Wealth, Warmth, and Well-Being: Whether Happiness is Relative or Absolute Depends on Whether It is About Money, Acquisition, or Consumption', *Journal of Marketing Research* 46, no. 3 (2009): 396–409.

7. How to Be Humble

1 www.cnn.com/2004/TECH/space/07/21/apollo.crew/

2 Don A. Moore, *Perfectly Confident: How to Calibrate Your Decisions Wisely* (New York: HarperCollins, 2020), 22.

3 Ola Svenson, 'Are We All Less Risky and More Skillful Than Our Fellow Drivers?', *Acta Psychologica* 47, no. 2 (1981): 143–8.

4 Moore, *Perfectly Confident*, 22–3.

5 www.imdb.com/title/tt0090525/

6 Aristotle, *Nicomachean Ethics*, trans. Terence Irwin, 2nd edn (Indianapolis: Hackett, 1999), 24.

7 Ibid., 29.

8 Sarah Lichtenstein, Baruch Fischhoff, and Lawrence D. Phillips, 'Calibration of Probabilities: The State of the Art to 1980', in *Judgment Under Uncertainty: Heuristics and Biases*, ed. Amos Tversky, Daniel Kahneman, and Paul Slovic (Cambridge: Cambridge University Press, 1982), 306–34.

9 Baruch Fischhoff, Paul Slovic, and Sarah Lichtenstein, 'Knowing with Certainty: The Appropriateness of Extreme Confidence', *Journal of*

Experimental Psychology: Human Perception and Performance 3, no. 4 (1977): 554.

10 Baruch Fischhoff, 'Debiasing', in Daniel Khaneman, Paul Slovic, and Amos Tversky (eds.), *Judgment Under Uncertainty: Heuristics and Biases* (Cambridge: Cambridge University Press, 1982): 422–44, 432.

11 Stuart Oskamp, 'Overconfidence in Case-Study Judgments', *Journal of Consulting Psychology* 29, no. 3 (1965): 261–5.

12 Lichtenstein, Fischhoff, and Phillips, 'Calibration of Probabilities', 437.

13 J. J. Christensen-Szalanski and J. B. Bushyhead, 'Physicians' Use of Probabilistic Information in a Real Clinical Setting', *Journal of Experimental Psychology: Human Perception and Performance* 7, no. 4 (1981): 928–35.

14 Fischhoff, Slovic, and Lichtenstein, 'Knowing with Certainty'.

15 Brad M. Barber and Terrance Odean, 'Trading is Hazardous to Your Wealth: The Common Stock Investment Performance of Individual Investors', *Journal of Finance* 55, no. 2 (2000): 773–806.

16 Brad M. Barber and Terrance Odean, 'Boys Will be Boys: Gender, Overconfidence, and Common Stock Investment', *Quarterly Journal of Economics* 116, no. 1 (2001): 261–92.

17 Moore, *Perfectly Confident*, 36–37.

18 www.biblegateway.com/verse/en/Proverbs%2016:18

19 Moore, *Perfectly Confident*, 38.

20 Ibid., 170.

21 Andrew Leedham, *Unstoppable Self-Confidence: How to Create the Indestructible Natural Confidence of the 1% Who Achieve Their Goals, Create Success on Demand and Live Life on Their Terms* (London: Unstoppable Media Group, 2019).

22 Erik Angner, 'Economists as Experts: Overconfidence in Theory and Practice', *Journal of Economic Methodology* 13, no. 1 (2006): 14.

23 https://quoteinvestigator.com/2019/04/10/one-handed/

24 Raymond S. Nickerson, 'Confirmation Bias: A Ubiquitous Phenomenon in Many Guises', *Review of General Psychology* 2, no. 2 (1998): 175–220.

25 Matthew Rabin, 'Psychology and Economics', *Journal of Economic Literature* 36, no. 1 (1998): 27.

26 Baruch Fischhoff, 'Hindsight ≠ Foresight: The Effect of Outcome Knowledge on Judgment Under Uncertainty', *Journal of Experimental Psychology: Human Perception and Performance* 1, no. 3 (1975): 288–99.

27 Rabin, 'Psychology and Economics', 28.

28 Justin Kruger and David Dunning, 'Unskilled and Unaware of It: How Difficulties in Recognizing One's Own Incompetence Lead to Inflated Self-Assessments', *Journal of Personality and Social Psychology* 77, no. 6 (1999): 1121–34.

29 Ibid., 1130.

30 Ibid.

31 David Dunning, 'The Dunning–Kruger Effect and Its Discontents', *The Psychologist* 35 (April 2022): 2–3.

32 John Stuart Mill, *J. S. Mill: 'On Liberty' and Other Writings* (Cambridge: Cambridge University Press, 1989), 21.

33 Allan H. Murphy and Robert L. Winkler, 'Probability Forecasting in Meteorology', *Journal of the American Statistical Association* 79, no. 387 (1984): 489–500.

34 Gideon Keren, 'Facing Uncertainty in the Game of Bridge: A Calibration Study', *Organizational Behavior and Human Decision Processes* 39, no. 1 (1987): 98–114.

35 Lichtenstein, Fischhoff, and Phillips, 'Calibration of Probabilities'.

36 Sarah Lichtenstein and Baruch Fischhoff, 'Training for Calibration', *Organizational Behavior and Human Performance* 26, no. 2 (1980): 149–71.

37 Philip E. Tetlock, 'Theory-Driven Reasoning About Plausible Pasts and Probable Futures in World Politics: Are We Prisoners of Our Preconceptions?', *American Journal of Political Science* 43, no. 2 (1999): 351.

38 Asher Koriat, Sarah Lichtenstein, and Baruch Fischhoff, 'Reasons for Confidence', *Journal of Experimental Psychology: Human Learning and Memory* 6, no. 2 (1980): 107–18.

39 Ibid., 117.

40 Moore, *Perfectly Confident*, 51.

41 Ibid., 169.

42 Ibid.

43 www.berkshirehathaway.com/letters/1996.html

44 www.tilsonfunds.com/BuffettNotreDame.pdf

45 Ibid.

46 Ibid.

47 Angner, 'Economists as Experts: Overconfidence in Theory and Practice'.

48 Ken Binmore, 'Why Experiment in Economics?', *Economic Journal* 109, no. 453 (1999): F17.

49 Robbins, *An Essay*, 1932, 119.

8. How to Get Rich

1 www.bankrate.com/banking/savings/emergency-savings-survey-july-2021/

2 Angner, *A Course in Behavioral Economics*, sec. 8.2.

3 www.spglobal.com/marketintelligence/en/news-insights/latest-news-headlines/s-p-500-returns-to-halve-in-coming-decade-8211-goldman-sachs-59439981

4 The proposition read: 'In general, absent any inside information, an equity investor can expect to do better by holding a well-diversified, low-fee, passive index fund than by holding a few stocks.' In the 2019 survey, 57 per cent strongly agreed, 36 per cent agreed and 7 per cent did not answer. No one was uncertain or disagreed. See www.igmchicago.org/surveys/diversified-investing-2/

5 Deirdre N. McCloskey, *If You're So Smart: The Narrative of Economic Expertise* (Chicago: University of Chicago Press, 1990), 112.

6 Barber and Odean, 'Trading is Hazardous to Your Wealth'.

7 www.bankrate.com/banking/savings/credit-card-debt-emergency-savings-2021/

8 https://edition.cnn.com/2021/11/09/economy/fed-household-debt-inflation/index.html

9 www.bea.gov/news/2021/personal-income-and-outlays-november-2021

10 www.statista.com/statistics/817911/number-of-non-business-bankruptcies-in-the-united-states/

11 www.biblegateway.com/verse/en/Proverbs%2022%3A7

12 www.cnbc.com/2021/02/16/map-shows-typical-payday-loan-rate-in-each-state.html

13 http://thresholdresistance.com/2015/04/16/mcdonalds-new-third-pounder-may-not-add-up/

14 Annamaria Lusardi and Olivia S. Mitchell, 'The Economic Importance of Financial Literacy: Theory and Evidence', *Journal of Economic Literature* 52, no. 1 (2014): 5–44.

15 Ibid., 10.

16 The correct answers are 1(a), 2(c), and 3(b).

17 See chapter 7.

18 Lusardi and Mitchell, 'The Economic Importance of Financial Literacy', 17.

19 Ibid., sec. 5.

20 Paul J. Yakoboski, Annamaria Lusardi, and Andrea Hasler, 'Financial Literacy and Well-Being in a Five Generation America: The 2021 TIAA Institute-GFLEC Personal Finance Index', October 2021, 20.

21 Tim Kaiser et al., 'Financial Education Affects Financial Knowledge and Downstream Behaviors', *Journal of Financial Economics* 145, no. 2 (2021): 255–72.

22 Ibid., 16.

23 Ibid., 15.

24 Lusardi and Mitchell, 'The Economic Importance of Financial Literacy', 15.

25 www.ft.com/content/b6a8107c-99f4-4a43-8adc-9686e6bd603e

26 Lusardi and Mitchell, 'The Economic Importance of Financial Literacy', 5–6.

27 Robert J. Shiller, *Narrative Economics: How Stories Go Viral and Drive Major Economic Events* (Princeton: Princeton University Press, 2019).

28 Angner, *A Course in Behavioral Economics*, 114.

9. How to Build Community

1 Peter Brusewitz, and Åse Lo Skarsgård, 'Simskolan och barnen som drunknade', in *Stora Rör: Berättelser och hågkomster*, ed. Elisabeth Nilsson, Åse Lo Skarsgård, and Karl Arne Eriksson (Högsrum: Högsrums hembygdsförening, 2014), 37–8.

2 Elinor Ostrom, *Understanding Institutional Diversity* (Princeton: Princeton University Press, 2005), 3; Vlad Tarko, *Elinor Ostrom: An Intellectual Biography* (London: Rowman & Littlefield International, 2017), 6.

3 Ostrom, *Understanding Institutional Diversity*, 3.

4 Tarko, *Elinor Ostrom*, 15.

5 Elinor Ostrom, *Governing the Commons: The Evolution of Institutions for Collective Action* (Cambridge: Cambridge University Press, 1990).

6 Tarko, *Elinor Ostrom*, 20.

7 Sara Hornborg and Henrik Svedäng, 'Baltic Cod Fisheries – Current Status and Future Opportunities' (RISE Report, 2019).

8 https://news.yahoo.com/iceland-tries-bring-back-trees-razed-vikings-031502923.html

9 Jacob Dembitzer et al., 'Levantine Overkill: 1.5 Million Years of Hunting Down the Body Size Distribution', *Quaternary Science Reviews* 276 (2022): 107316.

10 Ostrom, *Governing the Commons*, ch. 1.

11 Ibid., 3–5.

12 Garrett Hardin, 'The Tragedy of the Commons', *Science* 162, no. 3859 (1968): 1243–8; Ostrom, *Governing the Commons*, 2–3.

13 Elinor Ostrom, 'Beyond Markets and States: Polycentric Governance of Complex Economic Systems', *American Economic Review* 100, no. 3 (2010): 644–5.

14 Ostrom, *Governing the Commons*, 3.

15 Ibid., 6.

16 Ibid., 18–20.

17 Ibid., 21.

18 Ostrom, 'Beyond Markets and States', 642.

19 Ostrom, *Governing the Commons*, 15.

20 Ostrom, 'Beyond Markets and States'.

21 Ostrom, *Governing the Commons*, xiii.

22 Ibid., 88–102; cf. Ostrom, 'Beyond Markets and States', 652–3.

23 Ostrom, 'Beyond Markets and States', 643.

24 Ostrom, *Understanding Institutional Diversity*, 283ff.

25 Ostrom, *Governing the Commons*, 12–13; Tarko, *Elinor Ostrom*, 89–92.

26 Ostrom, *Governing the Commons*, 10; Tarko, *Elinor Ostrom*, 87–89.

27 Ostrom, 'Beyond Markets and States', 664.

28 Tarko, *Elinor Ostrom*, 7; cf. Steele, 'Choice Models', in Cartwright and Montuschi (eds.), *Philosophy of Social Science*, 203–4.

29 Ostrom, 'Beyond Markets and States', 665.

30 Tarko, *Elinor Ostrom*, 16.

10. Conclusion

1 www.npr.org/sections/money/2020/01/07/793855832/economics-still-has-a-diversity-problem

2 Amanda Bayer, Syon P. Bhanot, and Fernando Lozano, 'Does Simple Information Provision Lead to More Diverse Classrooms? Evidence from a Field Experiment on Undergraduate Economics', *AEA Papers and Proceedings* 109 (2019): 110–14.

3 Marion Fourcade, Etienne Ollion, and Yann Algan, 'The Superiority of Economists', *Journal of Economic Perspectives* 29, no. 1 (2015): 89–114.

4 Hayek, 'The Trend of Economic Thinking', 137.

5 Steven D. Levitt and Stephen J. Dubner, *Freakonomics: A Rogue Economist Explores the Hidden Side of Everything* (New York: William Morrow, 2005); Tim Harford, *The Undercover Economist: Exposing Why the Rich are Rich, the Poor are Poor – and Why You Can Never Buy a Decent Used Car!* (Oxford: Oxford University Press, 2006).

6 Joan Robinson, *Contributions to Modern Economics* (Oxford: Blackwell, 1978), 75.

7 www.aeaweb.org/research/charts/an-empirical-turn-in-economics-research

8 Erik Angner, 'We're All Behavioral Economists Now', *Journal of Economic Methodology* 26, no. 3 (2019): 195–207.

9 Robbins, *An Essay*, vii.

Further Reading

1 The CORE Team, ed., *The Economy* (Oxford: Oxford University Press, 2017), www.core-econ.org/the-economy/

2 Daron Acemoglu, David Laibson, and John List, *Economics, Global Edition*, 3rd edn (Harlow: Pearson, 2021); Betsey Stevenson and Justin Wolfers, *Principles of Economics* (New York: Worth, 2020).

3 Diane Coyle, *The Soulful Science: What Economists Really Do and Why It Matters*, revised edn (Princeton: Princeton University Press, 2009); Diane Coyle, *GDP: A Brief But Affectionate History* (Princeton: Princeton University Press, 2014); Diane Coyle, *Cogs and Monsters: What Economics is, and What It Should Be* (Princeton: Princeton University Press, 2021).

4 James R. Otteson, *Seven Deadly Economic Sins: Obstacles to Prosperity and Happiness Every Citizen Should Know* (Cambridge: Cambridge University Press, 2021).

5 Steven G. Medema and Warren J. Samuels, eds., *The History of Economic Thought: A Reader*, 2nd edn (London: Routledge, 2013).

6 Julian Reiss, *Philosophy of Economics: A Contemporary Introduction* (New York: Routledge, 2013); Conrad Heilmann and Julian Reiss, eds., *The Routledge Handbook of Philosophy of Economics* (New York: Routledge, 2021).

7 Zoë Hitzig, *Mezzanine: Poems* (New York: HarperCollins, 2021).

Bibliography

Acemoglu, Daron, David Laibson, and John List. *Economics, Global Edition*, 3rd edn, Harlow: Pearson, 2021.

Andersson, Julius J. 'Carbon Taxes and CO_2 Emissions: Sweden as a Case Study', *American Economic Journal: Economic Policy* 11, no. 4 (2019): 1–30. https://doi.org/10.1257/pol.20170144.

Angner, Erik. 'Economists as Experts: Overconfidence in Theory and Practice', *Journal of Economic Methodology* 13, no. 1 (2006): 1–24. https://doi.org/10.1080/13501780600566271.

———. 'The Evolution of Eupathics: The Historical Roots of Subjective Measures of Wellbeing', *International Journal of Wellbeing* 1, no. 1 (2011): 4–41. https://doi.org/10.5502/ijw.v1i1.14.

———. 'We're All Behavioral Economists Now', *Journal of Economic Methodology* 26, no. 3 (2019): 195–207. https://doi.org/10.1080/1350178X.2019.1625210.

———. *A Course in Behavioral Economics*, 3rd edn, London: Red Globe Press, 2021.

Aristotle. *Nicomachean Ethics*, trans. Terence Irwin, 2nd edn, Indianapolis: Hackett, 1999.

Banerjee, Abhijit V., and Esther Duflo. *Poor Economics: A Radical Rethinking of the Way to Fight Global Poverty*, New York: PublicAffairs, 2011.

———. *Good Economics for Hard Times: Better Answers to Our Biggest Problems*, New York: Allen Lane, 2019.

Barber, Brad M., and Terrance Odean. 'Trading is Hazardous to Your Wealth: The Common Stock Investment Performance of Individual Investors', *Journal of Finance* 55, no. 2 (2000): 773–806. https://doi.org/10.1111/0022-1082.00226.

———. 'Boys Will be Boys: Gender, Overconfidence, and Common Stock Investment', *Quarterly Journal of Economics* 116, no. 1 (2001): 261–92. https://doi.org/10.1162/003355301556400.

Bayer, Amanda, Syon P. Bhanot, and Fernando Lozano. 'Does Simple Information Provision Lead to More Diverse Classrooms? Evidence from a Field Experiment on Undergraduate Economics', *AEA Papers and Proceedings* 109 (2019): 110–14. https://doi.org/10.1257/pandp.2019 1097.

Bentham, Jeremy. *An Introduction to the Principles of Morals and Legislation*, new edn, Oxford: Clarendon Press, 1823.

———. 'Principles of the Civil Code', in *The Works of Jeremy Bentham*, ed. John Bowring, vol. 1, New York: Russell & Russell, 1962: 297–364.

———. 'Offences Against One's Self: Paederasty Part 1', ed. Louis Crompton, *Journal of Homosexuality* 4, no. 1 (1978): 389–402. https://doi.org/10.1300/J082v03n04_07.

Bicchieri, Cristina. *The Grammar of Society: The Nature and Dynamics of Social Norms*, Cambridge: Cambridge University Press, 2005.

———. 'Norms, Conventions, and the Power of Expectations', in *Philosophy of Social Science: A New Introduction*, ed. Nancy Cartwright and Eleonora Montuschi, Oxford: Oxford University Press, 2014: 208–29.

———. *Norms in the Wild: How to Diagnose, Measure, and Change Social Norms*, Oxford: Oxford University Press, 2017.

Binmore, Ken. 'Why Experiment in Economics?' *Economic Journal* 109, no. 453 (1999): F16–F24. https://doi.org/10.1111/1468-0297.00399.

Bourne, Ryan. *Economics in One Virus: An Introduction to Economic Reasoning Through COVID-19*, Washington, DC: Cato Institute, 2021.

Brusewitz, Peter, and Åse Lo Skarsgård. 'Simskolan och barnen som drunknade', in *Stora Rör: Berättelser och hågkomster*, ed. Elisabeth Nilsson, Åse Lo Skarsgård, and Karl Arne Eriksson, Högsrum: Högsrums hembygdsförening, 2014: 37–8.

Camerer, Colin F., Anna Dreber, Eskil Forsell, et al. 'Evaluating Replicability of Laboratory Experiments in Economics', *Science* 351, no. 6280 (2016): 1433–6. https://doi.org/10.1126/science.aaf0918.

Caplan, Bryan. *Selfish Reasons to Have More Kids: Why Being a Great Parent is Less Work and More Fun Than You Think*, New York: Basic Books, 2012.

Caplan, Bryan Douglas, and Zach Weinersmith. *Open Borders: The Science and Ethics of Immigration*, New York: First Second, 2019.

Carlyle, Thomas. *Occasional Discourse on the [N-Word] Question*, London: Thomas Bosworth, 1853.

Centola, Damon et al., 'Experimental Evidence for Tipping Points in Social Convention', *Science* 360, no. 6393 (2018): 1116–19. https://doi.org/10.1126/science.aas8827.

Christensen-Szalanski, J. J., and J. B. Bushyhead. 'Physician's Use of Probabilistic Information in a Real Clinical Setting', *Journal of Experimental Psychology: Human Perception and Performance* 7, no. 4 (1981): 928–35. https://doi.org/10/dksmph.

Coleman, William Oliver. *Economics and Its Enemies: Two Centuries of Anti-Economics*, London: Palgrave Macmillan, 2002.

Comte, Auguste. *A General View of Positivism*, 2nd edn, trans. J. H. Bridges, London: Trübner and Co., 1865.

Cook, Laurel Aynne, and Raika Sadeghein. 'Effects of Perceived Scarcity on Financial Decision Making', *Journal of Public Policy & Marketing* 37, no. 1 (2018): 68–87. https://doi.org/10.1509/jppm.16.157.

CORE Team, ed. *The Economy*, Oxford: Oxford University Press, 2017. www.core-econ.org/the-economy/.

Coyle, Diane. *The Soulful Science: What Economists Really Do and Why It Matters*, revised edn, Princeton: Princeton University Press, 2009.

———. *GDP: A Brief But Affectionate History*, Princeton: Princeton University Press, 2014.

———. *Cogs and Monsters: What Economics is, and What It Should Be*, Princeton: Princeton University Press, 2021.

Dembitzer, Jacob, Ran Barkai, Miki Ben-Dor, and Shai Meiri. 'Levantine Overkill: 1.5 Million Years of Hunting Down the Body Size Distribution', *Quaternary Science Reviews* 276 (2022): 107316. https://doi.org/10.1016/j.quascirev.2021.107316.

Douglas, Heather. 'Values in Science', in *The Oxford Handbook of Philosophy of Science*, ed. Paul Humphries, Oxford: Oxford University Press, 2016: 609–30. https://doi.org/10.1093/oxfordhb/9780199368815.013.28.

Dunning, David. 'The Dunning–Kruger Effect and Its Discontents', *The Psychologist* 35 (April 2022): 2–3. www.bps.org.uk/psychologist/dunning-kruger-effect-and-its-discontents.

Easterlin, Richard A. 'Does Economic Growth Improve the Human Lot? Some Empirical Evidence', in *Nations and Households in Economic Growth: Essays in Honor of Moses Abramovitz*, ed. Paul A. David and Melvin W. Reder, New York: Academic Press, 1974: 89–125.

Ebenstein, Alan O. *Friedrich Hayek: A Biography*, New York: Palgrave, 2001.

Fischhoff, Baruch. 'Hindsight ≠ Foresight: The Effect of Outcome Knowledge on Judgment Under Uncertainty', *Journal of Experimental Psychology: Human Perception and Performance* 1, no. 3 (1975): 288–99. https://doi.org/10.1037/0096-1523.1.3.288.

———. 'Debiasing', in *Judgment Under Uncertainty: Heuristics and Biases*, eds. Daniel Kahneman, Paul Slovic, and Amos Tversky (Cambridge: Cambridge University Press, 1982): 422–44. https://doi.org/10.1017/CBO9780511809477.032.

Fischhoff, Baruch, Paul Slovic, and Sarah Lichtenstein. 'Knowing with Certainty: The Appropriateness of Extreme Confidence', *Journal of Experimental Psychology: Human Perception and Performance* 3, no. 4 (1977): 552–64. https://doi.org/10.1037/0096-1523.3.4.552.

Fourcade, Marion, Etienne Ollion, and Yann Algan. 'The Superiority of Economists', *Journal of Economic Perspectives* 29, no. 1 (2015): 89–114. https://doi.org/10.1257/jep.29.1.89.

Franklin, Benjamin. *The Private Correspondence of Benjamin Franklin*, ed. William Temple Franklin, 2nd edn, London: Henry Colburn, 1817.

Frederick, Shane, and George Loewenstein. 'Hedonic Adaptation', in *Well-Being: The Foundations of Hedonic Psychology*, ed. Daniel Kahneman, Ed Diener, and Norbert Schwarz, New York: Russell Sage Foundation, 1999: 302–29.

Gertner, Jon. 'The Futile Pursuit of Happiness', *New York Times Magazine*, 7 September 2003. www.nytimes.com/2003/09/07/magazine/the-futile-pursuit-of-happiness.html.

Golden, Lonnie, and Barbara Wiens-Tuers. 'To Your Happiness? Extra Hours of Labor Supply and Worker Well-Being', *Journal of Socio-Economics* 35, no. 2 (2006): 382–97. https://doi.org/10.1016/j.socec.2005.11.039.

Gradisar, Michael et al. 'Behavioural Interventions for Infant Sleep Problems: A Randomized Controlled Trial', *Pediatrics* 137, no. 6 (2016). https://doi.org/10.1542/peds.2015-1486.

Guala, Francesco. 'Building Economic Machines: The FCC Auctions', *Studies in History and Philosophy of Science Part A* 32, no. 3 (2001): 453–77. https://doi.org/10.1016/s0039-3681(01)00008-5.

Hardin, Garrett. 'The Tragedy of the Commons', *Science* 162, no. 3859 (1968): 1243–8. https://doi.org/10.1126/science.162.3859.1243.

Harford, Tim. *The Undercover Economist: Exposing Why the Rich are Rich, the Poor are Poor – and Why You Can Never Buy a Decent Used Car!* Oxford: Oxford University Press, 2006.

Hart, Hornell. *Chart for Happiness*, New York: Macmillan, 1940.

Haushofer, Johannes, and Jeremy Shapiro. 'The Short-Term Impact of Unconditional Cash Transfers to the Poor: Experimental Evidence from Kenya', *Quarterly Journal of Economics* 131, no. 4 (2016): 1973–2042. https://doi.org/10.1093/qje/qjw025.

Hayek, Friedrich A. 'The Trend of Economic Thinking', *Economica*, no. 40 (1933): 121–37. https://doi.org/10.2307/2548761.

———. *Studies in Philosophy, Politics and Economics*, London: Routledge & Kegan Paul, 1967.

———. *Law, Legislation, and Liberty, Vol. 3: The Political Order of a Free People*, Chicago: University of Chicago Press, 1979.

Heilmann, Conrad, and Julian Reiss, eds. *The Routledge Handbook of Philosophy of Economics*, New York: Routledge, 2021.

Helliwell, John, Richard Layard, Jeffrey Sachs, and Emmanuel De Neve, eds. *World Happiness Report 2021*, New York: Sustainable Development Solutions Network, 2021.

Herrnstein, Richard J., and Charles Murray. *The Bell Curve: Intelligence and Class Structure in American Life*, New York: Free Press, 1996.

Heyne, Paul T., Peter J. Boettke, and David L. Prychitko. *The Economic Way of Thinking*, 11th edn, Upper Saddle River: Prentice Hall, 2006.

Hitzig, Zoë. *Mezzanine: Poems*, New York: HarperCollins, 2021.

Hornborg, Sara, and Henrik Svedäng. 'Baltic Cod Fisheries – Current Status and Future Opportunities', RISE Report, 2019. http://urn.kb.se/resolve?urn=urn:nbn:se:ri:diva-38343.

Hsee, Christopher K., Yang Yang, Naihe Li, and Luxi Shen. 'Wealth, Warmth, and Well-Being: Whether Happiness is Relative or Absolute Depends on Whether It is about Money, Acquisition, or Consumption', *Journal of Marketing Research* 46, no. 3 (2009): 396–409. https://doi.org/10/dgfc7x.

Jones, David S., and Scott H. Podolsky. 'The History and Fate of the Gold Standard', *The Lancet* 385, no. 9977 (2015): 1502–3. https://doi.org/10.1016/S0140-6736(15)60742-5.

Kahneman, Daniel, and Angus Deaton. 'High Income Improves Evaluation of Life But Not Emotional Well-Being', *Proceedings of the National Academy of Sciences* 107, no. 38 (2010): 16489–93. https://doi.org/10.1073/pnas.1011492107.

Kaiser, Tim, Annamaria Lusardi, Lukas Menkhoff, and Carly Urban. 'Financial Education Affects Financial Knowledge and Downstream Behaviors', *Journal of Financial Economics* 145, no. 2 (2021): 255–72. https://doi.org/10.1016/j.jfineco.2021.09.022.

Keren, Gideon. 'Facing Uncertainty in the Game of Bridge: A Calibration Study', *Organizational Behavior and Human Decision Processes* 39, no. 1 (1987): 98–114. https://doi.org/10.1016/0749-5978(87)90047-1.

Kirwan, Desmond. 'We Need to Change the Way We Talk About Climate Change', *Behavioural Scientist*, 11 October 2021. https://behavioralscientist.org/we-need-to-change-the-way-we-talk-about-climate-change/.

Koriat, Asher, Sarah Lichtenstein, and Baruch Fischhoff. 'Reasons for Confidence', *Journal of Experimental Psychology: Human Learning and Memory* 6, no. 2 (1980): 107–18. https://doi.org/10.1037/0278-7393.6.2.107.

Kruger, Justin, and David Dunning. 'Unskilled and Unaware of It: How Difficulties in Recognizing One's Own Incompetence Lead to Inflated Self-Assessments', *Journal of Personality and Social Psychology* 77, no. 6 (1999): 1121–34. https://doi.org/10.1037/0022-3514.77.6.1121.

Kumar, Amit, Matthew A. Killingsworth, and Thomas Gilovich. 'Waiting for Merlot: Anticipatory Consumption of Experiential and Material Purchases', *Psychological Science* 25, no. 10 (2014): 1924–31. https://doi.org/10.1177/0956797614546556.

Leedham, Andrew. *Unstoppable Self-Confidence: How to Create the Indestructible Natural Confidence of the 1% Who Achieve Their Goals, Create Success on Demand and Live Life on Their Terms*, London: Unstoppable Media Group, 2019.

Levitt, Steven D., and Stephen J. Dubner. *Freakonomics: A Rogue Economist Explores the Hidden Side of Everything*, New York: William Morrow, 2005.

Levy, David M., and Sandra J. Peart. 'The Secret History of the Dismal Science. Part I. Economics, Religion and Race in the 19th Century', *EconLib* (blog) 22 January 2001. https://www.econlib.org/library/Columns/LevyPeartdismal.html.

———. *The Street Porter and the Philosopher: Conversations on Analytical Egalitarianism*, Ann Arbor: University of Michigan Press, 2009.

Lichtenstein, Sarah, and Baruch Fischhoff. 'Training for Calibration', *Organizational Behavior and Human Performance* 26, no. 2 (1980): 149–71. https://doi.org/10.1016/0030-5073(80)90052-5.

Lichtenstein, Sarah, Baruch Fischhoff, and Lawrence D. Phillips. 'Calibration of Probabilities: The State of the Art to 1980', in *Judgment Under Uncertainty: Heuristics and Biases*, ed. Amos Tversky, Daniel Kahneman, and Paul Slovic, Cambridge: Cambridge University Press, 1982: 306–34. https://doi.org/10.1017/CBO9780511809477.023.

Lundborg, Petter, Erik Plug, and Astrid Würtz Rasmussen. 'Can Women Have Children and a Career? IV Evidence from IVF Treatments', *American Economic Review* 107, no. 6 (2017): 1611–37. https://doi.org/10.1257/aer.20141467.

Lusardi, Annamaria, and Olivia S. Mitchell. 'The Economic Importance of Financial Literacy: Theory and Evidence', *Journal of Economic Literature* 52, no. 1 (2014): 5–44. https://doi.org/10.1257/jel.52.1.5.

Macchia, Lucía, and Ashley V. Whillans. 'Leisure Beliefs and the Subjective Well-Being of Nations', *Journal of Positive Psychology* 16, no. 2 (2021): 198–206. https://doi.org/10.1080/17439760.2019.1689413.

Marshall, Alfred. *Principles of Economics: An Introductory Volume*, 8th edn, London: Macmillan, 1920.

Marx, Karl. *The German Ideology: Including Theses on Feuerbach and Introduction to The Critique of Political Economy*, Amherst: Prometheus Books, 1998.

McCloskey, Deirdre N. *If You're So Smart: The Narrative of Economic Expertise*, Chicago: University of Chicago Press, 1990.

Medema, Steven G., and Warren J. Samuels, eds. *The History of Economic Thought: A Reader*, 2nd edn, London: Routledge, 2013.

Mill, John Stuart. 'The Negro Question', *Fraser's Magazine for Town and Country* 41 (1850): 25–31.

———. *The Subjection of Women*, London: Longmans, Green, Reader, and Dyer, 1869.

———. *Utilitarianism*, 7th edn, London: Longmans, Green and Co., 1879.

———. *J. S. Mill: 'On Liberty' and Other Writings*, Cambridge: Cambridge University Press, 1989.

Moore, Don A. *Perfectly Confident: How to Calibrate Your Decisions Wisely*, New York: HarperCollins, 2020.

Mullainathan, Sendhil, and Eldar Shafir. *Scarcity: The New Science of Having Less and How It Defines Our Lives*, New York: Henry Holt and Co., 2013.

Murphy, Allan H., and Robert L. Winkler. 'Probability Forecasting in Meteorology', *Journal of the American Statistical Association* 79, no. 387 (1984): 489–500. https://doi.org/10.2307/2288395.

Myers, David G. *The Pursuit of Happiness: Who is Happy – and Why*, New York: William Morrow, 1992.

Neyer, Ava. 'I Read All the Baby Sleep Books', *Huffington Post* (blog), 6 December 2017. www.huffpost.com/entry/i-read-all-the-baby-sleep-advice-books_b_3143253.

Nickerson, Raymond S. 'Confirmation Bias: A Ubiquitous Phenomenon in Many Guises', *Review of General Psychology* 2, no. 2 (1998): 175–220. https://doi.org/10.1037/1089-2680.2.2.175.

O'Donnell, Michael, Amelia S. Dev, Stephen Antonoplis, et al. 'Empirical Audit and Review and an Assessment of Evidentiary Value in Research on the Psychological Consequences of Scarcity', *Proceedings of the National Academy of Sciences* 118, no. 44 (2021): e2103313118. https://doi.org/10.1073/pnas.2103313118.

Oskamp, Stuart. 'Overconfidence in Case-Study Judgments', *Journal of Consulting Psychology* 29, no. 3 (1965): 261–5. https://doi.org/10.1037/h0022125.

Oster, Emily. *Expecting Better: Why the Conventional Pregnancy Wisdom is Wrong – and What You Really Need to Know*, London: Penguin, 2014.

——. *Cribsheet: A Data-Driven Guide to Better, More Relaxed Parenting, from Birth to Preschool*, New York: Penguin, 2020.

Ostrom, Elinor. *Governing the Commons: The Evolution of Institutions for Collective Action*, Cambridge: Cambridge University Press, 1990.

——. *Understanding Institutional Diversity*, Princeton: Princeton University Press, 2005.

——. 'Beyond Markets and States: Polycentric Governance of Complex Economic Systems', *American Economic Review* 100, no. 3 (2010): 641–72. https://doi.org/10.1257/aer.100.3.641.

Otteson, James R. *Seven Deadly Economic Sins: Obstacles to Prosperity and Happiness Every Citizen Should Know*, Cambridge: Cambridge University Press, 2021.

Pigou, Arthur C. *The Economics of Welfare*, 4th edn, London: Macmillan, 1932.

Rabin, Matthew. 'Psychology and Economics', *Journal of Economic Literature* 36, no. 1 (1998): 11–46. http://www.jstor.org/stable/2564950.

Reiss, Julian. *Philosophy of Economics: A Contemporary Introduction*, New York: Routledge, 2013.

Robbins, Lionel. *An Essay on the Nature and Significance of Economic Science*, London: Macmillan, 1932.

Robinson, Joan. *Contributions to Modern Economics*, Oxford: Blackwell, 1978.

Ross, Don. 'Economic Theory, Anti-Economics, and Political Ideology', in *Philosophy of Economics*, ed. Uskali Mäki, Amsterdam: North-Holland, 2012, 241–85. https://doi.org/10.1016/B978-0-444-51676-3.50010-5.

Roth, Alvin E. *Who Gets What – and Why: The New Economics of Matchmaking and Market Design*, Boston: Houghton Mifflin Harcourt, 2015.

Rubinstein, Ariel. *Economic Fables*, Cambridge: Open Book Publishers, 2012.

Scitovsky, Tibor. *The Joyless Economy: The Psychology of Human Satisfaction*, revised edn, New York: Oxford University Press, 1992.

Seneca, Lucius Annaeus. *Dialogues and Essays*, trans. John Davie, ed. Tobias Reinhardt, Oxford: Oxford University Press, 2008.

Shiller, Robert J. *Narrative Economics: How Stories Go Viral and Drive Major Economic Events*, Princeton: Princeton University Press, 2019.

Smith, Adam. *An Inquiry into the Nature and Causes of the Wealth of Nations*, 5th edn, ed. Edwin Cannan, Chicago: University of Chicago Press, 1976.

———. *The Theory of Moral Sentiments*, 6th edn, ed. Knud Haakonssen, Cambridge: Cambridge University Press, 2002.

Steele, Katie. 'Choice Models', in *Philosophy of Social Science: A New Introduction*, ed. Nancy Cartwright and Eleonora Montuschi, Oxford: Oxford University Press, 2014: 185–207.

Stevenson, Betsey, and Justin Wolfers. 'Economic Growth and Subjective Well-Being: Reassessing the Easterlin Paradox', *Brookings Papers on Economic Activity* (Spring 2008): 1–87. https://doi.org/10.1353/eca.0.0001.

———. *Principles of Economics*, New York: Worth, 2020.

Svenson, Ola. 'Are We All Less Risky and More Skillful Than Our Fellow Drivers?' *Acta Psychologica* 47, no. 2 (1981): 143–8. https://doi.org/10.1016/0001-6918(81)90005-6.

Tarko, Vlad. *Elinor Ostrom: An Intellectual Biography*, London: Rowman & Littlefield International, 2017.

Tetlock, Philip E. 'Theory-Driven Reasoning About Plausible Pasts and Probable Futures in World Politics: Are We Prisoners of Our Preconceptions?' *American Journal of Political Science* 43, no. 2 (1999): 335–66. https://doi.org/10.2307/2991798.

Wrosch, Carsten, et al. 'Adaptive Self-Regulation of Unattainable Goals: Goal Disengagement, Goal Reengagement, and Subjective Well-Being', *Personality and Social Psychology Bulletin* 29, no. 12 (2003): 1494–1508. https://doi.org/10/cjmb8f.

Yakoboski, Paul J., Annamaria Lusardi, and Andrea Hasler. 'Financial Literacy and Well-Being in a Five Generation America: The 2021 TIAA Institute-GFLEC Personal Finance Index' (October 2021). www.tiaainstitute.org/publication/financial-literacy-and-well-being-five-generation-america.

Index